LIVING WITH FAITH AND PATIENCE

LIVING WITH FAITH AND PATIENCE

Sai Baba's Teachings
in the Light of Advaita

GAUTAM SACHDEVA

in conversation with
Nikhil Kripalani

JAICO PUBLISHING HOUSE
Ahmedabad Bangalore Chennai
Delhi Hyderabad Kolkata Mumbai

Published by Jaico Publishing House
A-2 Jash Chambers, 7-A Sir Phirozshah Mehta Road
Fort, Mumbai - 400 001
jaicopub@jaicobooks.com
www.jaicobooks.com

© 2025 by Gautam Sachdeva

LIVING WITH FAITH AND PATIENCE
ISBN 978-93-49358-22-5

First Jaico Impression: 2025

No part of this book may be reproduced or utilized in
any form or by any means, electronic or
mechanical including photocopying, recording or by any
information storage and retrieval system,
without permission in writing from the publishers.

Printed by
Thomson Press India Limited, New Delhi

I give people what they want so that they may want what I want to give them.

—Sai Baba

Contents

Preface xi
Acknowledgements xiii
Introduction xv

1. Living the Teachings of Shirdi Sai Baba 1
2. How Does One Truly Surrender? 16
3. The Deeper Meaning of Shraddha and Saburi 28
4. Committing to One Spiritual Path 35
5. The Pitfall of Hankering After Miracles 42
6. Being the Black Sheep 49
7. The Blessings of Guru Purnima 1 (Gautam's Talk) 57
8. Our Relationship with Sai Baba's Messengers 61
9. Going to Shirdi with the Right Intent 73
10. Business in Sai Baba's Name 81
11. True Surrender to Sai Baba 87
12. Signs of Spiritual Progress 96
13. Spiritual Journeys at the Office Desk 103
14. Meditation on Faith (Gautam's Talk) 119
15. Awakening During the Pandemic 121
16. Living the Teachings During Turbulent Times —Part I 125
17. Living the Teachings During Turbulent Times —Part II 132
18. Blessings in Disguise 138

CONTENTS

19.	Staying Conscious Through Uncertain Times	145
20.	Insights into the Lives of Sai Baba's Staunch Devotees	154
21.	The Blessings of Guru Purnima 2 (Gautam's Talk)	163
22.	Self-Knowledge—the True Wealth	165
23.	Spiritual Friendship and the Spiritual Ego	174
24.	The Law of Attraction and True Surrender	182
25.	How to Know Baba's Will	190
26.	Seekers, Disciples and Devotees	199
27.	Do We Really Treat Others as Equals?	207
28.	Surrender—the True Prayer (Gautam's Talk)	213
29.	How Baba Instilled Humility in His Devotees	218
30.	Attitude and Free Will	224
31.	Serving Baba—the Highest Sadhana	230
32.	Baba's Explanation of Rnanubandhan	238
33.	Have You Already Made up Your Mind?	244
34.	The Thinking Mind and the Working Mind	250
35.	The Middle Path (Gautam's Talk)	259
36.	Baba's Teaching on Non-doership	262
37.	Sai Baba's Prophetic Words: A Wake-up Call	270
38.	How to Reflect on the Sai Satcharita	275
39.	The Satcharita Isn't a Pillow	278
40.	Climbing the Ladder of Consciousness	282
41.	Sai Baba's Emphasis on Reading the Pothis	286
42.	Missing the Point (Gautam's Talk)	291
43.	Am I Receptive to Sai Baba's Teachings?	294
44.	Developing One-Pointed Devotion to Baba	305
45.	Penetrating the Veil of Maya	314
46.	What Can We Learn from the Param Bhaktas?	324
47.	Getting Closer to God	333
48.	We See Things the Way We Are (Gautam's Talk)	342
49.	Traits of the Ego	345
50.	Reaction and Response	354

51. The Ego Loves to Feel Special—Part I	363
52. The Ego Loves to Feel Special—Part II (Gautam's Talk)	367
53. The Ego Wears a Mask	369
54. The Ego Loves to Criticize and Complain	375
55. Restlessness	380
56. Contemplating the Teachings (Gautam's Talk)	384
Appendix: Sai Baba of Shirdi—The Hidden Jewel of Advaita	387
Glossary	392
Disclaimer	404
Sai Baba's Original Paintings and Photographs	405
Podcasts	405

Preface

The last hundred years or so have seen an unprecedented and unparalleled rise in the popularity of Sri Sai Baba. While many would initially be drawn to *Baba* due to the miracles He was known for, in time, through His unique methods, He would direct them onto the path of *bhakti* (devotion). This phenomenon of gradual conversion to the sublime prevailed even before 1918 (when Baba took *Mahasamadhi*) and, by His benevolent grace, continues to date. He would say 'I give people what they want so that they may want what I want to give them,' meaning spiritual upliftment and *Self-realization*.

Sri Sai Baba taught through His *leelas* and seldom gave direct instructions. If one was spiritually ripe and earnest, one would be worthy of these subtle teachings. Although they might appear easy to comprehend, they were not, let alone embodying them.

In chapter three of the *Sai Satcharita*, *Ovi* 18–19, Sri Sai Baba says 'Listen to the stories with reverence; reflect upon them deeply. After reflection, contemplate them. This will bring great satisfaction. The mind will transcend the consciousness of the self, and the differentiated consciousness will dissolve. And by single-minded, absolute faith, the *chitta* (Heart) will become a mass of divine energy.'

This book aims to humbly offer guidance to devotees in the hope that they will be reminded of Baba's assurances and teachings. The talks within, encourage them to contemplate deeply on the life and teachings of this revered master, thereby enabling them to own the precious jewel of spiritual upliftment, which Baba has bequeathed them.

Gautam and I, far from calling ourselves devotees, are not even qualified to comment on Sri Sai Baba's teachings. Over the years, both of us would sometimes telephonically joke with each other that, perhaps, one or both of us were a dog or some creature that lived in Shirdi during Baba's time and were graced by the dust of His lotus feet.

We are very blessed and fortunate that, by Sri Sai Baba's grace, these series of talks took shape and significantly deepened the devotees' understanding of the teachings. Truly and humbly, we are not even His instruments, for it is He Himself who inspired it and got it done.

I was fortunate to have a close friendship with Gautam over the years and found that he was greatly blessed with the gift of explaining things very simply, his focus being the application of the teachings for attaining peace of mind in daily living. I am deeply grateful to him for having given us so much time over the years to help devotees delve deeper into the significance of the teachings.

I would also like to acknowledge Sunita Kripalani for her work in carefully captioning the talks before they were published. This was in the years long before technology evolved, and her work also often helped fact-check and scrutinize the content. This priceless work on the captions and transcripts later became the foundation for the book.

It is recommended that you read these chapters and watch the corresponding talks from the series *Living the Teachings of Sai Baba* if possible. [QR codes for the videos are provided as some of the titles as well as the sequence are different from that used in this book.] You will find that it will help you seriously reflect on the pointers shared in the talks. In turn, it will permeate your reading, contemplation and practice of Baba's teachings in everyday life.

We sincerely hope that you find this book helpful in deepening your faith, love and complete unconditional surrender to Lord Sri Sai Baba, making you truly eligible and worthy of attaining what He wishes to give you.

Om Shri Sainathaya Namaha.

—Nikhil Kripalani

Acknowledgements

I would like to express my heartfelt gratitude to my parents, Santosh and Ajeet Sachdeva, for taking me to Shirdi as a young child. Those early trips sowed some seeds that, unbeknown to me, would germinate decades later.

To my wife, Devika, for her care and compassion along our journey together.

To my sisters, Shibani and Nikki, for their support through the formative years as well as the times that followed.

To my editor, Mehernosh, for his painstaking and dedicated efforts (over many months) in transforming the video transcriptions into the edited book form that you are reading. It has been a pleasure working with him.

To Asha Jhaveri for generously supporting this project.

To Nikhil Kripalani for making our series on the YouTube channel Sai Baba's Devotee Speaks a joyful affair. I have learnt much from our exchanges across the interviews.

And finally, to all the viewers of the channel for writing to us and encouraging us to keep sharing our insights into Baba's teachings. It is their dedication to living the teachings of Sai Baba that has motivated us to do so.

Introduction

This book comprises a series of recorded conversations between Gautam Sachdeva and Nikhil Kripalani on the popular YouTube channel Sai Baba's Devotee Speaks. Nikhil interviews Gautam on various aspects of Sai Baba's teachings and the subtle spiritual import of His leelas. As Gautam's focus is on living the teachings of *Advaita*, all the talks are based on the impact of Sai Baba's teachings—from the *Advaitic* perspective—in our day-to-day life.

The fifty-six talks contained herein are carried out in simple language and have a conversational flow, covering topics such as *shraddha* and *saburi* (the hallmark of Baba's teachings), surrendering to Baba, spiritual progress, Self-knowledge, free will, serving Baba and *rnanubandhan*—something Baba often spoke about to stress its importance in our life. Some talks span the period of the Covid pandemic and subsequent lockdown, and delve into all the challenges faced by people in its wake as well as ways of overcoming them by living the teachings.

When the conversation veers towards Baba's *param bhaktas*, the reader can sense their devotional *bhava* for their *guru* whom they revere and consider above everything else. Something worth cultivating for those who are well and truly on the spiritual path.

The text contains a substantial number of non-English words and spiritual terminology in particular. Hence the reader (especially those who are unfamiliar with this terrain) will find it helpful to refer to the glossary at the end. All the first instances of the words therein appear in italics in the text (and vice versa in passages where the rest of the text is italicized).

The quotations in this book have come up spontaneously during the talks; they are not necessarily verbatim and cannot be definitively traced back to specific sources in some cases. Hence, citations have not been provided.

This compilation of talks is probably one of a kind in that Sai Baba's leelas and the teachings they illustrate have been approached in a way that's considerably distinct from the literature available on them.

Most present-day literature on Baba, particularly in Hindi, which has come to my notice, is based on facts narrated in the Sai Satcharita and other available books. To date, I have not come across any literature that reveals the philosophy behind Baba's actions and words, His way of life and living, and their analysis. Certainly, there is a need for writers, philosophers and researchers to delve deep into the life and leelas of Baba, the experiencing of Baba's Grace by unknown persons all over the world and the like. A mere narration of the miracles of Baba and the experiences of devotees will not suffice.

I am certain, in time to come, devotees will undertake a serious and deeper study of Baba and His leelas, and produce literature giving deeper significance to His actions and words.

—Scribblings of a Shirdi Sai Devotee,
Suresh Chandra Gupta

1

Living the Teachings of Shirdi Sai Baba

Nikhil: Today, we are interviewing Gautam Sachdeva, who has been a spiritual guide to me for more than eight years and comes from the Advaitic tradition and lineage of Sri Nisargadatta Maharaj. His teacher was Ramesh Balsekar*ji*, and Gautam's essential teaching is about peace of mind in daily living, with the focus being on how to live the teaching. I have benefited immensely from my association with Gautam, and I am very grateful for that.

I have requested Gautam to speak about Sai Baba's teachings to help devotees understand them deeply and imbibe them to attain peace of mind and equanimity in day-to-day living.

Gautam, the journey for most devotees on this path with Sai Baba typically begins with them being drawn to Baba by a miracle, a dream or a vision when He pulls them towards Him. That's essentially the common thread. Then it is followed by a further series of miracles that draw them to Shirdi, His life and His teachings. But somewhere down the line, I've noticed that many people write that their faith and their surrender are very dependent on favourable circumstances—that Baba does things in accordance with their will. In one of your talks, you mentioned true faith. Could we begin with you shedding some light on that?

Gautam: Sure. Nikhil, first of all, thank you for giving me this opportunity to talk about Shirdi Sai Baba's teachings. As you rightly said, there is so much material out there simply because of the miracles

Baba performed in His lifetime. As a ray of the Absolute, anything was possible in His domain. However, when I read the Sai Satcharita, I found that on one level there was the actual event of the miracle taking place, and on the other, there was a teaching being conveyed by each story, which seemed to directly impact daily living. So, because I was with a spiritual teacher [Ramesh Balsekar] for almost ten years, I started viewing the Sai Satcharita through the prism of Advaita, or non-duality, as it is called in the Western world. What I found was so pragmatic, but it had been hidden by the overwhelming evidence of miracles. I started underlining the expressions of Advaita uttered by Baba that really appealed to me and which I felt were within everybody's life experience. Through these non-dualistic gems, Baba delivers the greatest miracle of all—peace of mind.

People ask me about masters performing *siddhis*, yet there's this whole other layer of thought that says, 'Don't get stuck at the level of siddhis because they are mere experiences.' Even Nisargadatta Maharaj, in his younger days, used to perform certain siddhis for his devotees, but his guru, Siddharameshwar Maharaj, said, 'Look, don't get stuck at that level. You have to give them the message of Advaita.' And truly, peace of mind is the biggest miracle that Sai Baba gives through His teachings because that becomes a way of living, a way of being and a way of looking at yourself and the world around you.

So, through the stories, we can understand the core Advaitic message of such a Divine Being, whose very presence was venerated by Hindus as well as Muslims. That fact itself shows that He was non-denominational and that He was a guru to everyone unconditionally. Thus Baba's teachings had their origin in His own secular and selfless life, from which people can learn by example.

N: Yes. There are people who've had a vision: some sort of an experience. How do they understand what Baba is trying to convey? This is a common concern for many people. *How do I interpret this? How do I relate to it? What is Baba trying to tell me?* What would you say to devotees who have experienced this?

G: The very fact that they've had a dream or a vision means that it is not their doing but Baba's. That is how He has pulled them to Him.

Now they have to trust that force, which has pulled them without their free will, to do its job. We tend to analyse and seek the meaning of what we have seen or what we have experienced, but that force is so powerful that, if it could come to us without our knowledge and pull us in, we must trust it to take us all the way.

When you have such a vision or a dream, or whatever it may be, you get the answers once the mind becomes less caught up with the elation experienced by thinking, *I had this vision; I had the experience.* Since the 'me' feels great that God has chosen it to have a vision rather than someone else, it can strengthen the ego.

N: Exactly.

G: Yes. But to have the humility to understand that this vision happened without me doing anything is to trust that Source, which will show you the way. As my teacher would say, 'Never consider your glass half empty but half full. If God has brought you this far in your spiritual journey, why do you feel He will drop you here? He will hold your hand and take you home.' So, these are signs, not for the 'me' to take pride in but to see that life is taking a certain course through Baba's form, and you have to trust Baba to lead you along the way.

N: I have a question about this. There are certain practices Baba would advocate to devotees who followed the path of trust and surrender, such as *japa*, *dhyana* or even *Self-enquiry* at times. For those devotees who are sincerely committed to Baba and wish to go down the path of Self-realization, could you talk a little bit about practices that can help still the mind? Could you make some suggestions here?

G: Generally, masters like Baba saw the spiritual ripeness or inclination of the devotee and then prescribed what they felt was the right method for that specific person. Some were more inclined to bhakti, some to japa and some to Self-enquiry, while others, to a total understanding of what Baba was saying. For example, a *mantra japa*—the word '*mantra*', when broken up, means '*man*', or 'mind', and '*tra*', or 'freeing'—could help shift the energy of an overactive mind, involved only in mundane issues, to the mantra. This helps you move out of the regular pattern of thinking that you are embroiled in.

Someone may not have the inclination to practise Self-enquiry or understand Baba's other teachings but may find that they are very comfortable doing japa. So, different practices that best resonated with the individual devotee were prescribed, and they would all lead to the Source.

For instance, Baba would tell someone, and it is in the Satcharita, 'See Me in all beings.' Now one person may find that too abstract, but another might think, *Yes, what Baba is pointing to is that the same* Consciousness, *the same sense of the presence of being, functions through everyone.* That may be easy for that particular individual to understand. That person need not do japa because his life becomes the Living Teaching. He sees God in everyone. So that is what is meant by different practices for different temperaments or tendencies. It is not that we have to sequentially progress from one to the other.

Even Nisargadatta Maharaj would see the ripeness of the person who had come to him and then decide whether his *Jnana Yoga* talks were suitable for them or whether they should just do mantra japa. So that is what the master does.

N: A question arises in this regard. Now Sai Baba is not in physical form, yet many people regard Him as their main guru. How do they get guidance that is specific to them, so that they know they are on the right track?

G: The guidance will come. The point is that we have to be open to receiving it. There are some instances that everyone is familiar with, where Baba appears to certain people, after which they begin spreading Baba's message. The other instances are about those who don't have that connection. But Baba, being present in their life, brings about circumstances that would benefit them. The question is, Are we aware of the fact that these situations have been created for us? Or is our vision only on one track, waiting for some miracle to happen? It is only when we drop this narrow, conditioned vision, and are open and aware, that the Source, as represented by Baba, will step in to show us the way.

But we get so stuck on the thought *Baba will show me the way, Baba will show me the way,* that although Baba *is* showing you the way through something that happens in your life and which is coming your way as a gift, you remain blind to it. We remain unaware of this blessing because we have this fixed concept in our mind that it should come to us in a certain way; hence, we miss the opportunity.

N: Many devotees have experiences they believe Baba gave them. But how do you distinguish between a real experience and an imaginary one?

G: A real experience is an experience that comes to you. An imaginary one, in the sense you might be referring to, is that which I make myself believe is an experience. So, there's a very thin line here, and that is why this whole business of experiences is very tricky because 'All experiences come and go,' as masters like Ramana Maharshi or even Shirdi Sai Baba Himself said. 'You are the witness of whatever transpires,' is what Baba has said in the Satcharita. And 'whatever transpires' means all the pleasures and pains which come and go in life—all experiences. Because, for an experience to be registered, an experiencer has to be there. All experiences come and go because the state of the experiencer is temporal.

The mind is such that it tends to hook on to an experience, feels special about that experience and then wants to repeat that experience. Now that experience may or may not come again, and then you can get frustrated by that, making you think, *Oh, Baba came to me once in a dream; now I'm going to wait for Him to come another time!* But the bedrock of your life should be Baba's teachings. It should not be dependent on an experience you had of Baba. Otherwise, what is the point of a teaching if it doesn't impact your daily living? What is the point if it is stuck at the level of one experience you had? The value of the experience is tremendous because it's like a catalyst, but many of us tend to get stuck on the level of that experience.

N: This takes me to the next question. Sai Baba would often advocate the practice of Self-enquiry, saying, 'Ask yourself at all times, Who am I?' Could you talk a little bit about it in general and give us some guidance?

G: Sure. Self-enquiry is also mentioned in our scriptures, and after Baba, it has been taught by sages like Ramana Maharshi, who was known for his teaching of asking yourself, Who am I? Now this will appeal to those with a certain spiritual ripeness. It's not everyone's cup of tea. But what Baba is pointing to, or this enquiry of 'Who am I?' is pointing to, is to help us understand 'Who is this "me" that is living this life? Who is this person thinking this thought?' And when this enquiry of 'Who am I?' is undertaken, the understanding 'I am not this, I am not that,' starts sinking in. Why? Because I am the one aware of this. Who is the 'I' who is aware of this? There is no answer to this question as 'I' is not a thing—an object to be experienced. 'I' is the subject. The enquiry 'Who am I?' is meant to dissolve the constructs that we have created, which separate us from what *is* and from the world: this 'me' with its baggage of likes, dislikes, conditionings, feelings and emotions. It is designed to deconstruct this shell that we have created around us since childhood and take us back to that pure Being, that pure Source—that child consciousness which existed before the ego came in saying, *You and I are separate.*

So, this is what the enquiry 'Who am I?' does. And someone who can go deep into this enquiry will realize the absence of separation because the riddle of 'Who am I?' has been solved. So again, it is a practice, just like japa is a practice.

N: Sai Baba would say that one of the ten prerequisites for Self-realization is choosing what's right over what's pleasant. It seems that it's important for a devotee to be able to discern this in their day-to-day life. Even Ramakrishna Dev [Ramakrishna Paramahansa] made a clear distinction between worldliness and the path of God. It seems that discernment could be that fork or the starting point, where the devotee begins to be a witness and be aware. Could you speak a little bit about discernment as a practice and how devotees could implement it in their day-to-day lives?

G: See, there are many aspects of discernment, but we shall just touch upon one. Many of us, in fact, most of us, are so hardwired by conditioning that, based on our past experience, we react to different people the same way. We are in reaction mode rather than response mode. Now, in this case, what is discernment? Discernment is to understand that we are a result of our conditioning, and so is the other. That in itself is a level of discernment because you are no longer functioning on autopilot. With the understanding that the same Consciousness functions through each of us, as Baba has said, you accept others for who they are because God has made them, and likewise, you accept yourself too.

Earlier, you were going around pointing fingers, accusing, blaming and condemning people, but now you understand that such behaviour was improper. This understanding is discernment. So, you see that when you follow the teachings, discernment is initiated, and every aspect of life and of all kinds of relationships is seen in the light of discernment.

N: What you shared was discernment in relation to other people and events that are associated with them. Could we talk about discernment which need not have much to do with other people but more with everyday circumstances and the choices you make? Essentially, how can the devotee who is putting God first in his life, who is a serious aspirant, make choices which are favourable to the path rather than those which are not? For example, if you have to choose between peace of mind and lust or something that could lead you astray, as opposed to staying on the path, how do you discern when making these everyday decisions? Could you talk a little bit about *that* discernment?

G: Let's take desire, for example. Desire can arise, but suppressing desire is not the way. And indulging in it is not the way either. This is what the sages have advised. If we are discerning, when desire arises, the understanding arises at the same time that desire has arisen and whether it gets fulfilled or not is God's will. So, any involvement in the desire drops. That is how a desire arising is witnessed.

It could be something as simple as a desire for a cup of coffee. That's also a desire, right? But if for some reason, the coffee powder is over, you tend to vent your frustration by blaming a family member: 'Why isn't it stocked? I wanted to have a coffee, but now I can't have it.' And then the blame game begins. But if you have the understanding that the desire to have a coffee arose, which is fine, but it didn't get fulfilled because it was not meant to, then the hold that the desire has on you loses its grip. I have used a very soft desire, like a cup of coffee, but it would apply to any desire, like lust, as you said.

Allow the desire to come up because suppressing it is not going to work. But also let go of the attachment to the outcome because it is the 'I' wanting things to be a certain way and getting frustrated if they are not that way. The discernment in this case is allowing what has to come up to do so but with the understanding that it will get fulfilled only if it is meant to. So there is no frustration.

The other aspect of discernment is right thinking: 'Does my desire harm anyone?' If the answer is no and the understanding is there that it is a desire arising in the moment, there is nothing wrong with that. But sometimes you are so consumed by your desires that you don't even realize it could be harmful to someone else or yourself.

I keep pointing to this fact that Baba spoke about: 'Be a witness; let the world go topsy-turvy around you, but be a witness,' because there is a very deep teaching in that one line. And let the world go topsy-turvy does not refer to external events, because the world is inside you. He would even say that the *Bhagavad Gita* and *Kurukshetra* are inside you.

See, it's very simple. Right now, you are appearing outside me, but the fact is that you are in my field of consciousness. I am conscious that everything is appearing within that consciousness, including you and myself. It appears that I am speaking to you, but this voice which you are hearing now is being heard in your own consciousness. That is *maya*.

But we have lost touch with all of this because the sense of separation, which we have grown up with, is so strong. What was a simple structure in a life of duality—which is what life is: black and white, big and small, up and down, rich and poor, front and back—has become dualism. The 'me' and the 'other', the polar opposites of duality, have become 'me' versus the 'other'.

To understand what Baba's words mean, one has to live by them.

N: Absolutely. In this regard, I've received emails with a common theme, where people say they are living according to Baba's principles, such as 'Do your worldly duties, and keep your mind on Me.' Nevertheless, they find themselves leading a life which is pretty much immoral and not in alignment with Baba's teachings.

Could you shed some light on the deeper meaning of what Baba said [the statement mentioned above] to help devotees relate to it, with the emphasis being on whether they are living in harmony with Baba's teachings?

G: Sometimes it's not the time for the teachings to sink in. It is not that they have a choice as such, because the level of understanding or awareness is at a certain level. One can't say that they are voluntarily not following the teachings, but the teachings have not sunk in yet, if, for example, you harbour a desire that harms another. If you truly are living Baba's teachings, it would just not be possible.

So this is where being earnest and sincere in your practice, which all masters point to, gains relevance. What happens is that we segment our life, we segment our day. For instance, we may have a *puja* ritual with Baba in the temple, where we are full of bhakti, but the rest of the day, we are having fights with everyone. We don't get along with people.

Now if Baba has said, 'See Me in all beings,' what is true bhakti? It is to see God in everyone. What can be a higher bhakti than this? So then, bhakti is not just worshipping the *murti* at home or in the temple but actually living with bhakti by seeing God in all beings.

But when does this understanding arise? It arises when one is immersed in a master's teachings. It is a level of awareness that can speed up the process. But if it is not meant to happen, it won't.

A true *bhakta* of Shirdi Sai Baba, or any master, is one who follows the master's teachings and whose every breath, whose life force, is dedicated to the master and the teachings. Because they are not two. The form is of the formless. We tend to venerate only the form of the master. The guru is a projection of our Higher Self onto a form, so that also is not separate from us. But we are so conditioned by this world of forms and objects that everything is viewed as such.

It's as simple as saying the Sun is not apart from you. While it appears that the Sun rises and sets in the sky, it is all appearing in Consciousness, which is essentially what you are. That is how vast you

LIVING WITH FAITH AND PATIENCE

are; that is how vast Consciousness is. You will find Baba pointing to this in the Satcharita.

N: Could you give some general guidelines and pointers for people who spend more and more time with Baba, or whichever path they are on, to know if they are on the right track and making progress? Some signposts as indicators?

G: Ramana Maharshi was asked by someone how a person could know whether one acclaimed as a guru is a true guru. The master gave a very simple answer: the sense of peace you feel in the guru's presence and the degree of respect you feel for him is an indicator.

This word 'peace' is very important because that sense of peace which you feel is within you, and if you are a true devotee or a true disciple, that would be imbibed by you.

The point I'm trying to make is that your own life, and your attitude towards what happens in your life, will be an indication to you as to how close you are to the master's teachings: the degree of peace you feel in your life, your accepting people for who they are and the sense of respect you feel towards others. Someone was criticizing another guru to Nisargadatta Maharaj, and he replied, 'To criticize anything or anyone is to criticize the affairs of *Brahman*.'

To know the impact of the teachings is to see how they have influenced your daily living and, in turn, your acceptance, tolerance and compassion for people. Because we are not living in caves; we are living in a society, we are dealing with people. As Baba kept pointing out, all relationships are rnanubandhan, a cosmic debt of a former relationship. That is why He would keep emphasizing that even if you don't want to give money to a beggar who comes up to you, it's okay, but don't shout at the beggar as if he were a dog.

After living Baba's teachings, when you find that you experience a general sense of harmony with people, it does not mean you have to love everyone. There may be people you don't like, but you have the understanding that they are who they are, the way they have been made. And you naturally prefer the company of others to them, but you accept them for who they are.

You will see that your life has transformed as a result of the message of the master, and then you know that, yes, you are living the teachings. And your whole life, from the time you get up to the time you go to sleep, becomes a meditation on the teachings.

We think of meditation as a practice. We have to sit for half an hour, close our eyes and concentrate. My guru said, 'True meditation is witnessing whatever arises in life as movements in Consciousness.' For example, pleasure and pain come and go. It is witnessed, as Baba says.

The ground for meditation is life, and it becomes a way of being. Peace, equanimity and compassion are its characteristics. No blame, condemnation, hatred, malice, jealousy and envy.

Baba says, 'I am the Sole Doer. Nobody is the doer. The Lord is the Doer.'

Whereas pride and arrogance may have arisen earlier, prior to living the teachings, now, if I do something because of which society praises me, the humility and understanding is fully there that God gifted me a set of attributes as a result of which something useful got done, and so it was appreciated by society. What arises may be pleasure, because it feels good, but there is no pride and arrogance as it is clear to me that it is not my doing. These tendencies, as well as hatred and malice, start dropping away.

N: Sometimes if you experience this, maybe to a lesser degree, and you are pulled astray temporarily, you tend to be very hard on yourself: *I've been doing meditation, and I've been with Baba for so long, yet I had an episode of anger or outburst.* Could you shed some light on how to be in those moments?

G: We are not sages; it is human nature. You may follow a practice for years and, suddenly, an incident happens that disturbs your peace of mind. It's a happening. We take ownership of that and say, *I was not disturbed for all these years. But now I am disturbed by this happening. Why did I do it?* The fact is, you didn't. It happened in the moment.

So then, with this understanding, you don't set up these expectations that you have to be the perfect figure who will not make a wrong move and who will not say anything wrong. That puts a lot of pressure on you.

When we stop putting this demand on others as well as ourselves, life becomes free and joyful. Things may happen sometimes because we are human, but we are not claiming ownership of them. Because to claim ownership is then to get stuck again.

God has made us with all our imperfections. So, in a sense, we *are* perfect, because our imperfections are also made by God. Yet, we do what we think we should, to improve ourselves.

N: I remember you had mentioned once that when you were a child, you were taken to Baba, in Shirdi.

G: Yes.

N: So could you share a few personal experiences of your relationship with Baba?

G: See, I have not had many experiences, although He did come to me in a dream recently. When I was born, my father, especially, considered me a gift from Shirdi Sai Baba. I think I must have been really small, maybe two or three years old, when I was taken to Shirdi. The temple priest, who was on the podium, was taking babies from their parents, putting them at Baba's feet and then giving them back to the parents. This has been vividly etched in my memory. In that moment, I was aware of nothing else but being laid at Baba's feet and being handed back to my father.

But apart from that, I just feel that a lot of people in India, and Maharashtra especially, have grown up seeing Sai Baba's images in taxis and in temples dedicated to Him, built at street corners. He has truly become a part of us.

Plus, in my journey with spiritual masters, I was very drawn to the *Nath Yogis*, and they revere Lord Dattatreya. And there is a connection between Sai Baba and Dattatreya. The Nath Yogis consider Him a manifestation of Dattatreya; that is why He is called Sai Nath.

So I picked up these kinds of cues along the way, and with Sai Baba, because He is so all-pervasive, you keep finding these connections and stories and understanding aspects of Him as a truly Divine Being.

Just the other day, I was telling my mother that we were planning to have this interview, and she asked me, 'Did I tell you about my episode at the Shridi Sai Baba temple?'

'Which one?' I asked.
'About Baba's trunk.'
'No,' I replied.

Then my mother recounted that many years ago when she had gone with a friend of hers to the temple at *aarti* time, she was looking at the statue. She thought she saw a trunk on the murti, but she dismissed it because she felt that with the incense sticks, the *dhuni* and the lights of the *diyas*, sometimes the mind is tricked into creating patterns where none actually exist. She waited for the smoke to disperse; however, the vision persisted even after it had cleared. It was very perplexing for her.

After they stepped out, her friend wanted to buy some murtis from the shops in the vicinity. In one of the shops, my mother saw one small murti in a corner, almost leaping out, saying, 'Pick me up, pick me up.'

She wondered what it was and asked the shopkeeper about it. He replied, 'Ji, *yeh toh Sai Ganesh hai* [Ma'am, this is Sai Ganesh].' It was a statue of Sai Baba's with an elephant's trunk, like that of Ganapati.

She hadn't bought that statue, so I Googled images of 'Sai Ganesh.' Sure enough, I found Baba's images with a trunk.

So you see, all this is very symbolic. You could very well dismiss it by saying that someone had put Ganesh's face on a statue of Sai Baba's, just out of their creative imagination, but how do you explain the fact that my mother had a vision of the same image? That was *her* experience. I think it was very beautiful because a form called Sai Ganesh actually exists.

N: That's amazing. I think Baba is very . . . I would use the word 'cryptic'. A lot of His messages, His ways, His leelas were not very direct. He would use symbolism, which appeared in people's dreams and visions. Any reason?

G: Because He wants us to discern. He doesn't want to give us 'A for Apple'.

N: That's true.

One other question. Sai Baba is probably the most popular deity in India and pretty much in many parts of the world, especially where

Indians reside. Any reason why the teachings haven't spread in the West as much as they have spread through the path of Bhakti in India?

G: As you rightly said, Indians are Bhakti-oriented; the tradition is to visit temples and revere the deity's murti or one's guru. But the Western mind is more into enquiry, knowledge and thinking.

Now there's very little literature on what Baba has said about Jnana Yoga. But His leelas all point to that. Even the story of the two lizards, where He's sitting and someone sees a lizard on the wall and asks Him, 'This lizard is getting very excited. Why?'

And Baba replies, 'Its sister is coming.'

The next instant, a man comes along in his cart and puts a sack down, from which another lizard runs out and goes and meets the first one.

At one level, we can say, 'Look at Baba's leela. He knew that another lizard was going to come from some other town.'

However, the process of Jnana Yoga would be, What is behind this? What is the meaning of this? It is very clear. Baba is saying that anyone you meet in your life is because of rnanubandhan. The Universe conspires to bring about circumstances to make you meet them. In this case, it was two lizards. That was his vision, his enormity.

So now, what happens is that because the literature is mainly driven by these stories and incidents which evoke so much bhava and bhakti, because truly only God or the Absolute could do all this, the Westerners don't have much to look at unless they delve deeper.

I was with a master [Rameshji] who belonged to a lineage of Jnana Yoga masters, because of which my background is Jnana Yoga. When I read the Satcharita, I saw it through the prism of Jnana Yoga. And that is why I underlined all the things that appealed to me. I truly felt that living this is the highest form of bhakti because both paths are ultimately the same.

I do feel that, in time to come, the Western world is going to get more familiar with this master. I'll give you one example. It's only recently that a shrine has come up dedicated to Shirdi Sai Baba around Arunachala Hill in Tiruvannamalai, Tamil Nadu, which was not there earlier. And this is a place that Westerners frequent because of Ramana Maharshi's *ashram* located there.

And I feel that Sai Baba's message is going to spread far more than ever before in the years to come. That is why He said, 'My bones will speak from My tomb.' And He will come in any form: whether it is a vision, whether it is dreams or whether it is through Jnana Yoga. We don't know.

Ramana Maharshi and even Nisargadatta Maharaj had said very clearly that Baba was the Absolute.

So I do feel that it would be really wonderful if Sai Baba's devotees, like us, live His teachings in such a way that they have a direct impact on their daily living. I think that is a service we could render to Baba.

N: So that being said, we pray for His grace, that His will be done.

To view the corresponding video, scan the QR code.

2

How Does One Truly Surrender?

Nikhil: I would like to ask you some questions on surrender. Perhaps your answers could help devotees gain a correct and deeper understanding of what surrender truly means. How does one truly surrender to Sai Baba?

Gautam: Let's start by understanding what the word 'surrender' means. We hear people saying, 'This is my situation, and I have surrendered to it.' We need to look more closely at this.

In ancient Egyptian times, the hieroglyphs, or the symbols which were carved on the pyramids and temples, included a figure with its hands up, a symbol of surrender, and the depiction of which meant 'above the mind'. This indicates that it is not the thinking mind which can surrender. When the police say, 'Hands up', it means 'surrender', because your hands are up in the air with palms wide open and you can't use them. The Egyptian symbol is very much the same—above the mind.

What can one truly surrender? There is so much that happens in life over which we have no control at all. Most of it started from the time when we were young: the school we went to, the economic strata we were born into and the geographical location we were living in. All this, which was not in our control, shaped us; it became our conditioning.

Then a difficult situation happens—something adverse that we do not like—and we realize that no matter how hard we try, the situation is beyond our control. And we surrender.

So true surrender means this acceptance that whatever happens is God's will. In reality, you have nothing to surrender, because everything is given to you. What is yours to surrender if everything belongs to the Divine, to God? What can the individual surrender? The individual can only surrender their sense of doership: *I did this. I did not do this. This person did this to me, so I hate him. This person did not do this, so I don't like him.*

If you read the Sai Satcharita, you will see various pointers in the stories where this aspect of doership is pointed out. When we realize that neither we nor others do things, because it is God who is in charge of everything, we stop blaming, condemning, hating and judging. This is true surrender. We stop pointing a finger at individuals because we know that this is, as one says, Sai Baba's leela.

N: In this regard, Baba would ask us to see Him in every form, not as an act of doership but, essentially, to emphasize that He pervades all forms as Consciousness and to give us the understanding that we tend to reduce this Consciousness to I and me.

G: Absolutely! This is exactly what happens when one starts living the teachings. It's no longer just a concept or a theory or reading a book, such as the Sai Satcharita. When you can see that everyone in your life, especially people you don't like, are instruments of the Divine, instruments through whom Sai Baba operates, what happens? You start accepting people more and more, the way God has made them. You start accepting yourself the way you are made, and the inevitable result is a sense of peace and equanimity which permeates your daily living.

The example which I usually give concerns the kitchen. We have various gadgets, each designed to carry out their respective functions. The toaster makes toast, the juicer produces juice and the microwave heats the food. But without electricity, all these gadgets are dead instruments.

Similarly, it is Consciousness which animates us—the electricity, so to speak, which runs through all of us. And we are instruments through which Consciousness functions. When this understanding takes root, one starts seeing people through this new understanding. The focus shifts from individuals, with their respective characteristics, to an understanding that the same light, the light of Consciousness, shines through everyone. This is why Sai Baba has said, 'God is pure Consciousness.'

N: As a practice for devotees, especially those who are new to the teachings and Baba, could their taking this practice of just being aware of the 'I' or the 'me' when it arises in various forms be a good beginning point? Especially in situations where you think of yourself as the victim and would feel, *This happened to me*, *Someone hurt me* or *Why did this happen to me?*

G: It is an excellent beginning point. It is, at once, the beginning and the end.

Nisargadatta Maharaj gives us an excellent pointer on this practice. He says, 'Every time we are referring to the me—*This happened to me*—we are always referring back to the me.' So, he says, simply change it. 'Instead of thinking, *Something happened to me*, think, *Something happened*. Full stop.' He also advised changing the internal dialogue of *I see something* and *I hear something* to *Something is seen* and *Something is heard*.

What happens is that this intense focus on the me, which we are all living with, starts diminishing. The burden that the me carries of what the world has done to it, or of what it has done, starts becoming lighter.

If we consider how many times in a day we keep coming back to this me identity, it is astonishing! So that is why these teachings are presented to us. They diminish this sense of a separate identity, which is the me, with its sense of doership. When you think, *Something happened*, it becomes so much simpler to accept, rather than *Something happened to me, which should not have.*

N: For most people, the troubling point for them is their mind, their incessant thinking. However, if you have truly surrendered, that would subside majorly because you essentially surrender to the will of God, and life flows.

Could you suggest a few practices for this? For example, for someone who has thoughts which are assumptions? Could that person begin to question the reality of thoughts as a practice?

G: What needs to be looked at is the thinking mind. As my teacher, Rameshji, would say, there are two aspects of the mind: the working mind and the thinking mind. The working mind is needed to perform tasks. The thinking mind is that which goes into the dead past or an imaginary future—that is the problem.

Rameshji would give the example of a surgeon conducting an operation, which makes these concepts very clear. When the surgeon is conducting the operation, he is in the working mind mode. He is 'in the moment' because he has to do the incision precisely. All his years of experience are brought into play in that moment by the working mind to do the operation in the best possible way. Now this also includes all his past experience that he has available at hand. He dips into that experience, that knowledge, but his mind is focused on the surgery.

So this is a classic example of the working mind mode.

Now, supposing, just before the surgery, a colleague doctor comes and whispers in his ear, 'Hey, do you know that you are operating on a very important politician? You better be very careful because if you are not, then your career as a surgeon is finished.'

In this scenario, the surgeon may suddenly find himself thinking of an imaginary future: *What if I botch up this surgery? My career will go down the drain!* This is the thinking mind, which has now kicked in. The surgeon has projected himself into an imaginary future, and then the work that he would otherwise have done so efficiently is now jeopardized.

So the thinking mind is that which takes us away from the Now, and it is the thinking mind that needs to be curbed.

Coming back to your question, when we start witnessing, we can see that the mind is engaged in incessant thinking that is connected to the past or the future. Ninety per cent of the time, it is fear-based thinking: *What will happen to me?*

So it is just a simple seeing of a recurring pattern. It is not even a practice as such. It is not something one has to *work* on. Just that seeing is enough to create a gap between the incessant thinking and the one who is witnessing it.

That is why all the masters often stress the importance of not just reading their words but trying to live their teachings.

N: Some people who are in extreme agony write to me. They are either suffering a critical or terminal illness, or have lost everything. In situations like this, could you give some pointers?

G: I will give you an example of someone who wrote to me. We are talking of an extreme example. He is a young man who is working in Kabul, Afghanistan, running a hotel, and he has a staff of about a hundred people under him. He sent me an email, wherein he said, 'There are so many bombings going on all around that I don't know whether I'll be alive the next minute.' That is the situation, the extreme situation.

Now what happens when you practise Sai Baba's teachings or that of any other master, whom you relate to? You first accept the situation: *This is where I have been placed. If I was not meant to be here, I would not be here.*

This does not mean you like it; it is human nature. You may be uncomfortable with it, but acceptance is the first step. Thereafter, you just take this analysis step by step. In his case, let's say he has accepted that he does not know what the next moment brings. Sometimes, he is at peace. Sometimes, he gets frustrated. So what happens?

The witnessing of *I am at peace* happens as well as that of *Now I am feeling a bit tight and constricted and fearful*. That is when awareness starts kicking in. Otherwise, normally, what you do is, you are so engaged and entangled in this web of thinking that no other vision is possible. But with these teachings, you can see in a very objective way that this is what is happening. At some point, the thinking gets cut off, and you realize, *My God, the thinking mind was really galloping away.*

Now that cutting off is the grace. It is not you as the thinking mind who has cut off the thinking because you were too involved in the thinking. It is the grace, the light of awareness, which makes you realize that you were involved in that stream of thinking.

As this starts happening more and more, it results in a mind which is not engaged in excessive thinking—a mind at peace.

HOW DOES ONE TRULY SURRENDER?

N: I get emails from devotees who are either being harassed by a family member or are in difficult situations in general. Eckhart Tolle [the spiritual teacher well known for his bestseller *The Power of Now*] has spoken about three things you can do in a difficult situation: you can stay in the situation, walk away from it or try to change it. Could you talk about these three modes of resolving a problematic situation and their application in the lives of such devotees?

G: Let us go a bit laterally for now and talk about free will because that comes in here.

The masters have said that there are many aspects, such as our conditioning, our parents, the way we have been brought up, the school we went to and the religion we were born into, which are not in our control. We base our decisions on all this. Our decisions are based on what we think, and our thinking is based on how we have been shaped. So is it truly our decision? We think we are the doers of our actions, but it is not so.

Yet, a decision needs to be made. We cannot sit back and say, *I won't do anything; let God decide*, because that itself is doership.

Now coming to Eckhart Tolle, his book *The Power of Now* is an immense contribution to living life in the present moment. In the book, he has directly addressed this point: *Do I stay? Do I walk away? Or do I try to change it?* This will depend on how the individual is 'designed' to take each step. It has to be thought about and implemented. With the teaching, these options are seen objectively and not as a reaction to the situation. We could say we now respond rather than react to a situation.

Sai Baba has said that everyone comes together on account of rnanubandhan, the cosmic debt of a former relationship. What does it mean? It means, you first cross this hurdle. You accept that this person is an instrument of the Divine, which we've already covered. Once that is done, you see your options before you objectively because your thinking mind is no longer embroiled in the *bandhan*. And then a decision is taken based on true understanding and not as a reaction to the situation.

Ganapati's trunk represents the aligning of the third eye, the eye of wisdom, with the *Manipur Chakra*. When these two are balanced, proper decisions are taken, knowing that the results are not in one's control. The me is not caught in a *chakravyuh*-like situation, where it cannot see a way out, all the while getting sucked in.

There are very few devotees who are so committed to Baba that their whole existence is essentially Baba, and it is a privilege to even know them. Aai is one such example.

These devotees also have difficulties; it's not that they don't. Many things go wrong in their lives as well. But there is an underlying peace that they experience throughout that time as well.

N: Could you speak a little bit about them, the ones who have surrendered to Baba?

G: Yes. That brings us back to the main point—peace of mind. And these devotees are living examples of that. Because they have accepted that life means pleasure and pain. Many of us don't accept that. We run away from pain and only want pleasure all the time, which is not possible.

Just like a river has two banks, we have the banks of pleasure and pain. That is why Nisargadatta Maharaj said, 'Between the banks of pleasure and pain, the river of life flows,' which is, basically, everyone's life.

But we want to be a river with just one bank. It is not possible, because the design of life is duality. When we accept this duality of life, the very nature of life, that is the first step towards peace.

And then we have a master like Sai Baba who gives us so many more dimensions to access this peace.

N: Could you speak a little about that?

G: The Satcharita, which for me is the main work, contains stories operating at two levels. One level is the story itself, and the other level is the peace flowing through the story. When one starts reading it from the prism of the second level, one starts imbibing the peace.

Let's take someone like Aai, for instance. She has seen enough hardships in her life, right? But why has she not lost that sense of peace? It is not because of faith in the way we ordinary people think of faith. Our faith depends on getting the things we want. That is the honest truth. But true faith is the faith that whatever happens is the will of the Lord. Those with such faith are not setting up their will against God's will.

Heaven is to be found in the heart of the man who has total faith that whatever happens is God's will.

The Buddha said that *samsara* is *dukkha*. *Nirvana* is *Shanti*, and they are not two. Likewise, my teacher, Rameshji, would say that life is a prison. We are imprisoned in this body. We are imprisoned by our circumstances. But what we human beings do is we convert what is simple imprisonment into rigorous imprisonment. How? By having a sense of doership. By blaming, hating, condemning, judging and envying others, and feeling guilt and shame for ourselves.

Baba would say that one has to get rid of these tendencies. And all these drop away when you accept that nobody truly does anything. This is called living the teaching. The result is deep peace and equanimity in daily living. This is what Baba means when He says, 'I give people what they want so that they may want what I want to give them.'

N: When I see Aai as compared to some other devotee facing difficult situations that are similar, it seems like it is one's attitude and outlook on life which is very vital in facing them. Could we speak a little bit about how both will respond to the situations and if it is preordained?

Also, if an individual faces the same situation at different times in his life, his response to the event may be totally different as the understanding deepens. Could you speak on that aspect too?

G: I will bring in the example of Nisargadatta Maharaj again here because it beautifully illustrates the answer to your question.

Maharaj was very direct and to the point, and anger would arise every now and then because that was his nature. One day, somebody asked him a question during *satsang*, and he got angry. He said, 'You have been coming to me for so long, and you are asking me such a stupid question?'

So this man bowed down to Maharaj and said, 'But Maharaj, what can I do? God made me stupid.'

And in the next moment, Maharaj burst into laughter.

Now see, this is very important, referring back to your question, which is a very valid point. What we do is that we hold on to anger when it arises. We do not allow ourselves to laugh the next moment. Our mind says, *He made me angry. Now I must act angry, and I will be angry.*

With masters, what they see is that anger arose in their body just like it could arise in another body. So the anger is seen objectively, and then a story is not made around the anger. Each moment is honoured for what it brings. In Maharaj's case, the next moment brought laughter. He did not think, *This man has asked me this question. I got angry. Now I am going to be angry with him throughout the satsang. How dare he ask me this?* There was no such internal dialogue.

Similarly, in our lives, we will be faced with situations all the time, and we may react because we are not Buddhas. We may not be able to control our anger, for example, but with the light of the teachings and of understanding, the involvement in the emotion gets cut off. And that is when the Divine Light of peace shines through.

I will give you an example in a lighter vein.

Once, I was having coffee with two people. Twenty feet away, sitting at a table was a girl wearing a dress.

The person on my left commented, 'Oh, that's such a lovely yellow dress she is wearing.'

And the person on the right responded, 'Don't be silly. It is not a yellow dress. It is a light green dress.'

Now these two kept going on and on about whether the dress was yellow or green.

Finally, the person on my left asked me, 'Isn't the dress yellow?' I said, 'Yes.'

Then when the person on the right asked me, 'Don't you think it's green?' I said, 'Yes.'

Perplexed, they both asked, 'How can you say that the dress is both yellow as well as green?'

I said, 'Look, the two of you have been going on for the last five minutes about the colour of the dress, trying to prove to the other what colour it is. First of all, that girl is not concerned about your opinion about the colour of her dress. Secondly, one of you is seeing it as yellow through his eyes, and the other is seeing it as a shade of green through his eyes. Why don't you just accept that and let it go?'

You see, we are holding everything so tightly to us as if it is the truth. In this case, something as simple as the colour of a dress. But why not just accept that another's point of view can be equally valid as yours? You may not agree with it, but end it there.

Coming back to the teachings, Sai Baba has specifically said, 'Do not engage in slander; do not engage in criticism of others.' I can assure you that many of us who are Sai Baba's devotees do all that. That is our nature.

Exchanges such as this show Sai Baba lovers ways for the teachings to permeate into their cells. That is the beauty of this kind of sharing. Together, we can live the teachings of the masters.

N: Absolutely. And, in fact, once all this stuff that people hold on to falls away, then it frees them up to just *be*. And in that freer space of peace and joy that they begin to experience, they can divert their whole being to Baba as a form or as the formless aspect by doing *sadhana*, whether it's meditation or japa.

Could you talk a little bit about this?

G: The beauty is that this starts happening on its own. We started by saying that Sai Baba has said, 'God is pure Consciousness.' When we no longer focus on individuals, when we understand that it's the same Consciousness functioning through them, this is already happening.

Or you can replace each form with Sai Baba's form. That is also a very common spiritual practice. Why is it happening? It's because one is living the teachings.

It is no longer theory. It's no longer about reading a story in the Satcharita and keeping the book aside; it's about living it. When your mind, instead of being full of thinking, is replaced by thoughts of Sai Baba, of pure Consciousness, then the garbage has been substituted by them.

So it is a natural process. Eckhart Tolle calls it 'Living in the Now' because you are not doing anything to live in the Now, but living in the Now is *happening* because the thinking mind is not engaged in an imaginary future or dead past.

That is why, in some esoteric traditions, in the symbol of the Cross, the horizontal bar represents the dead past and the imaginary future, which is horizontal time. The vertical bar represents the present, which is vertical time. And where both intersect, that is, living in the moment; that is where they say, time stands still.

What does that mean? It means living in the Now.

So it happens.

Nisargadatta Maharaj was asked a question: 'Does it help to be in the presence of a sage?'

Maharaj kept silent for a bit and answered, 'The trees near a sandalwood tree in a forest start emitting the same fragrance.' This means that by just being in the company of a sage, one absorbs and imbibes his qualities.

Now with Sai Baba, how would that work? What does being in Sai Baba's company mean? Having His teachings in mind all the time or having His form in mind, if we prefer that mode. But it cannot be that you are in front of your temple for just fifteen minutes doing puja, and the rest of your day is a mess. Satsang with Sai Baba is with every breath and not as a practice in a corner. What you need to understand is that life, and living it, is meditation. It is not merely a practice. Mind you, I am not trying to negate that. But it is important that it should carry over into your daily living.

When you meditate sitting quietly for fifteen minutes or half an hour, how does that impact your whole day? In meditation, you are witnessing your thoughts. Witnessing is happening without doing anything. Just as you see traffic going by on the road, you are separate from the traffic, you are not running away with the cars, right? You are witnessing the traffic going by on the road.

In meditation, one is giving oneself the chance to witness the thoughts which are coming across the screen of Consciousness. In those fifteen minutes or half an hour, there is awareness of the thoughts, and their witnessing is happening. Now this goes very far because this awareness stays with you for the rest of the day—this separation between what is happening and being the witness of that.

That is why the masters say, 'You are not what happens, but you are the space in which things happen.'

HOW DOES ONE TRULY SURRENDER?

So, similarly, when Sai Baba's teachings are in your consciousness throughout the day, you will feel that you are handling situations differently than you were earlier because you have been living that understanding. That is the beauty of it.

To view the corresponding video, scan the QR code.

3

The Deeper Meaning of Shraddha and Saburi

Nikhil: Could you speak to us about Baba's core teaching of shraddha and saburi, and what devotees could imbibe from it?

Gautam: Sure. Many people have spoken about shraddha and saburi, so I don't have much to add to this. But, perhaps, your viewers could look a little deeper into these two words.

First, let us talk about 'saburi', which means 'patience'. Most of us are being patient impatiently because we desire a certain outcome. So Sai asks us to be patient.

Consequently, we make becoming patient into an exercise. But what Baba is referring to with the word 'patience', according to my understanding, brings us back to the point we were discussing. True patience means living in the NOW, living in the moment.

As [Nisargadatta] Maharaj said, the road is the goal; the journey of life itself is the goal. It's about how we are living it and not a goal to achieve in the end, towards which we are rushing at an insane speed, with our thoughts all over the place.

So when the word 'saburi' is used, it means 'living in the moment'. That is when we are truly patient. We have faith—coming to the word 'shraddha'—that whatever the outcome, all we can do is put in our best; the results are not in our control. In whose control are they? The Divine's, Sai Baba's. If we truly accept that the results are not in our control, what automatically happens is saburi, you see.

But what we do is that we are trying to wait for a particular outcome to happen according to our liking. That is why when we say that we are being patient, we have to look deeply to see whether we are really being patient or are merely telling ourselves that we are being patient.

Shraddha and saburi are intimately connected because, with true patience, the natural outcome is shraddha, or faith, that whatever is meant for my highest good is going to happen, not the faith that I will get what I want. Often, after getting what we desire, we realize that it is not good for us.

Let's say we are hankering after a specific relationship and we do manage to get into the relationship. Six months later, we realize that it's an incompatible relationship. That is the limitation of our thinking that we know what is good for us. This is a big problem because it is circling back to the me: *I know what is good for me.* Instead, leave it to the Lord to know what is good for you.

I received an email yesterday from a girl about her and a boy having a relationship, when another girl came into the picture. So now the boy is distracted. She wrote to me, 'Now, after understanding the teachings, I have the full acceptance that this happened because it had to happen. I am not blaming the second girl. I don't hate her. I have now seen that my relationship with this boy was great while it lasted. Whether or not it continues, because this new person has come on the scene, is God's will.'

This is called living the teaching. This girl said she has totally accepted that this was meant to happen; otherwise, it would not have happened. Now whichever way the boy moves, she is very clear that there is no blame. She is neither blaming him nor is she blaming the girl. But she will witness whether he stays in this relationship or moves away, and this will bring her peace of mind.

This is the essence of Baba's leelas. They are there for us to discover ourselves and understand what is happening. But we get stuck in reading them just as stories that have nothing to do with us. Although these stories are about what happened in Baba's life, they are opportunities given to us in a subtle manner to show us the way.

The beautiful messages which come through these stories are the key takeaways because the stories stay in one's mind. That is why

LIVING WITH FAITH AND PATIENCE

many spiritual masters have also given messages through stories. Plus, these were events that actually happened, and were written down. So for us, it is as if we were there at the time they happened. They are invaluable. But the point is, they must be constantly applied in our own lives.

Coming back to shraddha and saburi, these are important pointers, and they need to be thoroughly looked at and *lived* because we don't live with patience. Something comes into our mind and our thoughts run helter-skelter. But to live with patience is very crucial to the journey of self-discovery because, with true living, which is living with patience, comes the acceptance that this is His leela. Whatever is happening is meant to happen, and I have true faith that it is God who knows best and not this little me. That is when one starts living Sai Baba's teachings.

N: It seems like the biggest hurdle is this little me in everything. The lesser the identification with this me, the more the dropping off of the self-concern. Then the light of Consciousness will shine by itself.

G: Absolutely. And when does this little me come into being? The ego surfaces at the age of one-and-a-half or two years, when the baby realizes, *If I do something, I will get what I want.* Till then, the Universe provides for the baby; it gets its milk from the mother's breast.

But then the baby starts realizing, *If I cry, my mother will come running.* That is when the ego starts being formed. *If I do something, something will happen.*

So even the creation of the ego is not something we are responsible for; it is Consciousness becoming identified with a specific body and name as a separate entity. Thereafter, we start living life as this separate entity based on doership.

One example I give is of a child running around in the house. Now the nature of children is to run around, and the child knocks down an expensive object, a curio, which the parent paid a lot of money for.

So what happens? The parent screams at the child: 'What have you done? You should have been more careful!' But the child was just being a child. It knocked down an object accidentally, not knowing its value. The value is assigned by the parent who paid for that object.

This child now starts growing up thinking, *I did something bad.* And this conditioning starts becoming progressively stronger, with the child constantly thinking, *I did this and I didn't do that.*

We grow up with this sense of doership. The ego becomes encrusted with the notion *This is me. This is what I do, and this is how I am separate from others.* So we become these bundles of separate identities.

The journey of discovery is to discover that this sense of separation is not the truth—that if the concept of doership is dropped, everyone is seen as an instrument of the Divine. That is why my teacher, Rameshji, said, 'Love is the absence of separation, and separation is the absence of love.'

In a similar vein, when the great sage Ramana Maharshi was asked, 'How can one truly love another?' he replied, 'But there are no others.' What did he mean? What he meant was that everything is seen as Consciousness, as the Divine. In that sense, there is no separation.

Of course, in manifestation, we are separate objects. We are not merging into each other in a vibrational field and living a different reality. But we are living with this understanding, with this knowing, that there is truly no separation.

So that becomes the way by which we live our daily life because, ultimately, it boils down to peace of mind in daily living.

Nirvana is Shanti.

N: I have observed that people practise patience, or they think they do, but they have a desire or some wish they feel Baba will fulfil at some point in time. And they have the faith that Baba will do it. And He may, if it is good for them; if it is meant to happen, it will.

However, this personal me, which has decided it wants something, in a very subtle way, has not surrendered to Baba yet. It still says, *I will be patient, I will have faith,* but, in a way, this is very conditional.

Could you talk about how the devotee can see through this facade, so to speak, and start practising unconditional faith and patience?

G: Let's address this with an example.

Supposing, God forbid, you are really unwell. Really unwell, to the extent that the doctors say that it's a fifty-fifty chance. And let's say you are eighty-five years old. Now two things could happen. One, you have complete faith that Baba is going to make you okay. And the other, you have complete faith that whatever is best for you will happen.

Now, you see, the me has such tremendous faith that it will become okay and survive this illness. You may recover, but the rest of your life may be in bed. Whereas, in some circumstances, the best thing that could happen is that the ailing body comes to an end.

So, the limitation of the me is that you think you know what is best for you, and you will see it through; this is your goal, and this is where your faith rests.

But is it the best thing for you? Supposing life is such a burden for you from that point on, that you feel, *My God, why did I wish this?* Then you live to regret your wish.

When you have a specific faith based on what you think, there's always an underlying tension. That tension can become frustration and your faith begins to waver when you feel that time is passing by and you are not getting what you want.

Although you believe you have faith, it may not be true. You may just *think* you have faith. That is why we keep coming back again and again to the point that true faith is the total acceptance that whatever happens is God's will. With that true faith, you will not have sleepless nights.

N: In your example you raised a very important point about the possibility of one becoming bedridden. Baba would say that there were many devotees with ailments who would pray to Him to save them, even when He was in the body, and in some cases, they would pass away.

But only He could see their past lifetimes and their future incarnation, and that continuing this life would become an impediment to their progress.

G: There, you have it!

N: Exactly. So this is something people must understand for themselves and their loved ones: In the eventuality of a dear one's passing, the human mind cannot judge and understand what Baba knows, because He sees the whole picture, whereas we see a very limited vision—as if through a keyhole. It is only Baba who can see the whole picture, so one must have faith and trust in that.

G: Yes. My teacher used the example of a huge canvas or a huge painting. Since you are a painter, you will understand this.

Let's say it's a hundred feet in length, and it's in a museum. At night, you enter the premises using a small pen torch, and you walk across to look at the painting. You are only seeing that sliver of painting that is lit up, which is, let's say, a few inches, but everything else is dark, right?

So we individuals can see only that. We cannot see the bigger picture, the magnificent tapestry of Creation, which someone like Sai Baba can. We don't have that information with us, but we base all our wants, all our needs, on just that thin sliver we have seen.

That is why it is best that it is left to the masters and to God to take care of our journey of life.

I would like to give another example here. There is a book called *A Search in Secret India* by Paul Brunton, in which he mentions that he had gone to Varanasi, where he met India's leading astrologer at the time.

Brunton asked him, 'Do you read your own horoscope?'

The astrologer looked at Brunton and said, 'The day I started accepting that whatever happens is God's will, I stopped reading my horoscope.'

N: That sums it up.

I'd like to probe a little more into this for devotees—that only a master can see the full picture. If you consider everyday life events, even small things, you realize that you truly don't know what is good for yourself. Wouldn't that be almost like a clue to understanding that only Baba sees the bigger picture for you, and then, you could make this a sadhana?

G: It is no longer a practice; it becomes a way of living because you start looking at whatever happens in your day through this lens.

Take the example of driving. When you get your driver's licence, you're still new to driving; you're struggling through heavy traffic, you're nervous, you're tense. Now let's say four years have passed, and you're driving down the same road, which, four years ago, you were really stressed about driving down. You finish the journey and say, *My God, this drive was so peaceful, but when I started driving four years ago, it was so stressful.*

So also with these teachings. When you look back, you realize that you have changed. What you would have said or done or spoken in the past, without being exposed to the teachings, would be so different from what it is today. Then you look back and see how it has impacted your life.

Some people see this difference in a few months; others see it over a larger time frame, but the main thing is the seeing. That is the beauty. I think Baba is so compassionate that by exposing us to the teachings, He is giving us an opportunity for transformation. So let us translate them into experience and daily living, to walk the talk, as they say.

To view the corresponding video, scan the QR code.

4

Committing to One Spiritual Path

Nikhil: This particular discussion will be themed on the difference between spiritual seekers and devotees.

Many people come to the spiritual path, even Sai Baba's, and then they jump from one teaching or one teacher to another. And at the end of the journey, they stay committed to one master or one teaching, becoming that master's devotees.

Could you speak about this journey from being a seeker to a devotee, ending in commitment to only one master?

Gautam: At one of my talks, a gentleman in his late fifties told me that he had, since the last twenty to twenty-five years, tried many spiritual practices: *Reiki, Pranic Healing, Kriya Yoga,* and so on and so forth. Then he asked me, 'How will I know which is the path for me? When will I know where this journey will end?'

Now firstly, the very fact that he asked this question meant that his journey had not ended. But more importantly, did he know *what* he was looking for? Because if he was looking for something, and then he found it, then he would know that the journey was over.

Many of us don't ask ourselves what it is that we are looking for through these practices or teachings which we come across. Consequently, we start pursuing practice after practice because that is the nature of the ego—to acquire, to add more knowledge to the me, to do more things—in this case, spiritual things.

So once you ask yourself, *What is it that I am looking for?* and you get the answer, then you will know what to look for, and when you find it, the journey is over.

This is where things become extremely simple for us because what everyone is looking for, whether they know it or not, is peace of mind. Once you know what it is you're looking for, that is, peace of mind, look back on all the practices you have done so far. They may have brought to you different dimensions of awareness, knowledge, etc. But did any one of them give you more peace than the others? Ask yourself that question. And if your answer is *No, I am not at peace. I haven't found what I was looking for*, then continue the journey till you have found it.

Now regarding your question, once I know what a particular teaching is giving me, then that becomes my focus, my resting place. But if I don't know that, I am not going to know how it is impacting my life.

When Nisargadatta Maharaj was asked whether one should stick to one practice or try various paths, he gave a very simple answer: 'Do you get water by digging one deep well in one place, or many shallow wells all over the field?' So what he was pointing to was to stay with one teaching that gives you peace; resting in it, living it, breathing it.

Many of us don't allow ourselves this opportunity because the nature of the mind is to wander all over the place, including spiritual wandering. What happens is that we are operating at just a certain level. A seeker may just be curious, looking around, has a taste of things, is not sure, is unsettled, is exploring. Whereas a devotee is devoted to the teaching. Both ways are valid. But the point here is that one should not be lost in the jungle of everything available.

Masters say that when you stay focused on one path, which is giving you what you are looking for, then going deep into it is what is required. How? In daily living, not as a theory. This is important because, otherwise, your life may go by although this opportunity is available to you.

Let's take an example of a devotee of Sai Baba's. Something or someone may come along in his life, and he gets a taste through that teaching or that teacher, of the depth of peace which Sai Baba was referring to. He may have read about it in a book, but now he has got an experience of it through somebody. His mind might say, *Oh, I must ignore this because Sai Baba is my guru.* But, deep down, something touches him. This representation of Baba has come to give him the taste of that peace that Baba has been talking about because everything is Baba.

We have to be open and receptive, and see how the teaching comes back to us through whichever form it may choose. We shouldn't be dogmatic and say, 'That alone is the truth and this is not.' We cannot compartmentalize.

That is when the journey stays alive. There has to be fluidity. Water is fluid; it moves around the rocks. It does not push the rocks out of the way. Our lives have to be fluid, and we have to trust that the river is leading to the ocean; where else will it go?

That is the journey of life.

N: You've raised a very important point. A seeker, at some stage, will come to a teaching or a master, with whom they will experience peace. For example, if they follow Sai Baba, they will go to Shirdi and experience Baba's grace and feel peace. However, it's also a pivotal point. They can either continue running from one teacher, teaching and sadhana to the next, or once they feel this peace and change, stick to the master and the teachings.

Could you speak a little bit about that specific point in their journey?

G: This, again, is what we were talking about because it is only the wavering mind which does not stay in one place. When you have tasted peace, be it through Baba's teachings or any other teachings, you know what it is that you have tasted.

For instance, if you are a goldsmith, you would want to work with gold. You're not going to be happy with silver or copper.

In spiritual life, the gold we are referring to is peace of mind. When you come across the teaching that gives you that peace, automatically, you will not feel like going elsewhere. But if that teaching has not given you peace, then you will wander.

That is why it is very crucial to stay with the teaching once you get the taste of it because it has already brought you home. It is the wandering mind which goes all over the place.

I will give you my own example. I met my teacher at the beginning of 2000, and I felt it had a deep impact on my life. Over the next ten years, I met innumerable masters. I had the opportunity because I was in spiritual publishing, plus, somehow, I came across many spiritual masters on my journey, and I enjoyed meeting all of them. I imbibed a lot from them, but every time I met them, I knew that my home was at the feet of my master because his teaching had graced my life completely. So while I was happy to meet other teachers, it was also clear to me that I had found my pond of peace, and I automatically kept coming back to it.

If the mind does not know what it is looking for, it is going to be on this endless journey of going all over the place. If you have found your peace with Sai Baba's teachings, that doesn't mean you shut yourself off from what the world has to offer spiritually, but you know your resting place. You see, someone else can come along with a message of Sai Baba's, which you have not discovered yet in your readings or understanding of Sai Baba. As Sai Baba Himself says, 'Everyone is an instrument of Me.'

Thus, you keep yourself open to that dimension also, while knowing that you have found what you are looking for. You should be open and receptive. But let's say you are going to a particular living teacher today, and you come across another living teacher, and you are confused: *Is this one my teacher, or is that one my teacher?* That is the nature of the mind—to be confused. This confusion can go on and on. You may meet ten more teachers because you don't know the criteria on which you are asking the question. But if you ask yourself, *Whose teaching is a validation of my life's experience? I can see the events in my life through the prism of that teaching, and it makes total sense; it shines a light on who I am and what has happened to me since childhood,* you will get your answer.

So it could be the first teacher you meet or the second one. Deep down, you will know. Supposing you feel that the second teacher has really opened your eyes, it doesn't make the first teacher invalid because, in reality, it's one journey.

When someone asked my teacher, 'Is it possible to have many gurus?' he replied, 'Yes, but at any one point in time, you will have one guru. That is the first thing. You can't have two gurus at the same time. Secondly, eventually, you will know who your guru is.'

Supposing you have met three, four or five gurus, there will be one who has touched your heart the most. At that time, the seeking ends, and that is when you settle into that teaching. So this is a very important pointer for devotees of any master, that you have to be open, because now you know what it is that you're looking for.

It is not a judgement on your relationship with a particular teacher if you happen to resonate with someone else at a more intimate and deeper level because it is your personal journey. These are just milestones along the way. But it could be that you meet someone and you feel, *Now I am resting in peace, and I don't want to travel any further.*

N: As one is impacted by the teaching and the presence of a teacher, a sacred bond develops between them and the master. Then one almost forgets the teaching, forgets enlightenment, forgets wanting anything. It's a bond of pure love.

I would like you to talk about the aspect where a devotee begins to care for their master's well-being.

G: Why does this happen? Because the master or the guru is none other than the Higher Self of the disciple. My mother has seen this visually, where the Higher Self identifies with a form, which guides the person as a guru.

That is how the whole guru-disciple relationship comes into creation. There is no separation. It appears that there is a guru and a disciple. But from the guru's point of view, he does not see the disciple as separate from him. It is the disciple who makes that distinction initially.

The nature of the relationship with your Higher Self is by default one of love, and that love starts getting expressed in many ways, not only in the dualistic way of the me-and-the-other kind of love that we are so used to. It is truly the love of God, where you feel so connected. It's as if you are doing everything for your Self.

So if you are close to a living teacher and helping him in his tasks, that is one way it manifests. For me, it manifested in editing the books of my teacher: sitting with him and going through the manuscripts in detail. That was my way because that was my background; so, I could offer that skill set.

Some people may not have that background, and their love may be expressed in other ways, like taking care of the master's financial needs if required, offering their time for some service, and so on. But in whatever way it happens, it's a spontaneous outpouring of love. It is not that one is *doing* something.

This is called love in action because it is love for the Beloved, and that is a very intimate love. It is very deep because it's not love between two individuals.

That is why you see that in many cases where there are living masters, there are people around them who are offering some sort of support service or network.

I am sure now, in your case, if you take your channel for example, you must have encountered people from all over the world, considering it's a YouTube channel, who are coming together and offering support in whatever way they can because they have been moved by the teachings. So, ultimately, you are only moved if you feel something within yourself.

I'll give you this example.

Someone had come to me saying how the teaching has impacted them; how I have changed their life and so on. But one thing we must bear in mind is the example I have spoken of in the past: before email, you had the postman delivering letters to your house. So teachers are like postmen. They deliver a message to you, and you read the message. The message has an effect on your life. The teacher is the messenger, and the teacher himself was given a similar message through another messenger. Because he was influenced so much, it is out of love and compassion that he is passing it on.

And the message is ancient. The same message is coming down through various lineages, teachers and masters, and being delivered to your doorstep. This is the grace of the masters.

So when you read that letter and it opens your eyes to a different kind of reality, then you feel like giving all of yourself to that. And in that, you've already given yourself in terms of the teaching because it has impacted you through the form of the postman who delivered it. You realize that he carried with him this very important teaching.

So when you want to contribute, it has to come naturally. This happens on its own. You cannot force it, because it is only if the teaching has deeply changed your life that this spontaneous arising and giving will come up.

N: On this subject, just on an ending note, for seekers who are at the beginning of their journey, would you say it's of utmost importance to remember and know this pointer, that ultimately, you have to settle down on one path, one master, one teaching, and if you're fortunate enough that God has put you at the feet of a genuine master, you surrender there?

G: Yes, ultimately it is that, provided you know what you are looking for. Because you could be spending time at the feet of a master or with a certain teaching that is not delivering it to you.

You may think, *I must stick to one path*, because someone has put this idea in your head or something in your own mind tells you so, but if it is not influencing you and your life, it may be time to move on.

N: So once you find peace and it has a profound effect on you, then you stick to it. That's the bottom line.

G: It is not even an option. There is no doership involved. You will not feel the need to move out of it.

To view the corresponding video, scan the QR code.

5

The Pitfall of Hankering After Miracles

Nikhil: Sai Baba's miracles can become an obstacle if devotees start hankering for them.

Firstly, is that true? Could you speak on that, please?

Gautam: Miracles are a bit of a complex subject because, invariably, we humans classify miracles as something out of the ordinary and positive that happens to us, which would not have happened, were it not for divine intervention.

As other masters have pointed out—especially masters on the Advaita path, such as Nisargadatta Maharaj—what about the miracle of daily living? Life has decided to give you this wonderful day. Isn't that a miracle?

The Earth you are standing on is rotating on its axis as well as revolving around the Sun, at different speeds. The Sun is shining. The force of gravity is enabling you to be here. You're gifted with the senses. Isn't all that a miracle?

Isn't breathing a miracle? Are you able to control your breathing? Or does it happen? Isn't the blood coursing through your veins a miracle? Are you doing it? Or is there a Higher Force which is doing it?

The miracle of nature is protecting us, allowing us to exist, but that gets taken for granted. The me comes in and says, *Now, if this happens, I will consider it a miracle.*

So the lens has shifted focus onto the little me, which wants a certain outcome, which it knows is unlikely, but with its full faith, will make it likely. And then, when it happens once, the me starts hankering after what it has defined as a miracle. *We* have put the label of 'miracle' on it. God has not classified it as a miracle.

So we have to be very careful with the phenomenon of miracles because, then, we as individuals start looking for miracles in our life. But what about the larger picture? What if that which you consider a miracle is harming someone else unbeknown to you?

Our outlook is so narrow that our whole journey starts shifting towards trying to manifest miracles, which becomes me-centric, rather than embracing the miraculous Universe and existence, knowing that it is intelligent enough to take care of its Creation. That is the biggest miracle.

Miracles can strengthen the ego because you think that you know how to get miracles to happen in your life. There is a very popular book in the West, in the esoteric tradition, called *A Course in Miracles*. It's more than a thousand pages long. I have read it, and I found two sentences therein, both of which translate to 'The ultimate miracle is peace of mind.' I have even underlined them. And the teaching in that book, which also considers finding peace of mind through relationships a miracle, is astonishingly close to the Advaitic teachings. But, unfortunately, we are looking at *events* as miracles.

Finding Sai Baba in every form is a miracle. A true miracle. Sai Baba's teachings also ask us to look deeper and go within. That is where the miracles take place.

Let's say you are involved in a situation that you don't like, but you have the total acceptance that the other person is an instrument through which the situation is unfolding. When you start looking at things that way, that is a miracle.

Otherwise, we just live, waiting for signs and miracles to happen. We hope they will happen and are even convinced about it. But that is still operating in the dimension of something happening, which we perceive as miraculous.

Sometimes, Sai Baba's leela may happen. One does not even want it or think of it, but that happens by His will. And when a true miracle like that happens, something that He ordains, it will have a transformative effect on the devotees, provided they are receptive. But if the devotees have a fixed vision of what is a true miracle, it will not happen.

N: True. So in that case, when someone experiences an event of Baba's, first, why is He gracing a devotee with that, and second, how should the devotee be receptive? Some pointers on that?

G: The 'why' question cannot be answered. As my teacher said, a painting can never know why its painter painted it.

But the pointer is that a miracle does not require me to play any part in the miracle. That may sound a bit complex, but what it is pointing to is that it is the absence of the me with its sense of doership that enables miracles to happen. We need to get out of the way.

What happens is, we step in, and then we decide what we want as the outcome. The me becomes very convinced about it, whereas the reality is just the opposite. This wanting results in our imagining things and forcing perceptions, convincing ourselves that what happened is a miracle. We see things which, in reality, are not there.

People try to look for images or find something non-existent. So that is up to them and the journey they want to take. For example, someone may come across some image and spontaneously see Shiva in it, which is absolutely valid. Wonderful! But now they make it their mission to look at images everywhere to see if they can find forms of God in them. And when that does not happen, they get frustrated.

What is offered spontaneously is accepted and acknowledged by the person receiving it, whereas someone else may not see Shiva in that image. But it is valid for the one who saw it because, ultimately, it's what they have seen.

The me then wants to multiply that experience across various events, and then, instead of being focused on daily living and what life has to offer, it starts looking for images in which it can find forms of God, and that becomes its mission. So it's trying to repeat an experience which was not in its control in the first place. The first time it saw an image, and presuming it saw Shiva there, that was not in its control. Having had the experience, it wants to start controlling, having multiple experiences.

And that is the pitfall.

But supposing you had that experience and you acknowledged it thoughtfully and let go of it, if and when it were to happen again in the future, you would bow down to it and be grateful. Then you wouldn't start hunting for images which show forms of God.

However, that is what the human mind does due to the burden of memory. It has the memory of the first event, but it doesn't realize that it was not in its control.

So leave it to that same Force which brought about the first miracle for you, to do its job as and when it's meant to. You simply keep out of the way.

I have a friend who would say that every morning this was his only prayer: 'Today, I promise myself I will get out of my own way.'

N: Talking of that, I want to speak to you about desirelessness; when you have no desire whatsoever. In fact, the lack of desire is given to you.

I distinctly remember your sharing a story about Lord Krishna in one of your talks, where He took a farmer's cow away from him, and gave a rich man much more. Could you, if you don't mind, share that story?

G: That is a very common story, where I think Narada and Krishna visit two houses. At the first house, a rich man takes care of them, and the Lord says, 'I will bless you by giving you more riches.'

To which Narada responds, 'My Lord, you should have done the opposite. This guy has too much.'

And then they go to a poor farmer's house, who has only one cow, and Krishna tells him, 'I'll bless you by taking away your cow.' At this point, Narada is shocked.

So Krishna says, 'No, I have done the right thing because if I take away his last attachment, he will come closer to Me.'

This sounds very harsh, but what is the meaning behind this story? We get so identified and attached to objects due to maya.

You see? Now let me use a lateral example.

I know someone very wealthy, whose passion is to collect watches—expensive watches. Nothing wrong with it. You have the means, you like it. There's no judgement on that. But what happens is that every time he buys an expensive watch, in two weeks, the pleasure he derived from it is over. He sees another watch and wants to buy that. This is because he is deriving his sense of self from the watch.

So, at some point in his journey, when and if it is God's will, this person will himself reach the conclusion that acquiring objects is endless, and he will reach a point where, because of the surplus of wealth and objects, he will realize that these are not giving him true happiness in life. Then his spiritual journey will begin because he realizes that objects are transient and their value is short-lived. That has been his experience so far with each watch he has acquired. Sooner or later, a question arises: What is it that does not depend on an object, which I can derive value from?

So these stories point to that. Coming back to Krishna and the cow story, it is not that God is being cruel by taking the cow away. What God is trying to show is 'Look what you are identified with in your life and what you are deriving your sense of self from.'

That is why it is common that on the spiritual journey you start losing interest in material things, not as a deliberate act but because you know that they are not really valuable. You are searching for pure gold, but these toys do not give you the satisfaction of having it. Why do you think ashrams, for example, are simple places? Why does your room in the ashram not have curios and objects? Because the journey is now within; it is an internal journey, not an external one.

N: Then could one see this as a sign of progress as one matures in their devotion, and if Baba gives some signs, without one seeking them?

G: Absolutely. It is a sign of progress.

N: Especially on the Baba path.

G: It is very beautiful when that happens because it happens on its own.

N: So it is the journey from seeking to being given grace by Baba. We see it as that, and it's encouragement.

G: Totally.

N: For those devotees of Baba's who have heard stories about Him but have not experienced Him first-hand, it's very natural to feel, *Even I should get something.* Could you say something about that?

G: If you ask me, they are even luckier. Because, like we just discussed, those who have had an experience start hankering after it, and they think they are special compared to those who have not had those experiences. I have seen that also.

N: Could you speak a little more about this feeling of being someone special? Because that is essentially the pitfall.

G: It is the ego which feels special, and that is the pitfall. But if I am Sai Baba's devotee, and I don't need those miracles, yet I am firm in my belief, then that is being a true devotee. Because I know that Baba is with me. That is amazing. When one sees that, it is so beautiful.

It's all relative. Let's say if Baba comes to you in a dream, ultimately, it is your perception. And again, if He does not come to someone else, it doesn't mean He's not there for them. Maybe you needed this dream more than the other person who didn't have the dream.

It reminds me of something I read in a book on Sathya Sai Baba. A millionaire said that he started feeling very proud that Baba had put him in charge of the introductions before Baba's talks. So one day, he went and asked Baba something to this effect: 'I feel great when I am on stage with you, but why me? I mean, you've chosen me from all these people here. It's a great thing.'

And Baba told him, 'My son, you are only there because you need it more than all the others in the audience. Because if you didn't have that proximity to me, you would have been a mess. So don't fool yourself that you are special.'

But we take it the other way; we take it that the person who has had a vision is the special one. Being special comes from the ego because it means that the me, as separate from others, is more special.

But the truly special one is the one who is completely devoted to Baba, vision or no vision.

Can God differentiate between all His children as to who is more special than the other? But that is how we perceive it.

That is why, when someone asked Rameshji to sum up his teachings in one sentence, he said, 'Love each and every one *as if* you created them.'

And that includes people you don't like.

N: Put them first, at the top of the list.

To view the corresponding video, scan the QR code.

6

Being the Black Sheep

Nikhil: There are many devotees or spiritual aspirants, especially the young ones, who take to spirituality and start changing their lifestyle. They also lose interest in things that are typically worldly. Consequently, their families and the people around them cannot understand and accept these changes in their behaviour.

Naturally, this causes conflict between the seekers and their family members as the latter's expectations and projections are not complied with. They feel that they are losing their grip on the member who has turned spiritual, and this torments them.

Could we discuss this, please?

Gautam: Yes, it is extremely common.

For example, when you evolve on your spiritual journey, you find that you're losing interest in your current set of friends. You can no longer gossip with them and share common interests because these don't appeal to you anymore. So you feel isolated. Also, your friends stop calling you because they feel you have become a bore. But the consolation is that worldly things don't interest you anymore because your journey has become a spiritual one—your journey home, so to speak.

So I would say that the strength, when one loses one's circle of friends because of one's journey, is to know that what is not of primary importance to life and living is being dropped and that you are going after gold.

And it is painful. Why? Because these are our past identifications and conditionings which are being let go of. That is always a painful process. It is very rare that one is very happy that all that is going away.

So know that that, which one is identified with and is based on conditioning, is being moved aside. You are not even doing it. It's a natural part of the process of spiritual evolution.

Of course, this phenomenon becomes more complex with family as you are living with them. There is a lot of control being exercised by the parents and the siblings too, if one has them.

That is why, part of the reason that sages like Ramana Maharshi ran away from home was because they couldn't deal anymore with that dimension. Their path was clear to them.

So, yes, one can understand the parents' concern because they feel that their child is not going to be able to earn a living and survive in society. These are genuine concerns, also because the spiritual path tends to become an excuse for not doing anything. The ego tends to abuse this path. But the genuine aspirants know deep in their heart that their spiritual pursuit is authentic.

And if it is not, then you cannot fool yourself. You can deceive others for some time, but not yourself—not for long.

N: As we discussed in the earlier interview, there are signs by which you will know whether you are genuinely on the path. You lose interest in materialistic pursuits. Things of the world that exert a pull on the average person and which are usually fear-based start to dissipate.

But this doesn't sit well with the family members because they are concerned about the aspirant's survival. They do not understand that the devotee has completely surrendered to Baba.

G: Yes, but this is a delicate matter, like I said, because the spiritual path can be abused.

The fact is that I have to live and work in the world for my living unless I'm one of those rare cases who's happy living in an ashram for the rest of my life. But one needs to know for oneself.

Okay, let's not take such an extreme example. Let's say my family and I have different worldviews. I show no interest when they are discussing politics at the dinner table or talking about something which I don't resonate with at all. So I tell them: 'Look, this is no longer what I occupy my mind with, so please respect that. However, you are most welcome to engage in it among yourselves.'

It has to be a mutually understood relationship. It cannot be one of opposition where I say, 'Oh, now I don't want to be with you.' It cannot be one of exclusion. It has to be one of understanding and accepting that everyone is playing their role according to their blueprint.

Eckhart Tolle gives this beautiful example of two people in a relationship. When one of them is intensely agitated, what the other could do to prevent this reactivity in the form of an argument or conflict is be the witnessing presence. Because if one of the two is the witnessing presence, then there is no rebound possible. You can't argue with a fully conscious person.

So when a person is considered the black sheep of the family because of their spiritual leanings, it is a crucial part of their journey.

N: Yes.

G: Although it is painful, it is a learning for that person. Also, it's a pointer to them that now their journey is different. We must respect and accept that people are on their own journey.

A twenty-year-old boy wrote to me saying that he is now fully on the spiritual path; he's read books by all the masters, and he's loving it. But he says, 'I can't bear my friends because they all are going on drinking binges over weekends.'

So I answered, 'See, these are strong words. You must accept that they are on their journey like you are on your journey. Now, if you derive your sense of self from these relationships, you will still be in them because you're identified with them. Right? On the other hand, if you don't, then don't go out with them. But don't judge them.'

At that age, youngsters are dealing with so much in life already. Some people loosen up and speak more freely when they drink. So the relationship involves the feeling that the individual has after drinking. It's a very complex thing.

You may be on your spiritual journey and feel that you don't want to indulge in 'all this nonsense'. But you have to understand that their journey is theirs, and your journey is yours. You may have a preference, but you cannot start judging them and think that they are wasting their time. How do you know that? They will come on to their own spiritual journeys if and when they are destined to.

When we create this separation, because we are on a spiritual journey and our family or friends are not, we make ourselves stand on higher ground, thinking, *I am the spiritual one. My family does not understand it.* We have to be careful of this also.

N: Ram Dass, I think, had said something very relevant: 'If you feel you're so enlightened, go spend a week and live with your parents.'

This is very beautiful, I feel, because, regardless of whether the family accepts it or not, on one level, if the spiritual aspirant is sincere and they can go beyond reacting to a situation and they can stay conscious, something has to change.

The family will do everything possible to provoke a reaction from the aspirant, and handling this, in itself, can then become a sadhana by staying conscious and seeing it through.

I have seen this in many cases: if, due to sufficient trust in Baba, a genuine awakening in one member of the family happens, then a certain change in the family comes about in time.

G: Absolutely. Furthermore, our scriptures say that if one member of a family is awakened or enlightened, it impacts seven generations. And don't forget Maharaj's beautiful words when he was asked if there was any benefit of physically being near a guru. He replied that the trees around a sandalwood tree in the forest start emitting the same fragrance. [Refer to talk 2.]

Your forest is your home, and your family members are part of it. So the way you are is bound to affect those around you. If you are on the spiritual journey and you feel that others in your family are not, setting an example by the way you treat them and look at the relationship is bound to create an impact. When others around you see that you are more 'present', you are more accepting of situations, it is bound to influence them.

So rather than creating this divide of me versus them through an internal dialogue—*They are like this, I am like that*—just be a living example of the path you are following. Use your judgement to stay away and not engage in the daily drama of reactivity as it surfaces and, at the same time, be a beacon of change. Be the Sun, which shines its light equally on all. Try not to reserve your love for a specific family member or friend. Rather, give it even to someone you don't like. The people you don't like—those who push your buttons the most—are your greatest teachers. In fact, you should be more grateful to them because they are showing you aspects of your ego, of what bugs you. So, in a sense, it is a gift; an opportunity to look within.

N: It is a nice approach as it is a good chance to work on oneself.

One of the keywords here is 'non-reactivity'; as they say, '*Tali ek haath se nahin bajti* [It takes two hands to clap].'

Even in situations that are not spiritual, pressure from family and society is prevalent. Introverts are expected to talk and socialize, and live up to certain expectations.

G: Totally.

N: I think you raised something beautiful: realizing that everyone has their own views and that it's not about me versus you. It can become a different dynamic, where your point of view is communicated nicely and you are given your space. Everyone else can pursue their own way of life, and conflict is reduced. Otherwise, that burden of expectation becomes very difficult to handle.

G: That, and also one more point: as my guru said, parents need to understand that their children come with their own destinies. What parents do is they try to control the destiny of the child, which we can understand from a point of view of concern. But if parents are also aware of this, they can acknowledge the child's spiritual leanings and trust the Universe, that maybe this is the child's journey.

That is why, as part of the gurukul system in the olden days, a child's horoscope was consulted by astrologers to see its inclination and to guide the parents.

To exercise too much control over a child is to not accept that the Universe knows best and that your child will be taken care of, provided your basic concerns for the child are taken into consideration and explained to the child.

N: For some sincere devotees, these spiritual inclinations increase in intensity. I believe this is mentioned in *Autobiography of a Yogi*. Also in *The Gospel of Sri Ramakrishna*, Ramakrishna Dev talks about a specific prayer to God to reduce one's worldly responsibilities, so one can spend more time in devotion. Now this happens when there is sincere devotion, where it has crossed a particular threshold.

I have felt, and I have practised staying conscious and afloat in an undesirable situation by using all my energy to pray and surrender at Baba's feet, saying, *Baba, You know what is best, I wish to surrender to You, and I leave this at Your feet*, rather than trying to take the burden on myself, thinking, *Oh, I have to break these shackles that are binding me.*

Could you comment on that?

G: We tend to do that, but we have to be pragmatic in life. We have to trust that at the appropriate time, circumstances may change to make us comfortable where we are.

We must accept that this timing is not in our hands. In our endeavour to fast-forward the process, we try to blame people and impose our wishes on them.

For example, I have to earn a living and, at the same time, I don't want all these worldly responsibilities. But I have to acknowledge that I need to earn enough money and that maybe the undesirable situation is going to go on for some time. I have to trust that God knows best, and at the appropriate time, what has to happen will happen.

That is once again where shraddha and saburi come in because we get impatient on our spiritual journey; we get restless.

N: I see a very common pitfall among many spiritual aspirants: many of them have some specific goal in mind where they feel at some point they will reach some experience or some shift. Then what happens is that the journey is not as important as the end, whereas, I think that in a lot of the Zen traditions, they say the journey itself is the destination.

G: That is what [Nisargadatta] Maharaj said: 'The road is the goal.' [Refer to talk 3.]

Imagine you have a goal, and on that journey, you're trampling over everyone; you're complaining about situations and abusing people. What kind of a journey is that?

All our journeys have the same end—death. We're all heading there. What kind of relationships are there on your journey? Are they honoured relationships? Are you treading gently on the path? Are you treading in awareness? Or is your thinking mind full of garbage?

Are you walking, enjoying the scenery, the sky, the sea? Or while you are walking, your mind is full of thoughts and thinking incessantly about transient stuff, irrelevant stuff, what people did to you, what they said to you, why your life situation is this way, why it can't be that way; complain, complain, complain!

I know of a millionaire's daughter in Mumbai, whose life is a living complaint. Either she is complaining about how the waiters at a restaurant have not been trained properly, the air conditioning there or the food. Or she is complaining about the dirt in Mumbai, why her parents are so strict with her or a friend who doesn't respect their friendship, and so on.

Is your dialogue a dialogue of complaint? This means you want what *should be*, and you don't want what *is*. Sometimes, the 'what *is*' is not convenient, but that is what the journey is about—to accept it, regardless of what it is. Thereafter, we can do what we think and feel we should do.

N: Yes, and the ultimate freedom is acceptance.

G: Yes, Because to even accept that you don't like it is acceptance.

N: Exactly.

G: One doesn't have to like what *is*, but one has to accept that also.

N: I think it was Eckhart who said, 'The greatest source of peace is the acceptance of the unacceptable.' In this case, for a spiritual aspirant, it's very painful when they are sort of constrained in a way, but if that also is accepted, it will lead to peace.

G: Yes, but why? Because one is no longer involved in the non-acceptance. We tend to build stories around it, you see. That involvement cuts off. So even if you don't accept something, or you don't like something, it ends there.

N: I like this cute little example that Osho would share:

When you are driving, the dogs chase and bark at your car. So what you should do is just roll the window down and look at them. They will feel silly and walk away.

That's a beautiful metaphor for living without conflict. Whether you are a family member or a devotee, if you are not reactive, the issue falls away. Because the game only continues as long as either side is reactive.

To view the corresponding video, scan the QR code.

7

The Blessings of Guru Purnima 1 (Gautam's Talk)

Today, 5 July 2020, is *Guru Purnima*. It is the most auspicious day of the year, dedicated to the guru.

It is believed that on this day of Guru Purnima, the blessings of the masters, guides and teachers flow in abundance, and they are for the taking by the students, devotees and disciples. However big your bowl is, it will be filled with the guru's grace.

The word 'guru' has various meanings, but, fundamentally, it means 'the remover of ignorance'. 'Guru' also means 'heavy', in terms of spiritual weight.

For this podcast, I would like to share a quotation by Sant Dnyaneshwar on the guru–disciple relationship. He says, 'Alone, there is no happiness. Therefore, your consciousness assumes the form of guru and disciple.'

This simply means that true happiness is found in the sacred bond of the guru–disciple relationship.

So, the question we have to ask ourselves is, Are we happy with our relationship with the guru?

Now, for the Sai Baba's Devotee Speaks channel, on which this podcast is being aired, Shirdi Sai Baba is the guru figure. As disciples, as devotees, is our relationship with Him making us happy? Or are our lives miserable, our thought processes miserable, our relationships miserable? If so, our relationship with Sai is not bringing us happiness. It is a relationship based on wants, needs and demands, in many cases, from the guru. We have to reflect upon this.

True happiness is deep peace of mind which translates as a sense of calm and equanimity in dealing with life's situations. For many of us, our relationship with the guru is a bargain: *I want the guru to give me what I want because I think I need it.* Do you see how restrictive we as individuals are? Do we love the guru wholeheartedly, without any compromises, no matter what we are facing in our lives, no matter how hard the circumstances are, not blaming the guru for giving us hard circumstances and saying, *I really believe in you; when will my circumstances improve?* and so on? Do we offer complete, unconditional love, and surrender to whatever is happening in life?

If we are convinced that Sai is our guru, then it surely means that He is aware of whatever is happening in our life. He doesn't need to be told, you see.

So that is what Dnyaneshwar is pointing to. That true happiness cannot depend on the guru giving us what we want. True happiness is nothing but a deep, abiding peace so that whatever challenges we may face in life—financial, health-related or relationship-related—we have the faith that the guru will see us through it. But that does not mean that we will get the outcome we desire; that is the common mistake we make.

Life is like a journey across a river from one shore to the other in a boat, from birth to death. Now, either we sit alone in the boat without knowing how to row the boat and trying our best to deal with the currents as and when they arise, not knowing where we will land, or we trust the boatman whose intent it is to take us safely across to the other shore.

If the river is in spate, would you trust your own skills, not knowing how to navigate the boat? Or would you trust the boatman? It is the same while navigating through life. Wouldn't you trust a master to lead the way?

The current of life, the way the river flows, is not in our control. It comes from *Prarabdha Karma*. We have to face what we have to face. Even Sai Baba has said this. However, our attitude towards what we have to face *is* in our control.

Do we still get caught in old patterns, in action-reaction loops and so on, and make that journey to the other shore a challenging one, even more so than what it already is? Do we indulge in that?

It is as simple as that.

So, on Guru Purnima, we bow at the feet of the master because He is God in human form. We bow at the feet of the master in total surrender, saying, *Whatever happens in life, whatever has happened, is happening, and will happen, is by Your grace, so please be with me through this brief journey.*

That is all that is required.

As Sai Baba is not in the body, many of us have also come across teachers, guides and masters whom we have learnt from and who have made our life more meaningful, more simple, more clear.

We bow down to them.

What more could we ask for, if such Beings are present in our lives? So, we surrender to them, we thank them and we express gratitude to them for showing us the way to the *Sadguru*. And that is why the gratitude flows freely from the disciple to the guru, more so on this day than on other days. In return, as the saying goes, the more you give, the more you get.

So this is my message. These are my thoughts on Guru Purnima.

In my younger years, my connection with Sai Baba was very deep because, as a child, I was taken to Shirdi by my parents. And then that stopped happening for a long while. Nevertheless, every now and then, since the last few years, I make a day trip from Mumbai to Shirdi and back, to keep the connection going.

But what is known in the heart is that since childhood, He has never left me. It is as simple as that.

His message, 'Sabka Malik Ek', which means 'Everyone's God, or Master, is one', refers to the one Reality and not one particular God, which we always make the mistake of thinking because we think as individuals.

That message is even more potent and important today, seeing what we are all going through as one race, the race of human beings. We are all in a challenging situation where we have been brought down to our knees by a virus that is here to teach all of us some severe and challenging lessons, which are bound to be painful.

Therefore, this message of 'Sabka Malik Ek' cannot be more relevant than it is today.

God bless everyone. I love you all and wish you peace, harmony, happiness and joy in your journey ahead.

To view the corresponding video, scan the QR code.

8

Our Relationship with Sai Baba's Messengers

Nikhil: Although many devotees claim to get messages and guidance from Baba, only a few, such as Aai, are authentic.

I would like to probe into this so that devotees get pointers on what to look for within themselves as well as those whom they consider Baba's messengers and approach for guidance.

Gautam: This question has many aspects that need to be considered. It's not black and white. So we have to explore it in various ways.

Are those who are connected with Sai Baba and claim to be His messengers honest with themselves?

For example, I go through a phase of life where I am feeling so deeply connected with Sai Baba, that I get messages for myself as well as for other people. But it could also happen that, sometimes, those messages are not flowing from the Source. Yet, I give messages to people because now I am identified with a role; I am a messenger of Sai Baba's, and people are coming to me for guidance.

I have experienced this too, not with a messenger of Sai Baba's but that of another master, where it was very clear that the message was coming from what one could call the higher mind of that individual and not from the Source. One can sense the difference between the two.

So, on the part of the messenger, it is a disservice to the person who seeks help from them if only their higher mind is coming into play.

Now, unfortunately, this is quite likely not even conscious. Sometimes the messenger is not even aware that they are doing this. It's possible.

So what does this mean? This means that what is meant to happen will happen based on the destiny of the person who goes to someone to receive a message. What we are trying to point out here is that there is no foolproof method to determine who is the right messenger and who is not. It is a very individual experience.

Let's take an example. Someone with some undesirable traits gives me the most beautiful messages from Sai Baba. Now what? Do I keep my judgements of personality aside and take what comes to me because I resonate with it? That can also happen.

So this is what I mean. There are various aspects, but the intention rests with the messenger and not the person approaching them.

N: I beg to disagree here a little bit.

When someone goes to a messenger, if they are the kind of person who will go from A to B to C, like some people visit various astrologers, the time comes to question yourself why you are going and to also look within. Because if you are inauthentic, you will end up going from person to person. That is another aspect to consider.

G: True. We tend to use messengers as a crutch. Whenever any small worry crops up in life, we go running for a message. This dependency can get abused by the messenger.

I know someone who had a tarot reader as a guide, and for any small thing, she would call for guidance. Now, the tarot reader should also have the awareness that this is becoming a relationship of dependency and put an end to that. But that does not happen because, sometimes, they like the importance, they like the dependency, and of course, there's also money to be made, in which case, it has become a co-dependent relationship.

N: Exactly. Also, a guru and a messenger are very different.

For instance, Aai, in all humility, says, 'I'm the dust of Baba's feet.' She doesn't claim to be a guru.

But unfortunately, many of the messengers take on the role of the guru. Then Baba's devotees who approach them take them to be the master, which they are not.

I don't mean to hurt anyone's sentiments, but you cannot confuse someone who gets messages from Baba as Baba Himself or a guru. Because that throws you off track, and you may not even seek a master in that case.

G: Yes, it's an important point you have raised because there's only one word which comes up—'humility'. The hallmark of a guru is humility. If that is missing, then one whom you consider a guru is not a guru.

I would use the same measure for a messenger. The absence of humility is a good indicator for recognizing an inauthentic messenger. But make no mistake, the messenger might have quirks in their personality which you don't like, but still, humility could be there. And that is to be discerned by the person going to the messenger.

You mentioned a very beautiful example—that of Aai—because I have met her, and for me, she is the embodiment of humility. Someone who does not want to be put on a pedestal, who does not want to be known in society as being so-and-so; these are signs of humility.

In fact, I would go as far as to say that if a person is not concerned about whether one person shows up at their door or a thousand, that is a sign of humility.

One very important point I'd like to make here is that the guru is nothing but the Higher Self of the disciple. My mother, for example, saw this in her meditation. She saw the Higher Self come out of the person and project Itself onto another individual who took the form of the guru. She actually saw how the guru manifests, and that guru ultimately points the disciple to the Sadguru within. [Refer to talk 4.]

That is the mechanism of the process. Now, this is a very subtle process, and it is one of honouring, because the guru does not consider the disciple to be a disciple. A true guru does not say, 'I am your guru.'

Someone asked my spiritual guide, 'Are you my guru?'

And he replied, 'That is for you to decide. If you feel you are my disciple, then I am your guru.'

N: I feel that with the master–devotee relationship . . . Actually, there's no relationship. They are one.

G: Yes.

N: The problem is with the messengers: they sit on a pedestal, resulting in dependency on the part of the seeker, and that is when control comes into the relationship. This is not so with a real master whom you go to. There is no relationship. It is just oneness.

G: Absolutely. And what you have pointed out can even happen in other domains, like, for example, therapy, which is so big in the West.

N: Yes.

G: The therapist can end up controlling the patient.

N: I have met so many people who, on one hand, do get messages, which get validated by their experience, but on the other, they can see that they are being controlled.

Could you give pointers on how to manage that? Because it's a predicament for most people.

G: According to me, even a slight indication that you are being controlled is a good enough reason to exit that relationship. Were the guide a genuine guru or a sage, he would have the conviction that nothing is in his control. He would know that his next breath is not in his control. He knows that there is no control whatsoever over whatever the next moment brings. Therefore, it is not possible for the sage to have even the slightest control over any individual because his understanding is that there is a Higher Power.

So, if one does sense this control issue stepping into a relationship, it is a very clear sign that it is not an authentic relationship.

Yes, as you said, the function of the relationship is to get the message, and the message conveyed might be a very appropriate one. But this function that the relationship serves should end there. The dependency on the messenger to play a role which is more than that is doing injustice to both the messenger and the person coming to them.

N: Osho said something beautiful: 'To misguide someone on the spiritual path is worse than committing murder because if you kill someone, you kill them once. But if you misguide someone spiritually, they can go astray for lifetimes. So people must be aware.'

I'll give you my own example. Someone recently wrote to me as they wanted to meet Dharamdas Baba, and we were in contact for that specific reason. All of a sudden, I get this message saying that [Sai] Baba has said that in my past life, I was this particular individual who was in contact with Him, which I knew was not true, and ten other things.

So I very politely told them that the only reason for contact was Dharamdas Baba and that I respected that they had the sentiment to share the message, but I had not asked for it. I also requested them not to bring this up with me again. And we lost contact after that.

But the thought struck me that, instead of me, if it was someone else getting such information, it could be very misleading, especially when they have not asked for it, because there is this control element of 'I have got the message, and I am saying this to you.'

G: You are quite right. Unfortunately, a lot of this does happen. The only word of caution I have here is to keep alert. Supposing someone tells me that I was Sai Baba's closest disciple in His life, I feel good about it: 'Wow! I am special!'

So this is something you have to be careful about because, ultimately, what does it boil down to? Does it really matter? Or your life in this moment, does *that* matter?

N: Absolutely. And Ramana Maharshi said it is God's grace that you don't remember the past, for if you did, you would be finished.

G: Exactly.

N: So then why dwell on it?

G: That's why one should be alert about mistaking a messenger for a guru. The guru is one who shines a light on your path, the path of darkness, of maya; he is like the radiant Sun. These attributes are very different from that of a messenger. The messenger's role is to pass on the message, even though it may be an authentic message. The guru's role is different.

All that we have talked about are pointers to look at because these are separate functions, and if they merge into one, then what would it mean? If you accepted someone as your guru and he did not give you even a single message, would he still be your guru? Are you okay with that, or are you running after a guru who only gives messages?

N: Usually, it's the reverse—the guru empties you. He doesn't give you anything. I spoke to Dharamdas Baba, and he very clearly said that a living master is essential; there's no question of not having a living master on the spiritual path. By way of response, I said to Baba, 'An apprehension that devotees have is whether they are going to a genuine guru or not.'

So Baba, using the term 'TV gurus' to refer to those who want publicity, said, 'There is one thing you have to look for when you go to a real master. He has no need for you. The master has no worldly interest. He has no need to get people around him, unlike the TV gurus.'

So this is also something one needs to realize when one goes to a master: he doesn't need you and, hence, you must approach him with humility.

G: Yes, but more importantly, there's no such thing as the wrong guru, because every experience is a learning. Every experience will point you in the right direction.

N: Yes, you will have an experience according to where you are spiritually.

G: Correct. But the devotee needs to be very clear whether they are looking for a messenger or a guru. And in case he finds someone who is playing both roles, he now has a set of criteria at hand, you could say, to understand whether the person qualifies as a guru or a messenger.

N: One other thing I would like to touch upon is that hundreds of people send me emails saying they would like to meet Aai. But her poor health doesn't permit her to meet them. In fact, I had to plead with her to even talk on camera, which she was reluctant to do.

But I must say that out of the hundreds of emails I received, maybe two or three people asked about her health and offered to help her. So, if you go to an authentic messenger or a master, anybody who guides you on the path, it is important to look after their welfare.

That does not mean you give them money or do anything specific in that sense, but you must be concerned about their well-being. It's not about just going to them to receive messages.

When you come to someone like Aai, who is authentic, you must care for them because they are Baba's messengers and are very precious, very rare. But many come with a sense of entitlement. Baba and Aai are not your servants.

So there are very few who care, and they are the ones who get called and get to spend some time with Aai. Baba arranges that.

I just want to give this as a pointer, that you have to be aware of the fact that they don't need you, but you should at least be concerned about their welfare.

Robert Adams was very emphatic about this. He said the ones who take care of the master's welfare—as the master, in most cases, lacks body awareness—are the true devotees, and they are the ones who progress the most because they give up everything of their own and take care of the master. But this is very rare to see.

G: It is very rare, and it is a very important point as well as an important pointer. My guru, Ramesh Balsekar, lived till the age of ninety-two, and for two weeks, he was in hospital before he passed away. I went to see him for just five minutes at the hospital as I didn't want to disturb him. A couple from abroad had also come to visit him at the same time. When they came into the room, I told Rameshji that I would take my leave. But he asked me to wait for five minutes.

So I waited, and this couple who had come said, 'Oh, Ramesh Balsekar, we came from the US to see you. So sorry to see that you are in hospital like this.' And the lady even shed tears, you know.

LIVING WITH FAITH AND PATIENCE

So then I felt that it was time for me to leave.
Again, I excused myself, but Rameshji insisted that I wait.
You won't believe it! The next instance, they started talking about their problems to him. And I was saying to myself, *My God, this man is ninety-two, he's in hospital, his eyes are closing, and these people have absolutely no consideration for that!*

That is how entangled they were in their own problems. And Rameshji being Rameshji was answering them out of compassion.

N: Exactly.

G: You see, that is the load we put onto the guru. So this is just one example I'm giving about what you mentioned.

Now, what happens with us ordinary people? We'll take care of our parents, we'll take care of our children, because they are ours. But what about the guru? The guru is God in human form. This is not only what our scriptures say but also what the masters have said.

And if the thought *How can I be of service to my guru?* does not even arise, it means I have not accepted the fundamental relationship between a guru and his disciple. I am still viewing it as a relationship where I want to get something from it. That is really an unfortunate situation.

Wanting to do *seva* for the guru should arise spontaneously.

N: Exactly.

G: So, as you rightly said, you may be getting hundreds of emails, which is understandable because people are suffering so much; they are so taken up by their situation that the thought of serving the guru doesn't even arise. Rare is the one in whom the thought *How can I help?* arises, and the expression of that thought is actually what takes the disciple very far.

There is a famous disciple of Ramana Maharshi who took such good care of him. I've forgotten his name. Sri Ramana said that this man had reached his destination by just doing seva.

N: Yes. It was an attendant of Ramana Maharshi who fanned him for fifty years. They hardly spoke to each other. One day, the man just dropped dead, and Sri Ramana said he was not coming back.

G: Beautiful.

N: Service.

Guruji [Dharamdas Baba] also says the same thing—that service to the guru is higher than any sadhana.

G: And service can take many forms, depending on one's ability. You could serve the guru by spreading his teachings in some way, giving money if he requires it, taking care of his physical health or being in his proximity. There are various ways, and one chooses the way that one is naturally inclined to.

I would like to backtrack a bit, just to complete one point: the genuineness of gurus. In India, we have a well-established tradition of touching an elder's or a guru's feet as a mark of respect. Now, a genuine guru will not care a damn whether you touch his feet or not. Siddharameshwar Maharaj was once asked, 'How do you feel when people touch your feet?' He replied, 'Don't ask me, ask my feet. What have I got to do with it?'

I brought this up because it is part of our tradition. Some people view bowing down before someone as an act of subjugation. But touching the feet is a very beautiful ritual because one is offering one's ego at the feet of the master or the feet of the Source. That is the significance.

Secondly, it is said that energy that is emitted from the feet is the highest form of spiritual energy. That is why some masters don't allow you to touch their feet as they don't want their energy drained. Also, when a master passes away, you will see photographs taken of the feet. And it is the same reason that *padukas* are worshipped; the padukas soak in the energy of the master. So the feet are very crucial in that sense.

But beware of a master or his disciples who make you touch his feet forcefully. I met someone who ran away from an ashram in Nasik because they forced him to touch the feet of the master, and he was very uncomfortable with it.

So, there are no hard and fast rules about this because a genuine master will not care about such things.

I'll give you another example that is relevant in a similar kind of way. I think it was Swami Chidananda who was called to give a *pravachan*. When he arrived at the venue, he was surprised to see that although there was a big crowd, the seating arrangement made for him was at the same level as that of the crowd; there was no raised dais for him to sit atop. People at the back could hardly see him.

In the front row were various swamis, and he could hear them saying, 'Now we will see a display of Chidananda's ego.'

As they were hoping, the Swamiji declared, 'How dare you make me sit on the same level as that of the audience?'

Of course, the swamis were happy as their prediction seemed to be validated by Swami Chidananda's statement. They thought that his ego was hurt.

But Swamiji was no fool. He insisted that a raised platform be arranged for. Once that was done, he sat on it and addressed the gathering: 'I know many of you in the audience must have thought, *Look at this man's ego. He wants to sit on a higher level.* But I only wanted to point out one thing to you. It is not me as an individual who desires to be seen as being on a higher level. It is the teaching coming through me which deserves an elevated position. That must be respected.'

So Swamiji was giving a very important message: 'Respect the teaching. The master is an instrument.'

How many of us respect Baba's teachings? I'm coming back to what we started with. And how do you respect teachings? By living them. Simple.

N: Talking of that, on a closing note, the authentic messengers of Baba's, or the mediums—the instruments, I would say—of Baba's, through whom messages come through to us, are very rare. So it is also the responsibility of those who go to them to take care of them. And by care, I don't mean financial care or something like that, but they should at least be respectful. Respectful of their time, their energy. And not go with a sense of entitlement.

G: Yes.

N: Because they may not be gurus, but they are Baba's instruments, and respecting them is respecting Baba.

G: That is extremely important also because, unfortunately, we are so blinded by our suffering and our problems that all that goes out of the window. We just want to hold on to them because we see them as possible instruments to save us from our misery.

So one can't really be blamed, but as you said, one must go with more awareness because, after all, the messengers are contributing their time, their energy. It's not an easy task.

N: And in most cases, I have seen that when a message comes through the authentic instruments, it physically hits them [the messenger] like a bolt of lightning; it's a shock to their system.

G: Yes, it is draining. And don't forget, it is not for themselves; it is for others. The underlying principle is compassion.

N: So those who visit them must have the sensitivity to be respectful and make sure that they are not taken for granted.

G: Yes. Imagine an authentic messenger of Sai Baba's who has a timid disposition or who is gentle. Such a person may find it hard to tell a visitor, 'Look, I had said forty-five minutes, and now time is up,' because it's not their nature.

N: That is true.

G: Everyone is not like that. I know someone who is very clear that the reading is for forty-five minutes, and fifteen more minutes is this much extra.

So, as you said, a high degree of awareness is called for to see that you're not overstepping boundaries and that you're understanding there's a world beyond your world of misery and suffering.

N: Absolutely. Aai has said that one of the reasons she doesn't want to see anyone is because one out of a thousand who come to her really love Baba. Most of them just come for their own problems, and Baba is not their servant, for them to come and say, 'Oh, Baba, do this for me, do that for me.' Who are they to demand anything?

And what's worse is that they come with no consideration for her health and time, and sit before her for hours and complain, complain, complain. She told me, 'See, I am not Baba. It exhausts me physically;

it drains me. She also added that some of their problems are genuine, for instance, when someone's child is ill. So she says, 'Do you think I don't feel the pain? Every day, if a hundred people come and dump all their problems on me, imagine the emotional pain and turmoil it causes me!' This is one of the reasons why she doesn't see anybody anymore.

G: Let me tell you something that's related to this.

One lady came to my mother and poured her heart out to her about her disturbed childhood and how she had suffered through it. Later, my mother saw in her group meditation a subtle vision of a small baby coming out of this lady and falling at her [my mother's] feet.

I am bringing this up because thoughts have a form. We cannot see it; we don't have that subtle vision. That is why they say, 'Be careful of negative thoughts,' because all thoughts have a related form.

Now, can you imagine someone like Aai being bombarded by various thought forms, which are primarily thoughts of suffering? That is what they are receiving. It's just that with these eyes of duality, we cannot see it. Someone with the eye of singularity can have visions of that. So she must be going through a lot because she is at the receiving end.

Hence we have to be sensitive about these things.

If you ask me, the best guru or messenger is the one to whom you talk about all your problems, and the only answer you get from him is Silence.

To view the corresponding video, scan the QR code.

9

Going to Shirdi with the Right Intent

Nikhil: What is the right way for a devotee to be receptive when they go to Baba's shrine in Shirdi or when they go to any spiritual place, for that matter? Amid all the hustle and bustle that goes on at such places, how do you keep your focus on what is important? Could you shed some light on this, please?

Gautam: Sure. Firstly, the intent with which one is going is of primary importance. If someone says, '*Chalo, Shirdi chalay* [Come let's make a trip to Shirdi],' in an almost casual sort of way, as if they are going on a picnic, then they are going there with the intent of having an outing. But if one is going with the specific intent of devotion to Baba, then that must be in the heart throughout the journey; that must be the focus. Consequently, everything else becomes secondary.

We all know that it is very crowded and chaotic there. That is the way it is. You may complain all you want when you are there, but that complaint is only going to take you away from the intent. On the other hand, if you accept the situation knowing that you can't do much about it, you still have your intent at heart.

Unfortunately, it is chaotic, and it tends to take your thinking mind in all directions, away from your intent. And then all the questions come up: 'Why is it like this? Why is it not like that?'

It's very easy, if you are going in a group, to start gossiping and talking about irrelevant stuff. All this keeps you from focusing on the main purpose of your visit.

The intent normally is a strong one because it has pulled you there. In that sense, it's not even your intent because Baba Himself has said: 'Until I call you, you cannot come.'

Now how is one to honour that? By treating it as a social occasion? Or by criticizing and complaining? Or by being completely present with the intent of the visit?

There are various ways in which one can have the intent. One is a knowing in the heart. Another is the path of mantra japa so that the thinking mind is not all over the place. You chant a mantra, such as 'Om Sairam'. You are focused. That is the intent. That focus is very crucial.

This is how any spiritual journey needs to be made.

In Europe, there are pilgrimage centres—such as Lourdes, which I've been to—that are beautifully planned and organized. One does not have to deal with the chaos of the environment. But over here, we have to. We are a developing country with a huge population, and we are mostly poor. It is going to be chaotic. We cannot expect a miracle overnight.

So not being distracted and being single-minded is the approach to take when one approaches Shirdi.

Just imagine that Sai Baba is still there. What would be your approach? You would be so keen and eager to go and meet the master and sit at His feet. It's the same thing. There is no difference because the master has said, 'I am not the body.' So why not go thinking that He is actually there, alive, sitting there, and that you are going to see Him?

That should be the approach. But we tend to get distracted or think that it's just a *samadhi* and that He is not there in person. If the devotion is missing from our heart, the sacredness of the trip gets dissipated.

N: You made a very important point that the devotee must go there knowing that Baba is there now. It's not that He's not there because He has left His body.

And this also takes me to something slightly linked to this. I see many people criticize how things are structured there. But I always reflect on one thing: The whole place was set up by Baba's devotees years ago, over time. Now it is run by the government. But if devotees who have this feeling in their heart that Baba is there, go with the intention of serving Him in whatever way they wish, as I mentioned in the earlier interview, then the whole approach will change from one of criticism to one of service towards Baba.

G: Yes, and that will happen. Maharishi Mahesh Yogi proved that if a certain number of people meditate in a particular locality, the crime rate comes down there. Through the process of osmosis, of just having that common intent, change is brought about.

That will happen, I feel, over time. But right now, we are concerned with our individual journey to Baba's shrine. And what we have discussed are pointers to not get led astray by various distracting factors.

N: As you said, it's got a lot to do with one's intent. If a family or a group of friends go to the shrine, it would be best for one who is more keen on the sacredness of the visit than the others, to communicate: 'I am on a spiritual journey here; I would like my silence.' Because if you go into Baba's samadhi or *Dwarkamai*, these are very potent places to be receptive. But if there is this expectation from others to socialize, then the sanctity is trampled upon.

G: Yes, in fact, if you ask me, the intent is most potent if a group goes together in silence. You see, because then we are not wearing masks. Usually, we are talking because we are wearing social masks. I want to say things which you like and which you agree with; all that dynamic starts going on in a group.

That is why it is best to either go alone or with a like-minded friend. And if a group is like-minded, nothing like it. That would be ideal.

My understanding, which may not be everyone's, is that Sai Baba was also a Nath Yogi. Surprisingly, I have read in one place that He has said He was Kabir, and in another, that Kabir was His guru. I don't know which one is true. But that, for me, points to him being a Nath Yogi because Kabir revered Gorakhnath.

The dhuni is the sign of the Naths. Wherever the Naths are, there is a dhuni. It was very sacred for them. Somehow, my path led me to many Nath *sthans*, where there were living yogis, or which were abodes of yogis who had passed away, where the dhuni was always burning. One Nath Yogi told me that whenever you go, please present yourself before the dhuni because it records everything.

So then, how does one approach the dhuni in Dwarkamai? Do we go there saying, '*Arrey, yeh toh Sai Baba key time se dhuni chal raha hai toh usey dekhna hi chahiye* [We must take a look at the dhuni as it has been burning since Sai Baba's time]?'

Is that it? What does fire represent? It represents the force of life, the Sun, the *Kundalini*. Fire is a very important element. Fire is part and parcel of the practice of the Nath Yogis.

So when we are presenting ourselves before the dhuni, what is in our minds at that time? What are we offering the fire? Offering a coconut to the fire in a *havan* is the symbolic offering of the ego. What are we telling the fire to do to us to cleanse us? All this depends on our awareness when we are present before the dhuni.

But if you go there as if you are on a sightseeing trip, that this is Baba's dhuni, then you are not going to go very far spiritually. So the intent or the level of awareness, presence, or Being is very critical when you are in such a sacred place.

Let's talk about the stone on which Baba sat.

I'll tell you something. I was sitting on Marine Drive with a friend. He is a mantra expert, a Maharashtrian, and he goes around spreading the science of mantras all over Maharashtra. His name is Shankar Nikam. He once told me, 'Gautam, if I am chanting a particular mantra while I am sitting with you on the parapet here at Marine Drive, and after half an hour I get up and leave, you will sense the vibration of the mantra if you are sensitive enough.' That is the power of a mantra. Because a mantra is a vibration, someone who is chanting it all the time will leave an imprint.

Coming back to the stone on which Baba sat, can you imagine—whether you can see it or not, whether you can feel it or not—the vibration of that stone which was the seat of a master like Sai Baba? Can you even fathom that?

Now, when we are walking past the stone with our heads down, what is going on in our mind at that time? Are we open and receptive to the fact that on this stone sat this master? It should be as if He is still sitting there. Are we bowing down with that intent?

So everything has a significance. Otherwise, these things would not be there. The stone and the fire would not be in Dwarkamai. Also, the *chavadi* would not be there.

Our eyes of duality don't have this subtle vision, but it does not mean that what we don't see is not there. We need to be open, we need to be receptive, and we must not make the mistake of taking it to be a tourist destination.

N: Absolutely. In the olden days, people would travel only for pilgrimages. I am talking of a few hundred years ago. There was no concept of tourism then, and people made journeys, for instance, to Kailash or Kashi or any other place in the world that one went to on a pilgrimage. It was not easy. Usually, they had to walk great distances. So, right till they reached their destination, they underwent a process of purification.

G: Yes.

N: Now it is very easy; if you feel like going somewhere, you just book a ticket and go. But one must remember that in the past, people had no money. Often, they would undergo difficulties, such as illnesses. But they would go against all odds to reach the shrine.

G: Yes, you have raised a very beautiful point.

N: So, today, when you reach Dwarakamai after taking a flight, don't take it for granted.

I was talking to Dr Vinny Chitluri, the historian who has written extensively about Baba. She told me, 'I go to Kakasaheb Dixit's *wada*, and I pray to him: *How did you have the resolve to stay here when there were snakes and scorpions, with no electricity and various difficulties?*'

Now Baba was a master. He was beyond all this. But the intimate devotees who left their lives in Bombay [now Mumbai] or other cities, came there to be with Baba all the time. One must not forget those circumstances.

G: Very true. Now let's take the example of temples. Some are at heights, with steps leading up to them. There was a reason for everything. These steps played the role of opening the lower *chakras* as one walked up to the temple.

So can you imagine a pilgrimage, such as the one where many devotees from Mumbai walk for seven days to Shirdi! There's a reason for that, which takes us back to the olden days when bhakti and bhava prevailed.

What happens is that we, because of the level of comfort we are accustomed to—AC cars, AC buses—don't go through that process. So it tends to become a picnic.

N: Exactly. And if a difficulty does come your way, why not see it with the sentiment that years ago, this is how it used to be. Go with the determination that despite the difficulty, you will go and surrender to Baba. Do not think that Baba is putting an obstacle in your way.

Maybe, sometimes, your resolve is tested. I have had this experience when I was about to leave for [film] shoots. Some problems at home would get me thinking, *Should I leave or should I not?* But when I reflected on it, I thought that maybe it was a test of my resolve, and then I would go.

So, sometimes, situations may not be favourable or easy, but one must not adopt the attitude that Baba is putting an obstacle, for the wrong reason.

G: Right.

N: You are going to a sacred place and maybe it is to purify your intent. It should be seen from that perspective.

G: Absolutely. And it could be the other way also, that maybe a particular moment in time is not the right time to go. Then you have to use your discretion: *Is it a test, or am I not seeing something and maybe I need to go another time?* But it's not right to peg this on Baba and blame Him—*Baba, why are you making this so difficult for me?*

N: Yes.

G: This reminds me of a joke: St Theresa was working in a field, pushing a heavy wheelbarrow. She was so fed up with this heavy work that, perspiring, she looked up to the heavens above and asked Jesus, 'Why are You doing this to me? I mean, I am Your devotee, and You're making life so difficult for me!'

And Jesus replied, 'Don't worry, I ask this only of My friends.'

'No wonder You don't have any!' responded St Theresa in exasperation.

You see, we run away. When there's stuff we don't like, we run away.

N: I think people who are always complaining about difficulties don't seem to have any idea of what austerity is all about. Like that which Baba's devotees underwent when they lived with Him. Some didn't sleep the entire night for months. That's the kind of penance they have gone through over time. And not only Baba and Baba's devotees but also those on the spiritual path.

Today, it's very easy: you can watch a video on YouTube in a five-star hotel, which is fine. But those masters and their relationships with their devotees, the types of sadhana they underwent . . . I mean, they literally gave up everything to be on the path. Then to go on a pilgrimage as if it's a holiday, and also complain—that's not right.

G: Yes. That's unfortunately the world we live in today. It has become like that.

N: So, if one can go with the sentiment that it is a mark of respect to the master, that it is a sacred place . . .

G: Yes.

N: And if it is communicated within the group beforehand, that the intent is to be in silence, that could help.

G: Yes, and like I said, imagine Baba is physically sitting there, then would these complaints matter? They wouldn't matter. And Baba Himself has said, 'My bones will speak from My tomb.' [Refer to talk 1.] It means that He's there.

N: He is there; absolutely!

G: So, go knowing that. That's very important.

Not only that. An enlightened sage's body is considered the temple of the Living God. That is why sages were not cremated. The place where a sage's body was buried became a samadhi to be venerated by devotees. His vibration is present there. That is the importance of the place. You are actually in a throbbing, sacred, vibrational field when you are at a samadhi. And what it needs to do for you, that field knows best.

To view the corresponding video, scan the QR code.

10

Business in Sai Baba's Name

Nikhil: Today, I would like to discuss a slightly sensitive and rather unfortunate subject. There are people in Shirdi who make all sorts of claims about Baba and their being His messengers. They take gullible devotees, who come there with a devotional bhava, for a ride.

I want to share a few of these incidents and then let you comment on them.

Gautam: Sure.

N: On my trips to Shirdi, I happened to meet a few devotees who shared their negative experiences. What came up in common was that there are people in Dwarkamai who claim to have been there for twenty or thirty years and that they are Baba's intimate devotees. They have a few accomplices in their group who get hold of sincere devotees and tell them that so-and-so gets messages from Baba, which is not true. And at the end of it, they ask for financial favours.

I felt that without pointing a finger at anyone, it would be nice if we could give devotees certain pointers to look for so that while they are receptive at Baba's feet when they go there, they are not vulnerable to this sort of exploitation.

The fact is that out of the thousands who visit Shirdi every day, maybe a few have genuine feelings for Baba. Most people come with their demands and, unfortunately, they are the ones who fall prey to the exploiters.

So, if you could talk about this . . .

G: Yes, in fact, I wouldn't be surprised if many sincere devotees have stopped going to Shirdi due to all this nonsense going on there, because if they are truly living Baba's teachings and Baba is in their heart, they may feel that now it's best to stay away.

Again, it is a very sensitive topic, and I'll give you an example of what happened to me in childhood.

My mother took us to one *baba* at the appointed time, as we had to take prior permission. When we entered, we were very impressed because of the number of devotees there. One was massaging his feet, while another came and touched them in reverence. We had his *darshan* and took our leave.

After a few months, my mother happened to tell someone that we went and visited this baba, and that person disdainfully responded by saying, 'That fellow—he is not genuine.'

So my mother was very upset. 'How can you talk like this about a master?'

To prove his point, the person advised, 'All right. Go unannounced at the same hour on any other day, and see whether there are devotees; whether there is darshan happening.'

And so, we decided to go again without informing the baba. When we reached there, we were shocked to see that the environment was completely different. The 'master' was lying on his bed like a lord, and *parathas* were being served to him. There were no devotees there, and he was visibly shocked to see us. He got very upset and threw us out of the house, saying, 'You come only by appointment.'

N: That type of behaviour is a giveaway—a clear one.

G: But it's unfortunate because people are led astray. When money comes into the picture, I think it is a very important pointer. Financial favours, as you said. For me, that is a big red flag.

N: Absolutely.

G: I'm not saying that a spiritual master should not charge money. That's a separate topic of discussion. I'll give you an example. My spiritual guide spoke daily in his living room. And he said, 'Nobody is invited, everybody is welcome.' He didn't charge for giving talks at his house but people were free to give *dakshina*, which he would accept; everyone has expenses to be met.

If he was going on a retreat, there would be a charge because he was giving his time, and his travel and stay expenses were also to be taken care of. But in his living room, whether you were a taxi driver or a millionaire, you were treated equally, and it was up to you whether to give or not.

If there is a financial demand, it is a clear sign that the person is not genuine because what one gives from the heart is what the master wants. So can the master come to you in a form which is making a financial demand? I don't see that happening; that doesn't seem genuine.

N: Here, we are not even talking about masters; we are talking about people who claim to get messages and manipulate people.

G: Yes. That is part of the *mayajaal* today, unfortunately, and the more innocent-minded people, the simpler people, get trapped in this.

N: See, I look at it this way: if they are so close to Baba and get messages from Baba, Baba will take care of their welfare. They would not doubt that if they were genuine. The very fact that they need to manipulate people and swindle them off five thousand and ten thousand rupees indicates that it is a show that is being put up.

G: Yes.

N: I feel that, maybe, after watching this video, people can become more aware and alert, and if they are approached by someone, they can just say, 'No, thank you,' and be left in silence.

G: In fact, I would go as far as to say that they should ask upfront whether there is a monetary transaction involved, before taking the discussion any further. That would give them the answer.

N: In most cases, they loop you in with messages, and I feel that if you are clear in your intent, meaning you are there just to go to Baba, touch His feet and sit there, then any of these engagements would be almost like a distraction.

LIVING WITH FAITH AND PATIENCE

G: That's manipulation indeed. But what you conveyed is an ideal situation. Many people are going there to get rid of their suffering, and consequently, they are looking for such 'miracles' to happen. Now, in such instances, if they are very clear from the start that there is a transaction involved, they shouldn't engage. That helps.

I would like to give my own example of what happened recently in Mumbai.

Often, one sees a group of men, maybe two, three, or four, with a *chadar*, dressed in *kafnis*, or robes, going about asking for money, which they put into that chadar.

Now, very strangely, on a Saturday, I saw the same people in three different locations in South Mumbai. At one location, I crossed their path when they were asking people for money. Then I got into my car and went and stopped at another destination about fifteen minutes away—by car—and they happened to be there too. So, obviously, they were doing the rounds of South Mumbai.

Now, the third place I went to was opposite my home—the club— and when I came out, I saw them there too. So I knew that destiny was unfolding, you see, and they stopped and asked me for money. I put some money in the chadar.

Then the leader of the group said, 'You pull out more money from your wallet and touch it to the chadar, and I'll say a prayer.'

So I thought to myself, *All right, let me go along with it.* I pulled out a five hundred-rupee note, and I touched it to the chadar. Now, the minute I touched it to the chadar, his hand grabbed mine, and he said, 'I'm going to chant a mantra of Sai Baba's. Give me your name, your mother's name, your father's name,' etc. And I knew where this was heading because his grasp was very tight. But I said to myself, *All right, let destiny take its course.*

I was sincere in my intent. I noticed them, I gave them some money, he asked for more money, I pulled it out.

Now, as he was chanting, I lost interest because I knew that he was now just rambling, all the while eyeing the note. Yet, in my heart was the intent that I was giving the money to Sai Baba. After a while, I said, 'That's enough,' because he told me to touch the money to the chadar and that it would multiply and blah, blah, blah. I withdrew my hand but, very roughly and quickly, he yanked it and snatched the five hundred-rupee note; it could have been torn in the process. Then they started walking away hurriedly.

Now, this is the situation I was presented with. Can I say that anger arose within me? I'm not sure. Maybe irritation arose. But there was no involvement in it. I knew this was destined to happen, so it happened.

I had no intention of asking for the money back. I had no intention of stopping him. I had no intention of saying, 'How dare you?' But yes, I did notice that his eyes were red and that there was puffiness in his face—not what I would call pleasant signs. Once the money was snatched from my hand, I had the full understanding it was snatched in Baba's name, so I didn't care a damn. But I did say to him, 'Karma ka phal to sabko bhugatna hi hai [Everyone has to reap what they sow].' That's what escaped my lips.

So my understanding is that if you see Baba in everyone, in all incidents, you are not engaged in the thinking mind that says, *Why did this happen? How dare they do this? Who do they think they are?* That dialogue is finished. And these are tests for us, right?

But at the same time, what goes around comes around. If anyone is doing this in Baba's name, and although your understanding may be that Baba is operating through everyone—which God is; Consciousness is operating through everything and everyone—they will still have to bear the consequences of their actions, which is their destiny.

So when you come across such people in Shirdi, all you can do is be cautious. I know that's not much consolation. However, if you are taken for a ride, if money is taken from you, know truly well that this money would not leave your hand if it was not meant to. At least be thankful that it left your hand in Baba's name, and allow the laws of divine justice to take their course as far as the people involved in the transaction are concerned.

That is all I have to say.

LIVING WITH FAITH AND PATIENCE

To view the corresponding video, scan the QR code.

11

True Surrender to Sai Baba

Nikhil: What is the internal process of surrender to Baba that an ardent devotee of His goes through? What thought processes, emotional processes, or bhava does a devotee who has surrendered to Baba have amid life events, such as an illness or a loss, as compared with that of a beginner devotee or an average person?

If you could comment on this . . .

Gautam: True surrender is the total acceptance that everything is His will. That's it. The Bible says, 'Thy will be done,' which means, 'Not My will, O Lord, but Thine be done.' So, if we are totally surrendered to Baba, we would be living this, that whatever happens in life is God's will. Our God is Sai Baba. It is His will. This is true surrender.

Now, let's look at surrender. What can we surrender? We can only surrender what is ours. But is anything ours? From birth to death, what is truly ours?

If it's an object, we've got it from somewhere. If it's a relationship, it has come our way by way of karma, which is true of all relationships. Everything has come to us or has been given to us. Our pleasures have been given to us, our pains have been given to us, our *karmic* bonds have been given to us. Our breathing has been given to us. The blood coursing through our veins is given to us. Sitting here is given to us. We have not exercised any choice over all of that.

So can we really surrender any of this if it is not ours in the first place and is given to us by a Higher Force? Therefore, surrender is knowing that just as all this has been given to us, it can also be taken away from us. But we tend to grasp, we tend to clutch, we tend to hold tightly. We get identified with all these things; we don't want to let go. That is when surrender is difficult.

So true surrender is to accept that even loss is meant to happen. We may not like it, but we have to even surrender that feeling of not liking it to Baba. Any thought or emotion which is internal, even that has to be surrendered. Surrender is not only of external things, such as if something happens to me that I don't like, I have to surrender to it. That is just one aspect. But to surrender to each and every thought and offer it back to Baba, offer it to the Divine, *that* is living a life of surrender.

It is not easy because our surrender is selective. We are negotiating with Baba: *I am okay with surrendering this, but I don't want to surrender that.* Then that becomes a transaction, a negotiation.

If you have been living with the full understanding that everything is God's will, then you have been living a life of surrender.

N: Let's take an extreme example—that of Aai's. She has had excruciating back pain over the years, and I have tried many a time to get various doctors and therapists to treat her pain, but she never showed any interest; all she would say is 'Baba is my master. He will take care of me.'

I noticed that there was no fear or resistance in her at all. There was total trust, and that trust, for me, is love for Baba. It was so intense that she would almost not notice the pain, although everyone else would feel, *Oh, her condition is so bad.*

G: Yes.

N: I don't expect everyone to operate at that level of surrender, but they can at least take pointers from either Aai's example or that of many others, as to what are the internal processes that go on within a devotee during a tough situation.

For example, recently, Hema Ma's daughter had dengue, and I was in contact with her on the phone. I noticed that she was doing what was needed on the outside, like taking her daughter to the doctor and all of that. But internally, there was no turbulence. She said, 'I have left this matter at Baba's feet. He knows what is best.'

So, I felt that, perhaps, we can have this dialogue for Baba's followers to look into the mind and Being of these exceptional devotees so that they can apply what they discover to their own lives.

G: Yes. I think we can use these examples as you have mentioned two staunch devotees of Baba's.

Now, why are they able to deal with these situations? It is because they have the total acceptance that whatever happens is according to His will. So, Aai, for example, has the acceptance that if the body is meant to survive, it will survive. If it is not meant to, it is Baba's will. She is not attached to wanting to survive.

You see, when one is not attached to that, then you are fine with whatever happens.

Similarly, let's take Hema Ma's example. *Of course* she will think like a mother; her child is suffering from dengue. It's not that she will do nothing because she has surrendered, knowing that what has to happen will happen. But her faith is unshakable. I am not referring to her having the faith that her child will get okay and that everything will be bright sunshine, beautiful roses, and all that. I am referring to the steadfast faith that what is meant to happen will happen by Baba's grace because His eye is on the situation. That is the faith I am referring to. That is called surrender.

So when one is surrendered to that degree, the mind is not troubled beyond a point. Such a mind is still free compared to ordinary minds because of their degree of surrender. Baba told his devotees who were around Him: 'I cannot remove your suffering, but being near Me will dissipate it.' He said that because we have to go through our karmic blueprint and our journey of life. But the grace of the guru makes that journey easier.

There was a devotee of Baba's who lost his child, and Baba told him, 'Look, your child was meant to go as he had to bear the fruits of his karma. But by being near Me, you will find it easier to deal with the loss.'

These are extreme examples, and that is why such devotees have become living embodiments of the teaching. That is why you have them on your channel.

Now let us take ordinary people like us. What does surrender mean to us? We may not have the exalted position of seeing everything from the perspective of these rare devotees. Some of us may fear a situation and its outcome more than others.

What can we do? We can surrender that feeling of fear also to Baba, saying [for instance], *Baba, fear is arising. I am built that way. Maybe it is my conditioning because of what life dealt me when I was young, when things were taken away from me, my parent was taken away from me. It has led to fear in life. So I am in this situation. I know it's inevitable that something is going to happen. Fear is arising, and I offer that fear also to You because it is not my fear. So I'm offering that fear too at Your feet, in the hope that I'm able to handle the situation better, as well as my fear. Because if I could handle it on my own, then that would mean I don't need You.*

That is why it is said that we should offer every thought, every feeling, every emotion at the feet of the master. True surrender is to offer the sense of doership to God. And that is the message of the Bhagavad Gita: Krishna tells Arjuna that the deluded ego thinks, *I am the doer.* That sense of doership has to be offered, saying, *Lord, You are the one doing everything, including what is going on within this body-mind organism. It is all Your doing.* To offer *that* at the feet of the Lord is true surrender.

N: Could you share a prayer? By prayer, I don't mean a formal prayer that people generally associate the word with. I mean a prayer as a process. For instance, if you are in difficulty, you could pray to Baba, *Baba, only You know what is best for me. Please give me the strength to face this situation with dignity.* And you are not asking Baba to change the situation but to give you the strength to accept it fully and to see what is best for you.

Could you suggest certain prayers so that one could look within rather than react or give in to fear whenever it arises? How do you surrender it all at Baba's feet?

G: A genuine prayer, according to me, is one whereby we are not asking for something specific because we never know what is good for us in the first place. My teacher would say that a true prayer is one of gratitude which arises from the heart. Despite all that God has given us, we tend to focus on what is not given or what is taken away. But what about all that which has been given to us? Our life has been given to us. Should not a prayer of gratitude arise for that itself? Whatever love we have experienced has been given to us. Should not a prayer of gratitude arise? That is one kind of prayer.

Let me give you an example of another kind of prayer. When I was young, I would pray, *Please give me the strength to deal with life's situations,* because I realized early on that very little was in my control. Life was more pain and less pleasure. So how to deal with it? With peace, equanimity, calmness and tranquillity. That is what I was seeking from a young age. That was a prayer.

In the book *A Course in Miracles*, which is very popular in spiritual circles in the West, there's another beautiful prayer, which is almost like saying, *Dear God, please release my fear-based thoughts.* That is a genuine prayer because so much of our thinking is fear-based. It's about me. I want me to survive; me and my story, which is all fear-based. Why? Because I don't want to die. And that means the ego does not want to die. The Buddhists have said that all fears in life are ultimately the fear of death. The death of what? Not the death of the body, because the body, when it is dead, is dead. It is the me that is afraid of dying. The me with its sense of doership is what is afraid of death.

Dear Lord, please release all my fear-based thoughts is a prayer because you know you can't do it on your own. You are fear-based, so you offer it to the Higher Power to help you through your difficulty.

The other aspect is that there is no harm in praying for the health of loved ones as, of course, you would want everyone to be healthy—not only loved ones but everyone. That is a genuine prayer. You don't want people to suffer.

Whether the prayer is for someone's health or financial difficulties, whatever it may be, there is 'a felt oneness with Being', to use Eckhart Tolle's words. So someone else's suffering is your suffering. You don't want them to go through that.

When you have the understanding that we all have our destinies to play out, the prayer is meant to say, *Lord, please be as gentle as possible through their karmic journey.*

These are prayers from the heart. To pray for certain outcomes, for certain relationships you want in your life, for certain deals to happen in business . . . Okay, fair enough. That's also genuine because it's arising. But what we do is that we latch the prayer onto an outcome; we want a specific outcome.

So prayers which are not based on desired outcomes are the truly genuine ones, whereby you accept, *Yes, I want this, but I do know that whether or not I get it is Your will.*

N: When you truly go with the flow of life, accepting everything as it is, that is God's will in action. If something that you wish for comes unasked and naturally, then that is fine, but when there is resistance, then it is a sign for you to consider that maybe it is not meant to be. So you should not push it beyond a point. You may try it once or twice, but if it doesn't work, let it go.

Could that also be a pointer as so much of the suffering is due to people trying to swim against the tide? That causes more conflict.

G: Yes, by all means, try if you are determined. Like they say, for one who keeps trying, there is no failure. If that is your nature and you are determined for an outcome, keep trying. Your nature may be to try a hundred times, so keep trying as long as you are clear that your trying a hundred times does not guarantee the desired outcome.

We tend to believe that if we try, we will definitely get what we want. That is not true. That may happen in some instances. It will not happen in all instances. Some things are not meant to happen. To live with the understanding that some things are not meant to happen does not mean that you are living fatalistically. It is to live, knowing that if something is to happen, it will happen.

Ramana Maharshi said that what is meant to happen will happen, and what is not meant to happen, won't, try as you may. So the best course of action is to keep silent. And when he said to keep silent, he didn't only mean that one should remain quiet. He was mainly referring to the silence of the mind.

When you accept that what is meant to happen will happen and what is not meant to happen won't, the mind becomes automatically silent. Now, is that not a prayer? That is also a prayer. The best prayers are the silent ones.

To wish peace for all is a beautiful prayer because you are no longer focused only on the me. *For all.* That is a prayer.

Sai Baba's life was a living prayer. The fact that he could feel what someone was feeling hundreds of miles away was nothing less than a prayer.

N: Over time, having met devotees like Aai and those who have surrendered to Baba fully, one thing I felt is that in their lives, the karmic journey of what is meant to happen to the body on the outside does not change. Baba will reduce the intensity of their suffering; that is guaranteed. But on the outside, what is to happen will happen, and I used to reflect on how this is so.

And what I see, for instance, in Aai's case, is that physical pain is there. And that could be true of any devotee with the same karma. But because she has totally surrendered to Baba, her love for Him is so intense that her consciousness has merged into Him, so much so that when the painful event is happening, Baba raises her consciousness to such a level that the event is just an apparent drama, so to speak. Whereas in the case of an average person, they get totally pulled into the experience.

G: Yes, because we overlay what is pure physical pain with a lot of psychological pain. The devotee who has surrendered does not do that, so it is just the physical pain that they are dealing with; the pain in the moment. Whereas we have built a huge monument and story around the pain. That inflates our suffering, that inflates our pain. We ask questions, we try to reason it out, and we get caught in the wheels of the story of the pain.

To surrender means, as you said, to accept that the pain of the body is there, and it will take its course.

N: But even when the devotee is so absorbed in Baba that they transcend the consciousness of the body by His grace, to a certain extent, or a total extent, to the observer it looks as if they are suffering. But they are so absorbed in Baba! I think this is the final state of freedom, where you are free of the link to what is happening.

G: That is when you are not identified with the body anymore.

But let's not forget that the pain will make you cry out. You know, even Ramana Maharshi, when he was afflicted with cancer, cried out in pain, but there was no identification with the pain.

So it is rare that you will not feel physical pain, though there are masters and *siddhas* who are capable of that. Let's take Sai Baba's example. He used to perform a practice called Khanda Manda Yoga, which involved cutting off the limbs of the body and offering them to the fire, which was a test for the yogis, especially in the *Aghori* sadhana, to see how identified or disidentified they were with their bodies. And because fire represents purity, as a result of that act, it would regenerate the limbs.

And people saw this happening with Sai Baba, from what I have read.

These are extreme examples. But for us common people, even if we are not able to transcend the pain by going into states of samadhi, just the fact that our minds are not involved in a big story around the pain is of immense help. If we have totally surrendered and accepted it as Baba's will and that He has to take care of it, we may still feel the pain, but the drama with the pain is finished.

You've used the classic example of Aai. That is what has happened. And if she no longer even feels the physical pain, it means, as you said, her consciousness has reached that level of disidentification from the body.

N: She does feel the pain, but I meant something slightly different, where she's so absorbed in Baba that she doesn't notice it; that even through the pain, her love for Baba and her faith is so immense, that it overrides all that she is going through. As she says, it's just like a play. The body is meant to come to an end. It will happen, and nobody can be spared of this.

G: Yes, it's a free mind. Hers is a free mind.

N: As Ramakrishna Dev said, 'Suffering is of the body; none can escape it.'

To view the corresponding video, scan the QR code.

12

Signs of Spiritual Progress

Nikhil: What are the pointers or markers that devotees should look for, to know if they are making spiritual progress?

Gautam: This question is a crucial one and the answer is very simple. But you see, generally, people don't like simplicity. There is a saying—I think it is by the poet Walt Whitman—'The truth is simple. If it were complicated, everybody would get it.'

That's the problem. We make structures, theories, and concepts out of simple teachings. And Baba's is, by far, the simplest. But are we, Baba's followers, living that simplicity?

Such a simple question: What are the signs of spiritual progress? There is only one sign, and that is peace of mind in daily living. It is not about possessing siddhis or abilities, or of gradations in one's level of devotion to Sai. That all is excluded. It simply comes down to peace of mind in daily living.

And how do we know that we are at peace and, therefore, following Baba's teaching? Very simple. We have to accept the fundamental fact that everybody in our life—our family, friends, colleagues at work or strangers—is Sai Baba's instrument and that the same energy functions through everyone, bringing about what each one is designed to produce based on their genetics and their conditioning. With this understanding, the conflict ends.

You may not agree with someone, but you will agree to disagree. You will understand that someone else's view is as valid as yours. So you will not go about berating people or criticizing and condemning them like you used to earlier. Nisargadatta Maharaj said that to criticize anyone is to criticize the affairs of Brahman. [Refer to talk 1.]

And what is the result? Peace of mind. That is the sign of spiritual progress. This is a very underrated aspect of what happens in one's life when one truly follows the teaching.

When you are living the teaching, this process becomes automatic. Aspects of the thinking mind, such as ill will, spite, jealousy, envy, hatred, malice, blame and condemnation don't function anymore. You accept people for who they are. God has made them with their flaws, just like you have been made by the same Source with your flaws. So it comes down to acceptance. Accepting people the way they are, accepting yourself the way you are, and accepting that events in your life come to you as a part of the functioning of your destiny. Sometimes, pleasure; many times, pain. Accepting that life cannot be only pleasure, pleasure, pleasure and more pleasure. It is your own life experience. That is why Maharaj said, 'Between the banks of pleasure and pain, the river of life flows.' [Refer to talk 2.]

But what we do is we run away from pain and run after pleasures, thereby increasing our suffering.

Why did Sai Baba say that the two most important words of His teachings are 'shraddha' and 'saburi'? Because we know that we live a life of pain and suffering. Therefore, we should have faith and patience. That is what heals.

But the thinking mind, which is running into the past or the future all the time, is taking us away from our peace. So the sign of spiritual progress is the degree of shraddha and saburi that we experience in our lives and not just seeing them as concepts. It is living that teaching, living the faith—not the faith that I will get what I want but that whatever is meant to happen is for my highest good.

N: So, as you rightly said, ultimately, it is about living with shraddha and saburi in everyday life. There is something very peculiar I've seen about the Sai Baba path as I've explored other traditions also: people have experiences of Baba's miracles or dreams or visions, and unfortunately, they start to look at that as markers of progress.

Just so there's some awareness around this aspect, could you talk about it as it is very peculiar to Baba's path?

G: Sure. Sai Baba Himself has said, 'I give people what they want so that they may want what I want to give them.' [Refer to talk 2.] And He is referring to the ultimate: Self-realization, enlightenment, or Shanti; *Sukh-Shanti*, you could call it.

Now, the problem with experiences is that the ego gets hooked on the experience and feels special. *I had this experience; I had this vision of God; this was given to me.* But the point is that the ego comes in *after* the experience. The experience is not in your control.

Let's say one night you have a dream. Did you will the dream into existence, or did it just happen? But the next morning you wake up and say, *Wow! Sai Baba came to me in my dream and said this to me.*

And now what happens? Not only does the ego feel special, but it wants to repeat the experience and is now waiting for the next dream to happen. This is a classic pitfall on the spiritual journey. That is why the masters warn us not to get attached to experiences. It makes the ego feel special, which leads us astray.

Now, let us talk about what I feel is a great siddhi, which is peace of mind.

Let's assume you have two options placed before you. One is a life of ignorance and psychological suffering, of deeply divisive relationships, but you get many spiritual experiences in your life. And the other is a life of peace, calm, harmony and tranquillity; a life which is the absence of separation from others, but there are fewer experiences which you get. Now, which life would you choose?

If Sai Baba Himself came to you and offered you these two options and said, 'I will take away all the conflict in your mind, all these imaginary thoughts of what people did to you, what you did to people, what your future might be, and all that garbage of the thinking mind, so that from now on, till your last breath, you will have a clear mind. The light of clarity will shine through every moment of your life, and you accept your Prarabdha Karma, your destiny, the way it is.

'I can give you that life, or I can give you some experiences, but the rest of your life is going to be miserable in terms of psychological suffering and all the drama associated with the thinking mind.'

Which would you choose? Wouldn't the choice be obvious?

You see? So this is the issue with experiences. There is no end to having experiences in life.

Now, talking about deep sleep, we often wake up and say, 'I slept well.' The gift of deep sleep is so beautiful, right? You know it. And what is deep sleep? The absence of experience. In that sense, isn't that a better 'experience' than having experiences? That is the gift of deep sleep. That is why Ramana Maharshi said, 'Deep sleep is your natural state.' This is what he was pointing to.

N: Correct.

In your everyday life, you sit for meditation, you do your *bhajans*, you do your dhyana—everything. In time, if you are doing it correctly, you will wake up to a few things and act accordingly. For instance, you will be less reactive to a negative stimulus. You will have a much quieter mind.

Thinking, which is regarding some work and which is necessary, may happen; that is fine. But it's the unnecessary thinking that causes psychological suffering, as you say, which is the problem. That would reduce.

Then there are physical symptoms. I have met many devotees who have had phenomenal experiences. But when I sit with them, within two minutes, I can see there is a lot of restlessness.

Could you please talk about this?

G: You see, everything is the mind. I'll give you an example which veers slightly away from this. A boy who came to me said that he had accepted the teachings of the masters. He also added that his mind does not go into thinking of the past and the future. And he claimed to have achieved that feat by playing video games all the time.

Now that is missing the point because playing video games means the mind is still very active, whereas we are talking about a still mind—what Maharaj referred to as 'Conscious Presence' or abiding in one's Being. What Eckhart Tolle calls 'Being in the Now'.

Being in the Now is not something to be done as a major exercise. If your thinking mind is absent, you are being in the Now. You cannot not be present. But what happens is, one is not present consciously.

If someone is talking to you, and your mind is elsewhere, then you are not present.

So, the subsiding of the thinking mind leads to inner stillness.

Talking about agitation of the body, some bodies have more energy than others. Our blueprints are not the same. So, let's say I am someone with more energy. I go for a long walk, or a jog or whatever. I expend the energy in any way it needs to be expended. Right?

But then, the restless energy of the overactive thinking mind is not always expended. And that restlessness manifests in various ways.

Now someone with awareness can see that; they can see someone being fidgety, can see the eyes shifting, etc. So it is certainly not a judgement about that person, but one gets those cues.

N: Correct. I was saying that one can use these cues to self-reflect.

G: Absolutely.

N: I am assuming that if they are watching this, and they have come so far watching it, they are interested. So this would be important for them, right?

Two types of devotees could be on the Baba path for, let's say fifteen years: one who has had no experience of Baba or His miracles, and, on the other hand, one who has. But if they take these few suggestions and find stillness, then they will progress.

G: Yes. And I am here to defend those devotees who don't have these experiences. [Laughs.] Perhaps the viewers of your channel find my interviews not as *chamatkar*-filled as the others, but I firmly believe that Baba's teachings of Advaita are of the highest order. And that gets missed most often.

N: He lived it and demonstrated it.

G: Yes.

N: A dog is bitten or hit somewhere at a distance but He carries the wound. That's the highest form of teaching.

G: Yes. Now what is that? That everything is Me. 'M' caps, not lower case.

N: Correct.

G: That Oneness can only happen if one is established in the Absolute, which He was.

If we miss the teachings by way of His examples, and if we look at stories as just stories of Sai Baba's chamatkars, we get stuck with the chamatkars. We don't see the deeper meaning and significance of the stories. And stories are the best way to communicate. They are a very subtle form of teaching. We may be thinking this is a story we are reading, but it's actually operating at a vibrational level. Everything is vibrations.

I'll give you an example of my talk last Sunday, where someone mentioned that he gets visions of various deities. He said that he finds the experience beautiful. And then he asked me, 'What does it mean?'

I said, 'Look, firstly, the deity is a vibration.

'Ganapati Himself is actually a vibration when your *Ajna Chakra* synchronizes with your Manipur Chakra. That is why Ganapati's belly is huge and that is why He has a trunk. The *rishis* saw that when these two chakras are synchronized, one makes better decisions. One is more balanced and is able to deal with obstacles in a better way.'

So when one constantly looks at Ganapati and worships Him, one is imbibing those qualities vibrationally. It comes down to vibrations.

So there is very little that we actually see. That is, in fact, the play of maya. Things look one way but are operating at a different level.

Now the point is that we have someone like Sai Baba whose life is a living example of polar opposites. Calling a *masjid* Dwarakamai is one such example. All the polarities are being lived in the same moment. But if we miss that completely, then what is the point? I mean, can it be more obvious than that?

N: There's that saying: 'What's easy to do is also easy not to do.'

G: Exactly.

N: Maybe, at some point, I would like to go deeper into Eckhart Tolle's teachings of present-moment awareness because I feel it goes hand in hand with Baba's saburi, where, when you completely accept each moment as it is, that is present-moment awareness.

I feel there are some very beautiful pointers in Eckhart's teachings, which can take Baba's devotees—even those who have experiences—into that stillness, that ocean of Consciousness, which Baba is.

To view the corresponding video, scan the QR code.

13

Spiritual Journeys at the Office Desk

Nikhil: I would like to talk to you about your spiritual journey and your working life in the field of advertising and publishing, and how they have intertwined with each other. I feel it will offer devotees a very unique perspective because, in the course of your work, you have had the opportunity to meet many masters and teachers as well as devotees.

Despite your busy work life with all your responsibilities, you have been living the teaching. So if we can probe into this, I feel it would be a unique opportunity for devotees to get some pointers.

Gautam: Yes, very true. Because my teacher would say that work is a beautiful space to practise spiritual teachings. You deal with all sorts of people: suppliers, clients, colleagues, seniors, juniors . . . And it's fascinating because everything is about relationships and getting along with people, and getting work done.

You come to know how deeply you have absorbed a spiritual teaching only when you are out there in the world and not sitting in a cave.

So, yes, it has been a tremendous journey, a tremendous gift, and one I would love to share because of all that I have learnt from it.

I will never forget Sri Aurobindo's words. He said regarding *Karma Yoga* that meditation is fine because that's an internal journey. But what about meditation in daily living, when you're dealing with people, when you're dealing with work? That is also meditation.

You cannot exclude the external. It is *as* relevant if not more, than the internal. Why? Because, ultimately, every relationship is a reflection of yourself.

To start from the beginning, my journey began with a shift from advertising to publishing. When that happened, my mother had written . . . rather, she had drawn her spiritual experiences of awakening. And we wanted to share it with people who were going through similar experiences. It was like a road map of Kundalini awakening. A lot of books exist on the subject, but this was a visual journey because she *saw* the process of spiritual awakening.

That is when we thought that we should bring this out as a book. So we approached publishers, and many of them liked the book. However, given that the drawings were in colour, they wanted us to finance the publishing as the cost would be high. I thought to myself that since I have an ad agency and we've been doing colour brochures for our clients, rather than give someone else the money, why not do it ourselves? Which we eventually did, and it turned out to be quite a disaster, if I may say so, because it was a different ballgame altogether. You see, printing a book was very different from a brochure, and we didn't have the requisite knowledge. So we were also taken advantage of in the process.

When the book was ready and we went to the bookstores, especially the premium bookstores, they loved it because it was a colour production. It was well-presented and quite highly priced. They kept five copies each.

I also remember I went to one big book distributor who said that we should contact him again when we had a hundred titles for publication!

The bookstores that ordered the books, ordered five more copies because the initial five which we had given them had been sold. I was very grateful to God and asked them to give me the money for the first five copies. But we never got that money.

These events left me feeling pretty discouraged.

So there were various challenges, and I was convinced that I should not get into publishing again. But then one thing led to another, and we started publishing more books. And there were various learnings here, one of them being, Why did I continue despite it being so hard?

One day, while the advertising business was still functional, I was walking past the office reception when an elderly lady came in with a big cake, and I overheard her conversation with the receptionist. She said that a certain book had changed her life, and since the author seemed to be a foreigner and she didn't know how to contact him, she came to say thank you as she found our address in the book.

When I saw that, I was very moved because I realized that a book could change a person's life so much that she comes with a cake to say thank you. Whereas in the advertising business, if a client was happy, they didn't say thank you. They just paid your bills on time. That was it. Nothing beyond that. At least that was our experience.

I remember when I met Eckhart—I think it was in 1999 or 2000—I said, 'Eckhart, the advertising business is losing its grip on me.'

He gave me a two-word reply: 'Thank God!'

Because it was mostly about selling products to people that they don't need. That said, advertising does play a valid role, no doubt, but it was something I was not resonating with anymore.

So that is how the publishing journey began.

N: You were also blessed by a master. I think it was Gagangiri Maharaj who encouraged you to get into publishing.

G: Yes, because when he saw my mother's work, which I'm coming back to simply because it was the first book, he made it clear that it had to be shared. And he said, 'You do it.'

So I kind of felt that this was meant to be.

Early on, *The Times of India* was doing a big piece on 'spiritual businesses', so they called me for a telephonic interview. The lady at the other end asked me, 'Can you tell us something about your business plan?' I let out a laugh and replied, 'Only God knows.'

Not believing her ears, she said, 'Excuse me?'

I reiterated, a little differently this time: 'I don't have a business plan.'

She was shocked. 'You don't have a business plan!'

I said, 'I really don't. Things have just happened this way, and I'm going to follow it and see the course it takes.'

She promptly hung up, and that was the end of the interview.

But I truly believe that what is meant to happen will happen, and what is not meant to happen won't happen.

So through this journey of spiritual book publishing, as you said, I met wonderful masters as well as those who were not masters but who claimed to be masters, and I found it enriching.

Through this business, I got closer to my spiritual teacher, Ramesh Balsekar, as I helped him in editing and publishing his books. And his books were not as popular as, let's say, Eckhart's books, some of which we have published. So I would tell Rameshji that, thanks to Eckhart's books, we had the money to publish his books. You see, everything is so connected.

N: You've also had quite a few ups and downs. For instance, you mentioned once that in your advertising days, someone had refused to pay you, and you were forced to sit in their office and read a book there the whole day long till they made that payment.

G: Yes, that was a very interesting episode.

A big advertising client was not paying us, and we needed the money. Now, I was all of twenty-two or twenty-three. I had a staff of thirty people, and all of them were older than me. So I was really in a spot all around, and being the quiet type, I could not go and barge in and ask for my money. So what I decided to do was take the fattest book on my bookshelf. At that time, I was reading Robert Ludlum or something, so I picked up his fattest book, which I had read. I was determined that they should know that I was serious. So I went to their reception, met the secretary, and I said, 'Look, this money is owed to me. I will not survive without it, so I'm going to sit here till I get the money.'

The owners of the business didn't come out of their cabins to see me. For the first day, I sat from morning to evening reading my book. On the second day, they must have taken pity or felt bad because they offered me tea and all, I must say.

But, somehow, it worked. They said, 'Look, it's very embarrassing for us to see you sit here. The staff wonders what you are doing. So we'll give you your money. But you leave for now.' I stuck to my guns, saying, 'I won't leave till at least a part payment is made.' So that is how I eventually got paid.

I realized that I could do only that which was in my capacity. I felt deep down that I would not get this money because my nature was not to force it out of them, but thankfully, I got it.

But I was not so fortunate elsewhere. Our advertising agency eventually folded up because we had a huge bad debt. That money was not paid, and we had a general manager who was in cahoots with this client. He also embezzled some money and did things on the side, which he should not have done.

So that was also meant to happen. That closed down the ad business.

People advised me to file a case against him. Our lawyer said, 'You must go to court. This is wrong. We can prove it.'

But I asked myself if it was in my nature to do so. And this is what many people don't do.

Filing a case in the Indian courts meant going to court for perhaps twenty years. Was it really worth it? Did I have that kind of personality? I didn't. So I decided not to go to court.

People said that I was just trying to evade the situation by saying that it was my nature. But truly, I did feel that it was just not in my nature. And I knew that what was meant to happen happened, and destiny would take its course as far as the manager was concerned.

And I was so grateful that about twenty-five years after that incident, I came across a book, *Silence of the Heart*, by Robert Adams, wherein he advises you not to waste your time in court:

> Do not be for or against anything. Train yourself to observe, to watch, to look without any reaction. . . . Someone cheats you, and you're thinking of taking them to court to sue them. Think about this carefully. Is that what I really want to do? And then your ego will say, of course you do, you were cheated. . . . Say you did go to court and you won the case. You think this is good. But something will happen to even it out again. You'll have to go to court again and again and again. Sometimes you will win, sometimes you will lose.

I'm not saying that this applies to everyone. I'm referring to my situation; I did not have the bandwidth to deal with it.

I felt comforted reading Robert's book.

N: Generally, on the spiritual path, one tends to avoid conflict. Even Sai Baba would often mention, 'Don't get into conflict and argument. That hurts Me as well.' So it is not that you're escaping events, but you try and avoid a confrontation. This was a good living example in your case.

G: And why? Because conflict disturbs your peace.

N: True.

G: Nothing is as sacredly held as an opinion. So you don't want to engage beyond a point because points of view are often conflicting. You are no longer attached to your point of view. So you tend to walk away from conflicts. You tend to be less involved in the drama.

I met a clairvoyant in the UK many years ago—a lovely man. He told me, 'Gautam, the difference between you and me is this: suppose that we are walking by a pond and one is not quite sure whether it is clean or murky. I am someone who will just jump in, and you are someone who will say, "Is it really worth jumping in?" and you'll walk away.'

It is one's nature. If it is one's nature to avoid conflict, one avoids it.

So I have seen that this is something which pays off huge dividends. To avoid conflicts does not mean to escape them. Say what you have to, but to say the same thing a hundred times is not needed. However, many of us do that.

Thanks to advertising, I had these experiences. Thanks to the business folding up, I realized that when things are not meant to be, they are finished. There's no point in pointing fingers or accusing people. It was meant to happen.

So there were big lessons learned. When we are suffering in the process, we don't see it that way, but in retrospect, to even see that is a big gift. And this is what helped me in my book-publishing journey.

Many people would criticize masters and tell me to be wary of them. But the more the criticism, the more I would go to meet these masters. Because I realized that it was the critic's point of view. To be neutral and objective, I must reach my own conclusions.

When people criticize, they get stuck at the level of personality. Everyone has flaws, you see. So one is not looking at that aspect. One is looking at the bigger picture that is being offered. Is it of value to people? So you no longer operate based on personal likes and dislikes.

There may be a master who is considered very arrogant, and he *is* arrogant. But one should clearly see that it is an aspect of his personality. Yet when he speaks about a certain type of yoga or whatever it is, and he is brilliant, that is of tremendous value. So one learns to discriminate.

N: You've been a publisher, and you've met many masters. I have also met a few, and I have felt that all of them have ways to shake devotees up, which might be intentional. Sometimes they may do something—which I can't even say is part of their personality—to check why the devotee has come or to break their ego; they may do certain things that will go against the conditioning of the devotee.

For example, I think it was Ram Baba who had come to meet Sai Baba, and he saw Baba having onions, and he thought, *What will I learn from one who is eating this?* Baba read his mind and told him that only those who could process onions could have them. Ram Baba was taken aback.

The conditioned mind has an idea of a master, or what a master is, and it wants to see that on the outside. Whereas the master can break your idea or concept and do some sort of a leela. But I would say, it might not be their personality; it might just be so for that particular case.

G: It could very well be that also. We wouldn't know. Even Anandamayi Ma used to do the same thing. Someone with a big ego would come to see her, and she would tell that person to go clean the bathrooms or utensils or whatever.

So how this works is very strange, but the point is that we confuse the message for the messenger. The teachings are eternal. They have come from ancient times through the scriptures. So it is the teachings that are important.

In the olden days, when the postman came with a letter, did you just shake hands with him and send him off? Or did you take the letter and read what was in the letter? That is the message.

I learnt that because I met so many masters, yogis, psychics, astrologers . . . It just happened. I was not seeking them. And it was so clear to me what it was that drew me to the person. Or what didn't draw me. There was none of that conflict with liking some and not liking others.

There was a master who loved criticising my master. And I felt I was not reacting, because I just knew that this was the way he was. He was critical of all the masters. It had nothing to do with me. Someone asked me why I didn't defend my guru, but I didn't feel the need to do so because he's entitled to his point of view. What was I going to defend? I was not there to change his point of view. So let him say what he wants. Now, someone else would have walked away if it was unbearable. It was not an unbearable criticism, so I was there.

It's all very relative; there's no black and white.

But what I learnt is that, generally, spiritual egos are far bigger than normal egos. I've seen it not only in some masters but also in their disciples.

N: I remember having this discussion with you about many devotees who feel that they are ahead on the path and want to give advice which is not asked for. They try and impose their views on others.

Maybe while we are at it, we can probe into some examples.

G: Yes, because they think they know what is best. Whereas my teacher would say, 'Never give advice unless you are asked for it.' Because you don't know what is best.

Sometimes it does happen. I'll give you a classic example. One very big organization in South India, many years ago, split. Right through the middle, it split. I was at work, and I got a call from the faction which had separated from the existing organization. Theirs was the first call I received, and the lady on the line said, 'Gautam, this has happened. And I just thought I'd inform you that we are no longer associated with the master.'

I said, 'Fair enough, you must be having your reasons, and thank you for calling me.'

She replied, 'Yes, we just wanted you to know.' I don't know why me because I had no special connection with them, but maybe they thought being a spiritual book publisher and all that . . .

After two hours, I got a call from the master's faction informing me about what had happened. They were concerned, and they asked me what I thought of the situation.

And what I said to them was the result of a big lesson I had learnt from my auditor when I was twenty-four and had to take charge of the ad agency, as the senior management left to start their own agency. I was full of fear, thinking, *How will I be able to handle all this?*

And the auditor said to me, 'Look, Gautam, organizations are separate from individuals. As an auditor, I can tell you that nobody is indispensable.' And then he told me, to my shock, at that time, 'Your father died, and the ad agency continued despite that. That proves my point that nobody is indispensable. If the organization is meant to go on, it will go on.'

And I found myself saying the same words to this ashram head who called me. I said, 'Look, whatever has happened has happened. They may walk away with half the following, but if your ashram is meant to survive, it will survive.'

A simple life lesson—nobody is indispensable. And back to Ramana Maharshi's words: 'The Ordainer controls the fate of souls in accordance with their Prarabdha Karma. Whatever is destined not to happen will not happen, try as you may. Whatever is destined to happen will happen, do what you may to prevent it. This is certain. The best course, therefore, is to remain silent.'

So that was a pretty amazing thing for me to see that both sides called me, and what I said was only common sense.

N: When I last met you in Mumbai, you mentioned that the sales tax officers came to your office and gave you a big fat bill of something like eighteen lakhs to pay overnight, that too when you had done no wrong intentionally.

I think your sales tax consultant had made some errors over the years, and it was something that was beyond your control. But I was amazed to see your acceptance of the situation. There was no ill will towards the consultant, and you tried doing whatever you could do.

Could you speak about that? I felt that it was a very important aspect of the teaching being lived.

G: I tell anyone who has faced loss in life that when you have early setbacks in life, it will take you very far. Because then, the second time you are hit, you don't feel the impact that much.

In this case, we were not paying the correct sales tax, though it was based on our sales tax consultant's calculations. He misled us, albeit unintentionally. He just didn't understand our business.

The sales tax department randomly scrutinizes companies, and we came under their scanner. The amount they said we had to pay as a penalty and interest was a considerable one. Of course, for a small company like ours, it was a shock.

I was taken aback because this group of sales tax officers were so nice. They came into my cabin and they told me, 'Look, we can see when people are evading tax and when they have just filed it wrongly. We can see it on their face when we talk to them.' They felt bad about the whole thing.

I responded, 'We didn't know. We've been filing what our sales tax consultant told us to file.'

They even fixed a meeting, where the sales tax consultant was called to my office, and they asked him, 'What have you done? Because of you, this man is suffering.'

I was moved by their concern. But, at the same time, I knew that the money was meant to go. If it was not meant to go, it would not have gone. So my mind did not create a drama or stories about it.

And guess what happened after that? Despite the huge loss, the sales tax consultant sent me his bill. That is human nature. And I paid it.

So this teaching took me very far. Yes, the loss hit me hard, but I did not lose sleep, because I knew it was meant to go. How and why and when was irrelevant in the larger scheme of things.

And I must say that I've had other enlightening experiences.

Once my auditor told me that an income tax officer wanted to meet me. And I got very scared because 'meeting' means there's some trouble. You've done something wrong in your returns or filing or whatever. So I told my auditor I didn't want to meet the officer because I didn't know what to say in front of such people. I requested him to go on my behalf. He replied that the officer wanted to meet me specifically. I still insisted on not going to meet this man.

After repeated refusals on my part, my auditor finally informed me that the officer had decided to come over to my office to meet me. That got me really worried. I thought I was in big trouble. Who's heard of income tax officers coming to people's offices like that?

When the officer came, my auditor didn't accompany him because he had to fly out somewhere; so that made me very nervous. The man came, sat in front of me, and said, 'I only wanted to meet you to tell you that when your income tax papers came to me, I said to myself, *Oh, I know Yogi Impressions. I've read so many of their books.* So I just wanted to thank you for publishing them.'

It was a big lesson to me that reality is completely different from all the preconceived ideas and notions that we tend to harbour.

I had such a beautiful conversation with this man. It was a terminal illness that had brought him onto the spiritual path. He told me his story, and his parting line was one I will never forget: 'All I want is my life to be just a comma. I don't want to be a disturbance to anyone beyond that. I don't want any fuss or being in the limelight. I just want my life to be a gentle comma in the middle of a sentence.'

And that really touched me.

So these are the gifts I was gifted with, which would not have happened in the general course of business. It's only because I have been in spiritual book publishing that there have been so many instances, you know. It's just incredible.

I remember, in our early years, we received a manuscript which I really liked, and we decided to publish it. However, the author informed us that there was another publisher who was also interested in the same manuscript.

So I was disappointed, but I told her, 'Now it's for you to decide.'

Normally, a new author would be keen that their book gets published at the first available opportunity.

After some deliberation, she decided to get the book published by us. I asked her why she decided to go ahead with us. She replied, 'I had a dream. I dreamt that outside the publisher's window was a big tree.' She had once called me and asked me, 'Is there a tree outside your window?' I answered yes, thinking, *What a bizarre thing this woman is asking*! And I soon forgot about it. But the fact is that there was a tree outside the window of the office I had then.

So this incident proved to me that it was pure destiny. It was meant to be published by us, so she had a dream of a tree outside her publisher's window. Which is no guarantee that the book would sell well, by the way. That's the other thing, you know. We think that God has done this leela, so this book is going to be a bestseller. It was not a bestseller. All this incident proved was that we were meant to publish the book. But we tend to think that such incidents are a sign from God.

N: That is the tendency of the mind.

G: That is what it does. And thankfully, I've had enough experiences that prove the same.

But it's fascinating, you see.

N: I would like to cover that incident, what I call the Mooji Tea Incident, when we were in Tiruvannamalai together. We had gone to Mooji's house to meet him and they offered us tea.

On the second day too we were supposed to be visiting him again. I'm not sure if you remember. We all went to a cafe before going to his place and we had tea there. And I said, 'No, I don't want any, because we are going to Mooji's, and I'll have tea over there.'

And I distinctly remember that you looked at me, and said, 'Okay.' It was a peculiar sort of a look.

Later, when we left the place, we got a call to inform us that the meeting was cancelled and to come the next morning.

And then you told me, 'Listen, look back and see that you made this assumption that you would be going to Mooji's place and would have tea there.'

And that was a pivotal point, however simple it may have seemed, where I saw the assumptive nature of one's thoughts. And I truly realized that I didn't know anything, so how could I make an assumption?

It was very simple but really very profound.

G: Yes, that you should have tea when it is offered to you, because you may not get it again. [Laughs.]

N: Yes, absolutely.

G: I remember once, we had gone to the ashram of a very big scholar of the Gita and Vedanta, and I was quite looking forward to the visit. My friend and I were very courteously invited to have lunch with him.

From the start of that lunch to the end of it, he was criticizing each and every spiritual teacher in India. And there was no asking, 'Where are you from? What do you do?' or no sharing of anything of import, but only a barrage of criticism. I was so taken aback.

And then, you won't believe it. A few days later, I got a call that he had met with an accident and had to have umpteen stitches on his jaw. Who knows whether or not the two incidents were connected, in the larger scheme of things? It struck me that even a spiritual teacher of prominence and eminence was talking ill of others. And so I saw that even this happens on the spiritual path.

Someone else, a friend, was critical of the big gurus and went on and on about it. I just told her, 'You know, in the South, there are gurus who have done such tremendous work by setting up free hospitals for the needy, electricity and water in villages.' And maybe there was a bit of irritation in me when I said thereafter, 'If we did something like that, even on a very small scale, it would be so much more beautiful rather than just criticizing these masters.'

And that made her even more upset. 'How dare you tell me this?' Because a critical mind will not take any form of criticism about itself, but it is happy to criticize others.

So I have seen this also, that there's a lot of this happening all around, and these have been learning opportunities for me. It's quite fascinating that we tend to focus on only the negatives and ignore the positives.

N: I think one of the masters, I'm not sure if it was Ramakrishna Dev, said that the difference between man and God is such that if a man makes just one mistake, another man will look only at that. But if he does even one good thing, God will take note of it. I feel one can learn quite a lot from that difference in attitude.

G: Yes, it is the attitude which is the main thing.

N: Where you look at something good and you're grateful for that.

G: Yes, absolutely. That's crucial.

N: And then one other bit, which I feel would be very unique from your perspective is that you've met so many masters, pseudo-masters, and so many people on the path. There is this tendency that when one interacts with a group for the first time, they want to sort of convert you and pull you in. I'm sure you've experienced a lot of that.

G: Yes, many times.

N: So, how do you sort of assert your boundaries there?

G: See, I tend to have a more benevolent approach to this. Because of their love for their master and the teaching, they want to share both with others. So sometimes they tend to be pushy, you know. But people don't like being pushed.

However, with me, I'm not someone who would react to pushiness. I would just brush it aside, so it's okay.

But it is also, I think, something to be looked at by these devotees themselves. This need to bring others into the fold means not to accept that everyone is on their own journey, everyone has the master destined for them, and if that master happens to be their master, they will come into the fold.

That is why even someone like Sathya Sai Baba . . . I remember a book in which he is berating his main disciples about this by telling them not to go about canvassing to get people for his talk because they would come if they were destined to; God knows best. All it needs is an announcement, that's it.

This kind of overbearing attitude is happening a lot, unfortunately.

I think Ramakrishna said something so beautiful: when the flower blooms, the bees come. Nothing has to be done. It's as simple as that.

It is not only a big learning curve for the devotees who are doing this, but it is something which one has to learn from because you cannot force the hand of destiny.

Yes, if you have been impacted by your master, that spontaneous feeling to share the master with others is understandable. But beyond a point, if you ask me, that is a form of violence because you are trying to shape the hand of destiny. You have to trust that if the master's teaching is to reach out, it *will* reach out. Whether or not you put in that extra effort is really not relevant. Do what you can to share the teaching but not to convert people to the teaching.

Many times, I have been offered *mantra deeksha* and various other things. Or messages from the afterlife have been conveyed to me by others that, actually, my master is so-and-so and that this will be revealed in due course.

But be where your feet are right now. That is the biggest lesson.

That said, once again, this eagerness to convert everyone does show the love that the disciples have for the master and the teaching. That cannot be discounted.

On another note, I have enjoyed masters who are light-hearted and humorous. I think those are great qualities. Seriousness should not be there.

I remember reading about what Meher Baba would do. He was quite naughty. When he was travelling with his group by train, he would tell one devotee to shut the window as he was disturbed by the breeze. And that devotee would obediently do so. And then, when he wasn't looking, he would tell another devotee to open the window as he wanted to enjoy the breeze. And so, consequently, both disciples would get into a fight about whether the widow should be shut or open. And Baba would have a hearty laugh, you know. That was quite funny.

There was another incident when the train was already crowded, and they were approaching a crowded platform where hundreds of people were waiting to get onto the train. The disciples asked Baba, 'What do we do? It will be too crowded in here.'

He said, 'Don't worry; just get me a white chadar.'

When the train approached the station, Baba lay down and they put the chadar on him and started wailing and crying. Nobody got onto that coach; the scenario scared them as they thought it was a dead body. Then the train left, and Baba and his followers happily enjoyed the rest of the journey.

I think it's such fun, you know, this light-heartedness. That for me is a big sign. Humour is very important.

N: I think the master would be exempt from any karmic repercussions. But other people, if they try to do that . . . don't try that at home. [Laughs.]

G: I do enjoy good humour because life is already so serious. It's beautiful to be exposed to a master who's able to see the lighter side of life.

To view the corresponding video, scan the QR code.

14

Meditation on Faith (Gautam's Talk)

This is a meditation on faith, or rather, true faith.

We sit back and relax in a comfortable position, eyes preferably closed so that we are not distracted by the world outside. Open is fine too. As you wish.

We reflect on faith, the deeper meaning of faith. Not faith that I will get what I want. Faith that whatever happens is God's will. Whatever happens is Baba's will.

Faith that I don't know what is best for me. And so I trust a power far bigger than me that knows best. I go through life's journey with total faith that whatever happens in my life, whether I like it or not, is God's will. And it is this faith that gives me the strength to face life's challenges.

With such faith, there is no question of wondering *Why did this happen to me? Why did this not happen?* and so on. These questions have come to an end.

I now have the full faith that everything is ordained by God. Everything is ordained by Baba. He will give me the strength that I need when I need it.

This faith no longer shakes like a leaf in the breeze. Rather, it is like a large immovable rock on which I stand firmly with the conviction that I simply cannot understand the dynamics of the vast universal laws that are so complex, so perfect. It is impossible for my little mind to understand the connections, the various events that unfold in my life.

So I offer this faith at the Lord's feet, at Baba's feet.

And now I know. My heart is lighter now because space has been created for it to be filled with the light of total faith. I know that heaven is to be found in the heart of the man who knows that whatever happens is God's will.

All the questions I used to ask myself have dropped away. My mind is now free of that dialogue. For I have accepted God's will. I have accepted Baba's will.

I now always consider my glass half full and not half empty for I know that if God has brought me so far in life, He will hold my hand and take me further. Baba will always be holding my hand. I don't need proof of that, for I have total faith.

To view the corresponding video, scan the QR code.

15

Awakening During the Pandemic

Nikhil: We are here once again after, I think, a long eight or nine months, and the current global situation is unprecedented. No one would have even thought in their wildest dreams that the whole world would be locked down.

So it would be nice to talk to you about how people and devotees may have been affected under these circumstances.

Gautam: Yes.

I can't remember when we last met, but obviously, it was before the pandemic situation.

It's amazing because it shows us that so little is in our control. Even people who felt confident about being in control of their lives have now seen that if God wills something, there's nothing that anyone can do about it.

There's a big lesson here: devotees who live with this understanding that even the next breath is not in their control are the ones who can face such challenges because they are rooted in the teachings of the guru.

So the pandemic is a test of the sincerity of a true devotee.

Nobody saw this coming, including astrologers. In the last hundred years, maybe a bit less than that, one has not seen this kind of global collective suffering, physically and psychologically.

That is why I feel that Sai Baba's teachings are so relevant in these extreme situations. And let's not forget that the Satcharita begins with a cholera epidemic. So, isn't this a significant pointer as to how relevant the Satcharita is today?

N: Yes, you are absolutely right about that. It's not a coincidence that the first chapter of the Satcharita deals with an epidemic situation.

Also, I found that the grinding carried out by Sai Baba in the story is symbolic of being centred—and the centre is Baba. The avalanche of catastrophes for those who are not centred in Him by means of remembrance or sadhana is going to prove to be overwhelming. I say this because I have seen people who have been impacted by the teachings when they have gone through difficult times. Externally, although it might seem that they are having a rough time, within themselves, they are centred, and their faith is untouched, because of which their experience is very different from that of someone who may not have had an equally trying time but who may have been scarred quite badly psychologically.

G: Yes, and that is why, as I have said before, it is suffering and loss that bring people onto the path. This is a fact of life. When everything is going smoothly, why would you think of God?

There's so much suffering today as a result of the current situation. One example is job losses. Another one is the psychological suffering that people, who have been in the same space with each other all the time, have had to endure. Families have got stuck together. For instance, under normal circumstances, the man of the house would go to work and not see his family members for a large part of the day.

Now two things tend to happen in such a situation. One is that you start searching for the deeper meaning of life: *What is the meaning of all this?* That is the spiritual journey.

If you are already on the spiritual journey, let's say you are already following Baba's teachings, the opportunity is now provided to delve deeper.

But there's one more scenario where there's just endless suffering because you want to escape from what's happening and live in an imaginary future. For such people, the suffering continues. They don't take to the spiritual path. Each according to their destiny.

And you mentioned faith. You see, the Faith Meditation [Refer to talk 14.] has struck a chord because it is not about faith depending on an outcome. It is faith that whatever happens, or whatever may happen, is His will. Now that is unshakable faith and not faith that depends on one thinking, for instance, *I am Baba's devotee, so nothing will happen to me, and I'll get what I want materially.* Baba Himself has said that you cannot escape Prarabdha Karma.

However, as you said, the grinding motion symbolizes holding onto the centre—and that centre is Baba. That is faith that whatever I am meant to face in life will be faced with the strength of my devotion to Baba.

And you also gave an example, if you can mention it here, about a lady who experienced this faith.

N: Yes.

She faced a very tragic loss. Her husband succumbed to Covid after having contracted it. She wrote to me saying that the loss was unbearable but it was the Faith Meditation that held her together and gave her the strength to accept that loss; it helped her stick to her faith. That's the main thing. And also that understanding, as you said, of Prarabdha, that everything is ordained by Him.

However, some people question how Baba could ordain something as terrible as this. Then I reflect on what you say and even what is said in the Satcharita. Kakasaheb Dixit once asked Baba to save someone, and Baba told him, 'See, if I save him now, in his next birth, it is going to hamper his spiritual life. Are you going to take that upon yourself?'

That's it. That understanding and the Faith Meditation then make you realize you don't know what is best for you.

G: We have tunnel vision, you see. We see things only from our point of view. This is good, this is bad. But the broader vision spanning across lifetimes is the vision that Baba has. It's like when you're driving a car, either you look at the car which is just in front of you or you look way ahead—ten cars ahead. That is the difference between Baba's vision and ours. And we tend to question Baba because our vision is so narrow.

So the faith is knowing that my intellect is limited, that there's a vast presence, a vast force, far more potent than mine, which is in charge of affairs.

The lady who lost her husband to Covid did not have the psychological suffering: *Why did Baba do this to me? How could He?* People do tend to complain like that. *I am Baba's devotee. Therefore, this should not have happened to me.* This is the psychological suffering created by conditional faith.

However, because she tapped into true faith, all this psychological suffering did not take place for this lady. It's a very important point.

To view the corresponding video, scan the QR code.

16

Living the Teachings During Turbulent Times—Part I

Nikhil: Today the whole world is in a frenzy due to the coronavirus pandemic. We put out a post a few days ago about Baba's guidance regarding the situation and how serious it actually is. Many devotees had certain questions and many people found themselves in a very peculiar scenario, being locked up at home for long periods. As the virus has progressed worldwide, I also see it as being a big mental challenge. Could you shed some light on that?

Gautam: Yes, certainly.

It is indeed an unprecedented time for all of us. Most of us have not seen an event like this in our lifetime. And as you have said just now, because of the lockdown, we are forced to sit at home, a scenario we have not envisioned ever before.

It also shows how little everything is in our control. If we haven't realized that by now, it is time to wake up to this reality. And yes, what *is* in our control is our attitude to the circumstances.

The insights and learnings that we will gain through this event can help us on our onward spiritual journey.

The other point I would like to add here is that this time which we have to ourselves is a time for introspection and reflection. It is not a time to think, *Oh God, how do I pass this time? How can I keep myself occupied?* Of course, that will be so at the mundane level. But rather than frittering this time away, seeing movie after movie on Netflix and making endless phone calls to friends and relatives, it is a time which has been offered to us to re-evaluate our life and our priorities. It is a time to go within.

A channel such as yours is a tool that can be so easily accessed and referred to in a time like this, and it proves to be of much benefit on our spiritual journey.

N: In times like this, Baba has specifically guided people to do mantra japa and chant the *Hanuman Chalisa* as well as the *Gayatri Mantra*. And this brings us to what you just said about putting this time to good use so that the mind doesn't get pulled into the collective fear. That is pretty probable in WhatsApp groups, where people are sharing stuff. On a practical note, yes, these groups keep you informed of the rules and regulations that are in effect, but beyond that, it can become very easy for people to get sucked into the collective paranoia that is prevailing.

G: Yes, that is very true because the content of our consciousness occupies the foremost space in our minds. If we are looking at WhatsApp forwards that are talking about all the ghastly scenarios or projections of numbers all the time, it is bound to create a fear which is disproportionate to what the reality is, and the reality itself is bad enough.

So a lot of psychological suffering gets not only created but perpetuated because that is the nature of the thinking mind. The thinking mind is always projecting into an imaginary future.

Now when we come to the Hanuman Chalisa, the Gayatri Mantra, etc., why are these suggestions not to be taken lightly? When you chant the mantra, it is shifting your focus from all that fear-based content on social media to itself. The thinking mind, which was galloping all over the place, now has a peg to hold on to. The rope of the horse gets tied to this peg. That is the advantage of the mantra and that is what is meant by 'freeing the mind'.

The other thing is that each mantra has a specific purpose to fulfil. For example, the Hanuman Chalisa is based on Hanuman, who is connected to the breath, or *prana*. So reciting the Chalisa helps you regulate your breath. When you are filled with fear, the breath is different from what it is when you are calm. So the Chalisa is doing much more than what you think it is doing.

We just think on one level that we must keep reciting it continuously. But the vibrations created by the chanting are bound to be beneficial.

N: When there was a cholera epidemic during Baba's time, He had offered all His devotees protection, and according to His messengers whom I have known, He had very specifically said, 'Nothing will touch My devotees. Those who have surrendered with complete faith will sail through.'

It brings me to my next point, which is very related to that incident. As you said, the thinking mind does go into an imaginary future. I was reflecting that when excessive information is presented to someone, their mind receives this information; however, they cannot differentiate between facts and imaginary information.

With this pandemic, if there is this excessive fear that is prevailing and people cannot manage it, I feel it is going to affect them on a physical as well as mental level because they will not know the difference between fiction and reality. Their minds go into a frenzy, and that might affect their immunity.

G: Yes, very true, but you see, that is the true meaning of faith in the guru or faith in Sai Baba. When you have faith and trust, you know that whatever is going to happen, as far as you are concerned, is for your higher good. You are taken care of in that sense. Also, you understand the futility of thinking endlessly about something that may or may not happen.

If you have embraced Sai Baba's teachings and lived them, the incessant chatter of the mind will stop. But if your mind is chattering away, it is a clear sign that the teachings have not been embraced. If you have unshakeable faith in Baba, you will not be stressed beyond a point.

N: Correct.

G: Of course, you will be stressed on the mundane level: *How do I get my vegetables? Will the milkman come?* etc. because, after all, those are the mechanics of daily living. But beyond that, the stories and projections will not happen.

So, I think that extreme times like these show us where we truly stand on our spiritual journey. In that sense, they are gifts being given to us.

Let's take a very simple example. All is fine in your house with your loved ones. You feel that prior to the pandemic, you were busy at work, but now you are getting time to spend with your loved ones. It's so nice.

But let a few days pass, and then, suddenly, the same ones you were so happy to be with now start getting on your nerves—and vice versa.

N: Many people in the past may have indulged in distractions, such as going to movies and outings, and they may not even have been aware of it. But now, not only are they locked in but they are locked in with people who may be difficult to be with.

So I have two specific questions to ask you:

First, if there is a sincere devotee and they are constrained in a small apartment with four or five other family members who may not be on the same path, any pointers for them to stay conscious?

And, second, if people get on each other's nerves then it sort of becomes a bit difficult for everyone involved.

G: There are two things here:

One is that we come to know in times like this how much we are identified with situations and things. How much are we identified with our work, for example? What happens now that we can't go to work? How much are we identified with our social environment? We used to meet so many people, so many friends. Now we are not able to meet them.

So now, when we are at home, we can truly see where we derive our identifications from, and we will be surprised to discover how much of the external environment we derive our sense of self from.

I know someone in his mid-sixties who didn't have much work to do even before the lockdown. His business had shut down, but he still had his office. He would go, open the office, sit there and switch on the TV as he couldn't bear to sit at home. You see, that is the degree of identification with one's job.

Someone may have derived their worth from all their friendships or the huge social circle they had, but where has all that gone now? They were deriving their sense of self from an external source.

I will mention one relevant incident.

A very big industrialist made a statement that a person's worth can be judged by the number of people who come to his funeral. Then this industrialist passed away, and hundreds of people showed up for the prayer service.

And you know why? He owed many of them money, so they thought they had better turn up in the hope that they would get something back, and the other half showed up because they were so relieved he was gone.

So the point is, when you are home, reflect on all this. Sit with a cup of coffee. Think about all that you were doing during the day and what you were dependent on because all that has been challenged now.

And you may think that this is only temporary, but who knows how long is 'temporary'? It may be temporary now. It can come back after a few months or years.

This is the time to evaluate your dependency and where you derive your sense of self from. And if you are a true bhakta of Baba's and His teachings, you will know what He says about where you should derive your sense of self from. He clearly says, 'Give it all to Me.'

So what does that mean? It means to derive your sense of self from the Source, from God, from Consciousness, and not from this externalized *tamasha* that has been going on in one's life.

Normally, people who are on the spiritual path, like the ones who are on your channel, already have this understanding of life, that it is transient, it is temporary; that is why the turning within has already happened.

N: Correct.

G: The second thing is that this opportunity has to be used to delve deeper into the teachings. It is for one's benefit. It doesn't mean you don't watch TV. It doesn't mean you punish yourself. Everything in moderation is fine. But yes, do sit back and re-evaluate your priorities, and your internal dialogue, and see when you are at peace and when you are not at peace, because, as the great sage Ramana Maharshi said, Self-realization is nothing but peace and equanimity.

N: Modern life is full of distractions, but the current situation takes us back to very simple, minimalistic living—everyone is pretty much in survival mode. This is another aspect of Baba's teaching or rather what He showed us. Baba's life was minimalistic; He hardly owned anything.

I was also reflecting on the act of sharing. Many may hoard groceries and things out of fear. But how many would truly care and share with people who are in need? In a safe way, of course, without breaking any norms. In this scenario, one would come to a very minimalistic way of living because if this goes on for much longer, many of the fancy extra frills will be taken away. One could also look at this aspect, how one adapts to this lifestyle.

G: Yes, true. It's a very important point, which has two facets:

One is that we will be surprised because now so much of our spending is cut out automatically; not going to restaurants, shopping excessively and suchlike. So much is cut out that it is a chance to realize that we have been excessive and how little is really needed to be happy.

N: Correct.

G: You see, this is a time to realize that. That is one thing.

The other thing is that if we see God in all beings, then even the thought of hoarding would not arise because when we are hoarding, we are taking away something from someone else. Yes, of course, we will keep something as a reserve. Everyone will do that. But if we are true devotees of Baba's, and we see Baba in everyone, then that excessive hoarding—which is fear-based and done with the attitude that I must protect myself, regardless of what others go through—is not possible.

So if we have a heightened sense of awareness, then we can see our traits and habits, and be honest with ourselves. This time can be utilized to observe our reactions and our thinking, in the light of the beautiful teachings.

N: Yes.

G: I still maintain that though there was so much bhakti around Sai Baba, His teachings were the highest form of Advaita, the absolute highest. A simple line such as 'See Me in all beings' is nothing but understanding that the same Consciousness functions through everyone. That is pure, non-dual teaching. So this is a chance to live that.

N: Wonderful. Thank you for shedding light on these important pointers.

G: My pleasure.

I would like to end on the note that we should give a thought to all those who have suffered because of this virus, all those who have lost their lives and all the caretakers who have risked their lives to look after the people who have been impacted by this virus. Let's not forget that we are all one family.

To view the corresponding video, scan the QR code.

17

Living the Teachings During Turbulent Times—Part II

Nikhil: Regarding a conversation I had with Hema Ma yesterday, I would like to share a small message from her, which pertains to the current pandemic situation. She said that Baba has specifically asked all devotees to take a little bit of *udi*, mix it with water and sprinkle it around the periphery of their houses if that is possible. If not, they can do so at the main door entrance and the windows. And this practice must be carried out every day.

Furthermore, the Gayatri Mantra should be chanted, continuously if possible, or at the very least, a recording of it should be played in the house all the time.

Baba has said that people don't realize the seriousness and the magnitude of this disease that is spreading. So one must practise these two things religiously.

Gautam: Yes, I think they are very interesting suggestions, so let's explore them a bit. Water carries vibrations. That is why, as you may be aware, the Golden Temple in Amritsar is surrounded by a body of water. That water has absorbed the vibrations of all the chanting that has gone on for hundreds of years in that temple. So the atmosphere gets charged.

That is why the suggestion of sprinkling water mixed with udi around the house is given because it means that the water is charged with Baba's vibrations. It's a very significant aspect as, let's not forget, the human body itself is seventy per cent water. So the content of our minds is equally important at a time like this because we are carrying those vibrations within us.

And of course, the Gayatri Mantra is so appropriate. Our minds are so preoccupied with all these fear-based concepts now, that the mantra will help to clear that vibration, not only from within ourselves but from our environment.

So these are two wonderful suggestions which have come through Hema Ma.

N: This takes me to a story in the Sai Satcharita about the cholera epidemic. Baba had ground wheat and asked the ladies to go around the village and sprinkle it all around. He had assured them that He was taking care of His devotees by protecting them from the disease and that nothing would touch the devotees who had faith; they would sail through.

G: Yes, it's mentioned in the first chapter of the Satcharita.

N: I also happened to read a story in the Sai Satcharita about Baba and Jawahar Ali, a *fakir*, who came to the village. He was quite a sweet talker and tried to play the role of Baba's guru. And Baba also played along.

I hope you have read the story.

G: Yes, I am quite familiar with it. It's a very important story. But go on.

N: I would like your views on the story and what devotees can take away from it as Baba played along, willingly becoming his disciple and knowing fully well that the fakir had his shortcomings.

G: Yes. There are various aspects to this most interesting story.

The first is that, as we all know, Baba had the unique gift of being able to see His rnanubandhan with individuals. He could just look at them and know for how many births they had been with Him. Other stories have also touched upon this subject.

So obviously, Baba knew His previous association with Jawahar Ali. Now in this incarnation, the karma had to play out. It is Baba's greatness that He saw the bondage of this relationship, and it needed to play out till the end. And Baba did what is required of any guru–disciple relationship. The guru is considered God. So He allowed Jawahar Ali to play that role. That is the bigness of Baba's heart.

It is even said in our scriptures that the guru is God in human form. I will tell you another interesting story as an aside.

In Paramahansa Yogananda's book *Autobiography of a Yogi*, there's a story about Mahavatar Babaji, the deathless Himalayan master. A disciple climbs mountain range upon mountain range to reach Babaji and finally manages to do so, exhausted. When he sees Babaji, he prostrates and says, 'Master, I have come.'

Mahavatar Babaji tells him, 'All right, if you want to be my disciple, then please go and jump off the cliff.'

The man is shocked, but he tells Babaji, 'You are my master, and I will do as I am told.' And he does that.

After he falls, Mahavatar Babaji goes and revives him, and says, 'You have passed the test.' And the test is this: if you consider the guru to be God in human form, then you have to follow His command.

Today, in many guru–disciple relationships, that does not happen. And if I recall correctly, Baba Himself has said that one needs a living guru. Am I right about that?

N: Absolutely.

G: Where does He say that? Could you remind me?

N: There is a chapter in which Baba mentions ten prerequisites for Self-realization, and the ninth one is the necessity of having a living guru. He said that the path is so full of obstacles that one can easily get deluded and fall. A living master who has reached the very end will safely guide you through this. Baba has said this very emphatically.

G: Okay. So we know that Baba did not need a guru like we need one. But He could see that a relationship was established here between a guru and a disciple, so He fulfilled that role to the hilt.

And I remember how this story ends: Jawahar Ali comes and falls at Baba's feet and says, 'I have now seen Your greatness.'

So it is a very important story. It shows that even someone of Baba's stature honoured this guru–disciple relationship for the period it lasted, which means He kept Jawahar Ali's self-proclaimed-guru-personality aside. People didn't like Jawahar Ali. But Baba was so refined that He kept that out of the way and allowed the relationship to fulfil itself, whereas we tend to criticize and complain even about our own gurus because we judge them as individuals; we do not consider them to be God in human form.

N: There are numerous stories of various sincere devotees going to masters who had their shortcomings or were not fully realized. The devotees were so guileless and their faith was so complete that, for example, the master may just casually tell them to take God's name to overcome their troubles, and that would actually happen because the devotees had complete faith, so much so that even the master would be taken aback and wonder how it happened.

There are so many stories I could cite, and there is so much to take away from this leela of Baba's, that I feel if the devotee is sincere and they look within themselves rather than look at the shortcomings in the master or anybody else, that will really take them a long way.

G: Yes, and the main thing here is that we tend to read these stories as nothing more than just interesting stories, which I have emphasized in earlier videos.

But I think through these stories, we have to look at our own life, as you rightly said, and what our relationship is, not only with our gurus but with everyone in our life because everyone is an aspect of the same Source.

So now, to digress a bit and move away from the guru–disciple relationship, if we truly have an understanding that everyone in our life is an instrument of the Divine, or an instrument of Baba's, then what happens?

We don't blame and condemn them for things they are supposed to have done, and we don't blame and condemn ourselves. Blame, condemnation, hatred, malice, jealousy and envy, which are based on the principle of doership, start dissolving with this understanding. We clearly see that everyone in our life, our closest ones and even the ones we do not like, are all aspects of the same Source. We become less critical and less judgemental because we understand that everyone has been shaped by their genetics and conditioning, just like we have been. There is a sense of acceptance that starts blossoming in our heart. Compassion starts arising, and that is truly the gift of the spiritual journey.

And that is why I keep emphasizing that whichever story one reads in the Sai Satcharita, one has to apply it to one's own life and daily living.

N: Absolutely. Another pointer I took away from the leela is that it was the pinnacle of saburi in action because Baba let life flow. He let the event roll out without any interference at all.

G: Yes, and there is a deeper aspect to saburi. Normally, in our relationships, when there is a blame game, when there is conflict, we are perpetuating the bondage. It's like a tennis match, you see. I hit the ball across the net, and you hit it back. This is the action-reaction loop. 'You said this to me, so I'm going to say this to you.'

However, when this pattern changes to just witnessing—and witnessing requires only one of the two people in the relationship—then can you have only one person playing tennis against himself? It's not possible. Our relationships are based on a karmic cycle, which keeps perpetuating itself over lifetimes. But if one of the two in a relationship has the awareness to just be a witness to what happens, then that cuts off the entanglement in the relationship.

I would say that true saburi leads to witnessing because then you are not frustrated and *trying* to be patient, whereas, in reality, you are boiling inside all the while. Saburi, true patience, is an aspect of witnessing.

N: In the current situation, many devotees may be stuck with family members, where the action-reaction loop would play out. But you have shared such an excellent pointer that it could help them be a witness to the situation.

G: I will give you a classic example.

About a week ago, when the lockdown began, I had a friend who called me and told me how much he was enjoying his time at home with his family and his children. And this same person called me two days ago and said how frustrated everyone is becoming with each other.

In a confined space, egos can get along with other egos only as long as they are within their comfort zone.

Now these are the opportunities given to you to look at how much of the teaching you are living in your everyday life. That's very important.

I would like to share a message with the audience: Please live these days in awareness because, then, your spiritual journey will reach very deep layers. So, even if frustration arises, because it is natural for egos to get frustrated, be a witness to it. Look at what your trigger points are.

That is the beauty of the journey of life. God has gifted humans with awareness. Human beings are the only species on the planet who are aware that they are aware.

Reflection, contemplation and introspection, without judging oneself or the other, that is what shraddha and saburi are about.

So hopefully, this time will be spent on these aspects of life and living, and not just in complaining: *Oh, I'm confined within my four walls. I'm stuck; I have nothing to do; no newspapers to read. I'm just switching TV channels all the time.*

It is so easy to see how the mind is dependent on all these external factors. If one brings awareness into just knowing that, then you can allow the mind to do what it wants to do because you are witnessing all its antics.

To view the corresponding video, scan the QR code.

18

Blessings in Disguise

Nikhil: Today, I would like to talk to you about how devotees can utilize this time [the pandemic lockdown period]. It's a blessing in disguise.

Gautam: Yes.

N: How can they use this time productively for their meditation, spiritual progress or other things that you could recommend?

G: The great masters, including Ramana Maharshi, have said that the ultimate purpose of life is Self-realization—the final goal. And now that so many of us are not in our usual routines, especially of working, all that time is freed up and can be utilized fruitfully by pursuing our spiritual path or interests. This is something we tend to ignore and neglect, but it is the foundation of our existence.

It is also interesting to see how so many of us fall back into the old patterns. For example, we may be in the habit of reading three or four newspapers every morning; many people do that. So now you will sit and read all three or four online versions of the newspaper. Or you will watch films endlessly on Netflix, etc. to pass the time.

But as you rightly said, this is an opportunity to break away from our patterns, or maybe contain them within reasonable limits because there is no end to indulging in them.

We have been forced to stay within four walls, so this is the time for introspection. It is the ideal opportunity to reflect on our life and what we have learnt on the spiritual journey. If you have a sadhana, then you can deepen that spiritual practice, such as meditation, or if you enjoy reading books, read more of them. This will give you some insights.

So there's so much that you can occupy yourself with, which will enrich your life when you come out of this phase. This time should be utilized optimally.

N: Sai Baba's devotees who have busy jobs under normal circumstances now find themselves working from home, and they have spare time because they don't have to travel. So this time could be well spent in Baba's worship, for instance, by performing aarti at home or by reading the Sai Satcharita to deepen their bond with Baba.

I remember reading an article of yours on your blog or website a long time ago called 'Clearing Sadhana'. It was about clearing one's home or space, or maybe doing little things like gardening or beautifying your surroundings.

So I feel that this extra time that one has could also be used in such peripheral things as well, besides one's spiritual practice.

G: That is true because your vibration is dependent on the content of your consciousness. If, during the day, you introduce these rituals such as aarti or just sitting in front of an altar for some time, your body cycle starts adjusting to that. That is why meditation teachers advise keeping a fixed time for your meditation. Don't do it one day at 7 a.m. and on another day at 3 p.m. because you're busy with other things. Discipline is necessary on the path, and we have so much time that we can manage that now. Then everything is set smoothly in motion.

So it is a good idea to intensify the sadhana. If you are reading the Sai Satcharita, for example, then do it devotedly. Keep a fixed time for it; don't do it only if you have extra time left over for it. That is doing injustice to it. Say to yourself, *Okay, I'll keep fifteen minutes aside at this time, just for reading the Satcharita. Nothing else will get in the way.*

Although you rightly said that some people are working from home, like I am, the fact is that business, in general, is down. There is much less to do in terms of work unless you are taking online classes in yoga or therapy or whatever. Generally speaking, we all have more time during this phase.

What's more, we have to see what has come up in reaction to this phase—the fears which have come up—because all that has to be looked at. There are reasons why these things happen; reasons which we cannot comprehend. But whatever surfaces in our mind is a reaction not only to what has happened but a reaction to the people we are 'caged in' with, even if they are beloved family members. What are the pain points? Which buttons are being pushed? All that has to be looked at because we tend to brush all this under the carpet as we are always in reaction mode.

Now is the time to be still and take a serious look at what's happening in your life. You will naturally be inclined to certain practices or certain things that you have picked up. So, certainly, do set up spiritual routines and bring in the spiritual vibration as that will not end when this phase is over. That will permeate your life beyond this period.

Just today, I spoke to two friends who were the last in line as far as meditation is concerned. They would laugh at it. But today, they said they had started meditating, for different reasons, and they were enjoying it after all their initial resistance. So this is time that is well utilized.

N: I have a small recommendation for devotees, a small tool that I've come across over the years. It's an app for the phone called Calm. It's a free download, and it has many built-in meditations. It's even got a timer and reminders, and it tracks your progress.

If someone wants a silent meditation, they could start with fifteen minutes, thirty minutes or whatever they are comfortable with. But what's beautiful is that it tracks your progress and gives you reminders.

So I would highly recommend this tool, at least for people who are beginning and who want the sort of discipline you mentioned.

G: Yes, that's a good suggestion.

Coming back to the article you mentioned on clearing sadhana, the original title of that essay, by the way, was 'Clearing the Clutter'. And I am sure that many of your audience have already been doing that during this time. When you are at home, it is the ideal time to go through your shelves, remove books which you are done with, go through your files and finish your filing. It's an opportunity to take care of the things you have been postponing. This, in itself, is a sadhana because you are so present while doing the activity.

Let's say you choose to clear one shelf in your cupboard. For once, you have all the time to look at that shelf in detail. Each and every item there. See whether it's valuable to you today. Or are you keeping it because it brings back an old memory? Or because you couldn't be bothered to give it away? Or because it's expensive and therefore you don't want to part with it?

So look at your relationship with the objects in your environment. It's a beautiful spiritual practice, actually. I'm not joking. Clearing space is a spiritual practice. You can say that the external is a reflection of the internal. When you declutter your external space, the internal space, which is your mind, is also decluttered. Why? Because there are fewer objects to take care of, fewer objects to think of and fewer objects to be identified with.

For example, you find five watches in your cupboard. Ask yourself whether you really need all five. Or is it time to give one or two away?

You may decide whatever you feel. I'm not saying it's necessary to give them away. But at least reflect on that; reflect on what has been acquired. Is it needed? Is it not needed?

Also, why are ashram rooms bare? Why are they so spartan? Simply because of the same reason—there's less attachment to objects in the environment. That space is not about objects and attachment to objects; it is about going within.

You will find a tremendous shift in your perception when you clear your environment. You will feel it internally. You will also start getting more and more aware of the thoughts in your mind because even thoughts are objects. They are formless objects, in a sense, but they are objects all the same.

So you will soon find that even that space, your mind, which used to be cluttered with so many thoughts, is getting cleared. It's quite beautiful.

N: Over the last few days, there has been one particular story of Baba's that has been surfacing from various sources. And I see its relevance to what we have been discussing. Baba gave one of His param bhaktas, Lakshmi Bai, nine coins, which are said to symbolize the nine types of devotion.

If devotees can delve into this story, they can see which aspects of their devotion they could work on, especially since they now have this extra time. For example, some devotees don't remember to offer food to Baba before they eat. To rectify that could become one goal. For others, it could be doing the four aartis every day. Each case will differ.

Since there is a lot of information online about the nine types of devotion and this particular story, I encourage devotees to read it and then introspect on their journey: where they are and how they could utilize this time.

If you remember, we had gone to visit a very intimate devotee of Baba's together, and we had seen the shrine she had made in her house. It was so beautiful, with a dedicated space for Baba. We could see very clearly that Baba took priority over everything else in her life.

G: Yes, it was indeed beautiful. And you see, the first thing one picks up is the vibration of the place because it represents the person who has been in that place; in this case, it was her. I think it was a meditation room which she had made. Besides Baba's murti, there were some paintings on the wall, from what I recall.

When you develop a space like that in a corner of your house, you can get nourishment from it. So I encourage everyone to do so, especially since, on Sai Baba's path, there's a lot of bhakti involved. And normally, I have seen that Baba's bhaktas have His paintings or murtis.

Why not make that space holy? See what you can do with it. See if you want to put more candles or incense, and organize it in such a way that you're not doing your normal activities in front of that altar. Develop that sacredness because it will permeate your entire house.

N: Absolutely. Especially in times like this, when you are locked in, it may be very depressing for many. So just having a *jyot* lit, or some incense or camphor, all twenty-four hours, may uplift your spirit.

We recently did a project called The Voice of Sai. The website is

Sai.fm, wherein we have twenty-four beautiful bhajans recorded by a devotee, whose voice is blessed by Baba.

G: Oh, I too must hear these!

N: Sure. So these bhajans could be played, the aartis could be done and that just reminds you constantly of Baba, whereby you are almost in communion with Him.

G: Furthermore, as we said in an earlier talk, chants, etc. purify the atmosphere. One is, of course, playing them so that one is focused, but it's working on multiple levels.

So, to sum this up, I think, because we are so used to 'doing', we just tend to be overly occupied, like I gave the example of reading multiple online newspapers. You are just acquiring news in different formats, or you're wondering what next you can watch on TV.

Everything should be in balance.

We all have a limited number of years on the planet. Our last breath is predetermined, so why not spend that time well? And if you are a Baba bhakta, what does it mean to spend that time well? It means to spend that time focused on Baba, either by worshipping His form, seeing Him in everyone or living His teachings. There are so many ways.

So, instead of frittering away time, set yourself a routine. By all means, take your walk on your terrace or in your compound, if you're allowed to. Read one or two papers, if you enjoy it; no harm.

Balance is key as well as earnestness in your devotion to the Divine. If that is kept in mind during this time, not only will it pass well, but like I say, from this point on, till your last day on the planet, you will look back and thank yourself for having given the time and space to your spiritual practice.

N: This time, as you said, will not come again. One can make the most of this opportunity to go deeper within because it doesn't come every day.

G: It doesn't come every ten years!

N: Exactly.

Also, for many people living in cities, it's a lot quieter. One can hear Nature, hear the birds. In many parts of the world, due to the lockdown, even the environment has become a lot cleaner and quieter. So, it's much more conducive to meditation.

To view the corresponding video, scan the QR code.

19

Staying Conscious Through Uncertain Times

Nikhil: We are facing challenging times right now. Covid has barely retreated, and there is a relapse. Then we have these other situations around the border. There's just so much chaos everywhere, there's so much loss, so much pain.

I felt that, specifically, Baba's devotees and, more generally, spiritual devotees all over the world are, perhaps, going to be more sensitive to what is going on collectively.

So could we discuss this as well as how to stay conscious during these difficult times?

Gautam: Sure. It is evident that no one saw this coming. No one thought a day would come when people all over the world would be confined to their homes under lockdown. These are unprecedented times that we are facing collectively, and we are dealing with the unknown.

What the ego fears the most is the unknown, and the collective fears have come to pass. Furthermore, economies are collapsing due to the lockdown. So it is certainly a dire situation because nothing is clear. Some countries have lifted the lockdown, others are saying a second wave is coming, and in some countries like ours, unfortunately, the cases are still on the rise.

So it is the most difficult of times in terms of collective challenges. Otherwise, as individuals, we have all faced our personal crises in life, which have made us come onto the spiritual path. But this is . . . you could call it collective karma.

I am reminded of something the sage Vimalananda pointed out. He said that in school you are told to study and prepare for exams, the date of which you are informed of in advance. But in life, you will only have surprise tests as you do not know what the next moment will bring. Then you will know how prepared you are and how well you are following your guru's teachings. You see, this is what it is—a surprise test for us.

There are people who are walking on the spiritual path, and then there are those who are still caught up in maya. You have mentioned spiritual devotees because they are more aware. So it is like walking on broken glass because you have the awareness, you have seen your patterns, you have seen your issues and you know that there is a Higher Power like Baba, but you still have to navigate through the world.

N: Yes.

G: What has been placed before you is the acid test of your faith. Now, how much you live the teachings will determine how you walk on the path.

Let us bring it down to very simple things. How are you at home with your loved ones? Are you taking your spouse for granted? How are you speaking to them? Are you verbally or emotionally violent?

You see, the lockdown can bring out aspects of the ego one didn't even know existed. So these are the tests which are put before the spiritual devotee. Either you go through them without awareness, with no consequent spiritual growth, or you go through them with the light of awareness.

Baba always used two words: shraddha and saburi. The point is, Are they just words that stay at the intellectual level, or are they words one is trying to live by? That is the test of faith.

N: Certain devotees are already beginning to face the brunt of this, unfortunately. Some of them have contracted Covid, and naturally, a certain degree of fear is felt by all concerned. There is a lot of pain when a loved one is infected or someone passes away from such a disease. In such circumstances, where there is so much pain and loss, and it's sudden, it's almost like the carpet has been pulled from under your feet.

So I wanted to ask you about how to accept a situation. As Eckhart Tolle said, accepting the unacceptable is a doorway to the greatest peace. In such cases, could you give a bit of guidance to the devotees?

G: You see, this is so with any illness. When we find that an illness has come upon us, it is as sudden as, let's say, being tested positive for coronavirus. Supposing the doctor has told you that you have high blood pressure, or, God forbid, test results indicate that you have a terminal illness, as you rightly said, the carpet is pulled from under your feet because your whole story of life and living is shaken to the core.

In such cases, what generally tends to happen is that the 'Why me?' syndrome kicks into place. *Why did God do this to me? I have not done any harm to anyone. Why do I have to suffer this karma?* That is the thinking mind.

But, as Baba has said, Prarabdha Karma has to be faced. The question is, With what attitude does one face it?

Now, unfortunately for us, with this pandemic, one more illness has now been added to the baggage of illnesses, and it is something that we can catch unknowingly. So that is now the destiny of the world, and how long this virus lasts, we don't know.

But the teaching stays the same: Why not accept what has happened as the will of the Divine, and, thereafter, do whatever is in your power to do? So that whole 'Why me?' self-talk of the thinking mind is finished if one is a follower of Baba's or any true master.

N: Yes.

G: The master's words cut off this unnecessary mental anguish. You already have the situation to deal with: the course of action to follow, the doctors to be consulted, and so on. All that still stays the same. The devout follower of Baba's also still has to do all that, but the difference is that the mind is not burdened beyond these things.

Many people turn to spirituality when they are confronted with an illness. They realize that life is short. They realize they were taking their lives for granted. So it is often loss which brings one to the spiritual path.

What is this loss? The loss of something, which hurts you. For instance, if you lose your job, the fear of survival arises. And then you ask yourself, *What is this life about? Is this life about jobs?*

Thus, the spiritual seeker is born.

That is why we are given these losses—so that we turn within.

But this sounds pretty unfortunate. Many people who attend my talks ask me, 'Why did God have to give us the hard way to come onto the spiritual path?' The point is that you would be completely lost in the cosmic illusion if things were not taken away from you. They are taken away to show you how transient everything is; how temporary, how fleeting.

There is no security in a changing world, and the ego is trying to find security all the time. Nature does not guarantee security. The seasons change; we don't have just one season throughout the year. Life is change. And so, not only is everything in our lives transient but our own lives are transient. I mean, even we come and go. That sense of security is a false sense of security, which we are trying to find with outside things.

So all this is a turning within—a looking inside, not outside.

N: I feel what is happening today is all the more the reason that people connected with Baba should focus more intensely than ever on their sadhana. Because it's so easy to get gripped by fear. Just ten minutes of watching the news can do it.

I think it was Sri Ramakrishna who said that you yourself are emptying a pot full of water by drilling a hole in it. So, with someone who does sadhana but, at the same time, watches the news or interacts with negative people, it is possible that they can get caught in a web of negativity.

Could you talk a little bit about how, during these times, devotees can stay more focused on their sadhana so that they can keep themselves afloat?

G: Yes.

If your audience has read *A New Earth* by Eckhart Tolle, he has a couple of pages dedicated to television. News feeds on fear. You will rarely see good news being a news item, right? It's all fear-based, and if you're watching TV and news all the time, the content therein is absorbed by your mind, and then that becomes your vibration.

All that negativity, the fear-mongering, the constant showing of images which are fear-based, are presented in a way that gets us hooked to the television. Then what is happening on the screen starts happening within us.

So it is very important to be selective about what our minds are being fed with because it affects our vibration. Will it be fear-based, toxic and negative, or will it bring us calm, peace and tranquillity? If you are watching television, please do so with awareness. Understand that if it is triggering all your fears, it is doing its job; they want you to watch the channel. The TRPs go up; you see the advertisements and they get their revenue through these ads.

N: Correct.

G: So please be careful, particularly because there is so much fake news around. What is true and what is not, we don't know as it is an unprecedented situation.

The same newspaper in the United States runs two different headlines in different parts of the country, depending on the readership profile. Can you believe that? That is the world we are living in now.

In this scenario, your sadhana should entail being aware. That should be your mantra. *What is this collective conditioning that I am feeding into and being fed into? Am I being vigilant, being aware, or am I getting sucked into a pattern, into conditioning, and just playing out a mass collective kind of fear-mongering?* For example, passing on WhatsApp messages all the time.

By all means, be vigilant. Read what the experts have to say and the advice that they have to offer. But if the consciousness gets overpowered by fear-based thinking, it will cripple one's life. The life energy, the life force, will get crippled. This is a very important point.

N: You know, things may get worse before they get better. You may start hearing of deaths or cases of Covid in your neighbourhood.

And, God forbid, there could be a community transmission. It can pull anyone down and, as I said earlier, spiritual seekers and devotees are sensitive people, maybe more sensitive than average people with their distractions.

So in such a scenario, I feel it is important to take care of your space. In one of the earlier podcasts, we got some insights into how advanced devotees have their shrines and their practices, such as having some bhajan going on or lighting camphor. So some work should be done to create positive energy in your space as you are confined at home and you have all this negativity around you.

G: Yes, that is true, but what is sadhana, and how can one immerse oneself in it? The purpose of sadhana is to rein in the thinking mind that is influenced by the media and is, thus, fearful. The ego is thriving because of this mind that is rampantly thinking and starts imagining future scenarios.

So let's say a guru advises us to do mantra japa, for example, 'Om Sairam.' The whole purpose of this is to shift the focus of the mind to the mantra so that it gets anchored and stops expending its energy.

Even if you look at terms like 'shraddha' and 'saburi', they are also aspects of sadhana. Faith, patience and perseverance are aspects of sadhana. So when the outside world is topsy-turvy, awareness is what creates the shield of protection for one whose thinking mind is not running all over the place.

There are rituals that you could do—anything which each individual perceives as positive, whether it is lighting lamps, camphor or incense. Some people may not believe in all that, but as long as your mind is not the devil's workshop, it's fine. The idle mind starts thinking unnecessary thoughts because it has nothing else to do.

N: Absolutely.

G: That is why Rameshji would say that if you have nothing to do, do social service. At least your mind will be focused, and you'll be helping people. Besides, your mind will not be creating stories and keep chattering all the time, as it is wont to do.

So the importance of sadhana becomes much more magnified when the outside world is going haywire because that is what will anchor you.

N: True.

I think, to sum it up, we could say that in times like this, do whatever you can to make your mind quiet; see to it that it doesn't do cartwheels, because it's only going to amplify, project and imagine a situation which, otherwise, may not even come true.

G: Yes, and coming back to where we started, this is obviously happening on a collective level because each and every country is affected by it.

Man thought he had full power over this place called Earth, but what has ultimately happened? A small virus has humbled mankind. So this is an opportunity for us to look at ourselves. What have we done to the environment collectively? We must explore our own selves and not just look at it as an external battle where there's the virus and we have to protect ourselves against it.

What is the larger picture? What is it showing us? Is it showing us that we are not really needed for the Earth to function?

N: Yes.

G: Of course, we aren't. [Laughs.]

It reminds me of something that happened in one of Nisargadatta Maharaj's satsangs. Someone asked him, 'Is there no salvation for the world?'

Maharaj replied, 'What business have you with saving the world, when all the world needs is to be saved from you.'

What was he pointing at? He was asking the person to first wake up to who they are as that will then be projected outwards into the world. Because, as within, so without; as in the microcosm, so in the macrocosm. Both are reflections of each other.

We are always externalising about what is wrong with our world. But what about ourselves? What about our mind? What about what's inside us?

So the grace of the master, the form of the master, the teachings of the master, the mantra of the master—these are all there to purify the mind.

N: Yes.

G: And when that is pure, when one follows the teachings, when the teachings are lived, then you find that you are operating more and more from the heart. And I don't mean the physical heart. What I mean is that you are living the teachings. It is no longer just a mental construct: *Baba talks about shraddha and saburi, so I must have shraddha and saburi.* But when it is lived, then it is living in the heart. That is the difference, you see.

N: This has been a very awakening talk, and I do hope everyone who hears you and this important message can devote as much time to living Baba's teachings because, with the amount of turbulence going on, these are very challenging times.

Collectively, as a community, whatever one can do to stay in touch with loved ones, with other devotees, to support each other, we must do. And ultimately, those who have faith will certainly sail through.

G: Yes, those are the words of the Mother of Pondicherry. She says, 'Two factors can get you through a situation. Have faith in the grace of the Divine, and have no fear.'

Now, I know it's easier said than done to say, 'Have no fear.' Therefore, what I say is that when fear arises, witness the fear. Don't fight it. Witness it, see it as a movement coming up and have faith that the grace is there for you. You will notice that slowly and steadily, the fear will no longer consume you, like it did earlier, because now there is a gap between the fear and the one who is witnessing it. So 'have no fear' actually means that you should witness the fear whenever it arises. Do not judge it. Do not say, *I should not be afraid,* and don't start that mental chatter all over again. Accept it. It is a movement in consciousness. It has arisen. Let it arise. Let it subside. Let it be.

We live by these words, by these teachings, knowing that the masters are there.

N: Yes. Wonderful. Thank you. As you said, the Master is there.

To view the corresponding video, scan the QR code.

20

Insights into the Lives of Sai Baba's Staunch Devotees

Nikhil: Some people ask me how I happened to meet Sai Baba's staunch devotees and how my relationship with them developed over time. So I felt that we could cover this in the podcast, and maybe people can pick up a few things that would help them on their spiritual journey.

Gautam: Sure. Even I would be interested in knowing about your visits to such devotees and how you came across each other.

N: It's really Baba's blessings. I guess one thing leads to another.

It started with Aai. At that time, I was very new to Baba and didn't know much about Him and His teachings, neither had I met many devotees. However, something very interesting happened last year.

Around August, when I met Hema Ma and some other staunch devotees, I was completely in awe of them, seeing their devotion and sentiment for Baba, so much so that even the miracles were not very significant in comparison. When you are in their presence, it is so overwhelming that you nearly start crying.

We went together to meet Hema Ma, which was quite a wonderful experience.

G: Yes, it was. You're right.

N: What I saw in common between these devotees was that their sentiment for Baba was above everything; I mean, unparalleled. And they were not really bothered about following a certain discipline.

I've been very blessed to meet quite a few more devotees whom we've not covered because many are not comfortable being on camera and in the limelight, which is understandable.

G: I'm sure. You see, the main thing here, as you said, is that it is overwhelming. Why is it so? The reason is that your heart opens up in their presence because their own hearts are open with their love for Baba.

I remember when we visited Hema Ma, we were quite late because of prior commitments, but she did not show any signs of irritation or impatience. That was very touching to see, as it was only due to her commitment to Baba and nothing else.

So that is what I mean when I constantly say, 'Are you living the teachings?'

You could sense how open and vulnerable Hema Ma was because of all that she had seen as well as people coming to her with all sorts of problems. That can only happen when one's heart is open, and the right word for that, as you have mentioned, is 'bhava'.

N: For all those staunch devotees whom I've met, Baba comes first. Talking of Hema Ma, even a day will not go by without her doing her first *Kakad Aarti* for Baba at around 3.00 a.m. in the freezing cold of the Delhi winter. She has severe back pain, because of which Baba has conveyed to her from the subtle realm not to do it, but she still does it.

And I feel that is the commitment that they have despite their busy work schedules. They don't live easy lives by any means. Many people have the misunderstanding that because they are so close to Baba, their lives are rosy. The truth is far from that.

G: It's usually the opposite, you know.

N: Yes. Apart from the fact that Baba comes first, I've always felt that a certain threshold is crossed in their devotion, which qualifies them as intimate devotees.

G: You say they are shining examples of this kind of devotion, this bhava, and that their lives are not rosy. The whole point is that no one guaranteed them, not even Baba, that their lives would be a bed of roses if they worshipped Him. Despite the hardships and the physical aches and pains, the devotion is still ongoing. That is a very important thing. We have mentioned it in some earlier talks also.

So your audience might find we are repeating this point, but it is a point which needs repetition.

N: Yes.

G: Because there is this misconception that if one has a certain time allocated to pay respect to the Divine, to Baba, then things will not go wrong in their life. That misconception has to be removed.

N: That, unfortunately, is quite prevalent, at least with the beginners, and that is the basis of a conditional relationship with Baba, which is then bound to be one where the boat is rocked when something goes wrong.

G: True.

N: The devotees I met also mentioned to me that Baba is particular about discipline and routine, and it is *Baba* who instils this. So when I got some time with them, I asked them about their journeys and how they got close to Baba. And they said that it happened over some time and that it was not by their will and strength that they've been able to be so devoted to Him. They had the initial yearning, and then Baba changed their routine and blessed them to be able to do the things they do by way of worship. I have met some who have very busy work lives and responsibilities, but they get up in the morning at four, do their aarti, their sadhana, and then go to work. So that also shows us another aspect: their worldly responsibilities are fulfilled without any compromise at all.

G: Yes. It is their bhava for Baba that makes them get up so early in the morning. So, in that sense, it is Baba's doing.

N: Yes, absolutely. And in fact, you mentioned earlier in one of the episodes that one must instil a sense of discipline and time. So it is inspiring that these are the two fundamental things that all the intimate devotees have in common.

G: Also, for some people, the opposite could happen.

I have a friend who is highly disciplined. He would generally wake up very early, follow a routine and be in bed by 10 p.m. He mentioned to me that his routine has gone haywire now [during the lockdown]. At first, he enjoyed waking up late for a few days and just watching movie after movie, but then he reached a point where he felt uncomfortable because his nature was to get up early. He loved the early mornings, but now, this lethargy was creeping in. And if he had continued with this deviation from routine, he would have become miserable. Therefore, he took the decision to wake up early again, and he was so thankful for that.

So you see, the thing is that lethargy and laziness come in when that discipline is not there. Discipline is indeed essential. Some people are not inclined to discipline, and they will find it hard.

But you can introduce discipline in your own way. We are not saying everyone has to get up early. If you can't get up early, don't. But then, during the course of the day, do some rituals, such as lighting a diya, performing a small aarti or sitting in contemplation at a particular time for a fixed duration. That also is a discipline. To introduce it in one form or another according to what suits the individual would be a big blessing because, during these days, where there's nothing much to do, if the patterns are set, that becomes the new conditioning and then that can continue beyond this period.

So, it is, in that sense, a gift.

N: Many of the devotees say that if you take one step towards Baba, He will take ten steps towards you.

G: Yes.

N: Here, Baba will only see one's intention, and if that is pure and one is sincere, then He will pull them towards Him.

G: True. But I keep coming back to the point that our sincerity is conditional. We are sincere only if good things happen to us. However, that should not be the case. It should be constant regardless of the ups and downs in one's life.

N: I would like to share an observation here that might be helpful to the listeners. All the devotees say that they see Baba as a family member. Their relationship with Baba is so deep that it is not biased at all. They are not bothered about miracles and all; these have no significance for them.

This relationship, which is so deep, is the most vital thing. It is unshakable.

G: Correct.

N: The way I look at it is that Baba is navigating all His devotees towards what He wants to give them. That is the goal. Unfortunately, for devotees who don't have that level of relationship established yet or who are not immersed in love and devotion towards Him, when something goes wrong, they may question His intentions. It is like throwing stones at the shepherd who is guiding the sheep safely, which is a shame.

G: Yes, that's true. It does happen a lot.

N: Yes. But I do feel that the relationship is key, although it could be different for different people. For instance, Aai said that she saw Baba as her grandfather. So when that relationship is so deeply rooted, then there is no question of conditional devotion.

Now I will come to something that was brought to my notice by Vinny Ma [Dr Vinny Chitluri]. Once, we went to Baba Iyer's cafe in Shirdi. He was a very sweet old man. After we started eating, she said, 'Oh my God! I have forgotten it again.'

And when I asked, 'What?' she replied, 'I find it very difficult to offer food to Baba. I admire those devotees who do it, and I keep telling Baba that I keep forgetting.'

What she said made me aware, and then I started observing it when I would go to meet Aai, Hema Ma or Veena Ma: the first thing they would do before eating anything is they would offer it to Baba. I did not follow this practice before this incident.

G: Right.

N: And then I saw that this is not so easy, initially at least. Because

I would say that food is the most basic instinct. Even sex and other things one can do without, but food is vital to our survival. Yet they first offer it to Baba—it's almost like a ceremony—and then they offer it to other members of the family.

I find it very beautiful, and now it has become a practice for me. I am so grateful to Vinny Ma for bringing it to my notice, after which I observed it in other devotees too.

G: Yes.

N: So, even this was another very important aspect—offering food to Baba. Sometimes one may forget to do it, but that is fine.

Even when they are travelling, it may be only a mental offering, but the fact that Baba comes before anything else is the essence of their life.

G: I would like to point out why offering food to Baba is important.

The sage is aware that when he is eating, he is not an individual who is eating the food. He is aware that if he were not conscious, he would not be able to eat.

So, in his case, is the food being taken by the individual or by Consciousness, which is being offered the food? The sage has the heightened awareness that when he is eating, the food is being offered to something as holy as his sense of presence and not him as an individual. We ordinary human beings don't have that awareness.

Therefore, when the food is made, we offer it to Baba first because He represents Consciousness, the Source, the Divine, and then we partake of it. So it is a very beautiful gesture on the part of the devotee, the whole point being that the food is offered to God first because God is Light, God is Consciousness, God is Being—call it by any name—and Baba represents That.

This small act tends to deflate the ego. The feeling *I am eating* goes out of the window. So, offering food is a beautiful spiritual practice that has been introduced. Many people offer it to their family deity also, but the result is the same.

N: Another thing I have observed with the devotees is that even when it comes to daily living and decision-making in their lives, everything happens by Baba's will. Not only is it a deep realization, but they will not take any decision or do anything without Baba's consent, because they know that only He knows.

G: Yes. They have accepted that their own will is too limited and that there is a Higher Force operating, which is far beyond their comprehension. Therefore, they have surrendered to that force. One can see that this is something that all the devotees you have spoken about have in common.

N: Yes.

G: Since you have brought up devotees such as Hema Ma, as an example, I must say that even I have visited some of them. I remember that Aai had a very simple, basic household. They have created shrines, each with a distinct flavour, in keeping with their respective personalities. I found that Hema Ma's shrine was quite overwhelming, whereas Aai's was minimalist, but both delivered a similar result in terms of the sanctity you felt in that environment. What was common were the vibrations, the sense of peace.

N: Yes.

G: So could you share something, since you must have been exposed to more of this and seen commonalities or gained insights in their sacred spaces?

N: Yes, certainly. It takes me back to the shoot I did in Shirdi with Vinny Ma. When we were shooting, I would trouble her and start filming with her at three in the morning, poor thing.

G: [Laughs.] Oh God!

N: Vinny Ma would leave the door open for me. I would go to her house at 2.30 a.m., and then she would come out at 3.00 a.m. I noticed that right in front of Baba's beautiful image, she had a little glass and it had something floating, which I had not seen before.

When I asked her about it she said, 'This is an *akhand jyot*, which stays lit in front of Baba for twenty-four hours.'

So I said, 'Oh, how do you do that?'

And she showed me. It was a simple little thing—a floating wick with aluminium. These wicks are readily available.

G: Yes.

N: I said, 'How amazing, I had never seen that at anyone else's shrine before.' I got some of these and started doing the same thing at home.

You know, I'll make a list of all these devotional rituals I've seen at various devotees' homes. They are very simple, and they don't cost much.

That was something I really liked. So in the office, as well as at the shrine at home, I put a few of these, which are lit twenty-four hours, and they don't need any monitoring. It reminds me of stories in the Satcharita about how Baba liked lighting diyas. It removes negativity, and when you know it's there twenty-four hours, it's very beautiful. It changes the aura of your home.

G: Correct.

N: Another devotee I met had camphor lit for a few hours every day in a little heater. And all of them had chants pertaining to Baba going on in the background. I felt these are things that build up the ambience. Also, they are very regular with certain things, such as the offering of flowers or food. Another thing I saw is that they all take udi when they leave their house. They are very particular about the use of udi, which they drink with water.

It would be very helpful for devotees if they go through this talk. They can add various things, whatever resonates with them, to their little altar at home.

G: I think that would be beautiful.

N: I'm eternally grateful to meet Baba's devotees who are so close to Him and are so humble. There is no trace of any bookish knowledge. They are not bothered about any outcome; they don't want anything. It is only and only love. That love is so overwhelming that, sometimes, they write poetry, and I ask them to read it. It's just one of the most beautiful experiences to spend time with them.

And I pray to Baba that we can get more time with them so that all other devotees can benefit from it. Seeing their example, that same kind of love and devotion towards Baba can be awakened.

G: Yes, and I think all that you are doing is unfolding by itself. You have brought to the channel these individuals you've come across *after* you have felt their genuineness through their devotion to Baba. It is significant that their innocence has been of prime importance.

N: I must say that since the channel is now gaining a bit of traction, there are people who do get in touch. However, whom we feature is something I'm very careful about. I don't invite somebody unless I know them and have spent time with them, because, as the saying goes, 'All that glitters is not gold.'

Any genuine devotee of Baba's, honestly, doesn't want to be in the limelight. I have literally had to plead with these devotees whom I have spoken about to come on the channel, so they are doing a very big service to Baba by agreeing to do so, not out of any personal interest but just because they feel that, maybe, their story might kindle a bit of hope or inspiration for others who are on their journey with Baba.

To view the corresponding video, scan the QR code.

21

The Blessings of Guru Purnima 2 (Gautam's Talk)

Namaste, everyone.

It's been a year since the last Guru Purnima, a year which nobody could have foreseen, with all the challenges and the ups and downs of coming out of the first wave, getting into a very intense second wave and serious crises for many individuals—job crisis, relationship crisis, and of course, health crisis.

Guru Purnima, for me, is a time to reflect on the guru's teachings and how much they have been lived, and to express my gratitude to the guru for lighting up my path.

Just a few days ago, I met a Sai Baba devotee who said that in the first lockdown, when he was at a crisis point, he had to reexamine his faith in Baba. Would his faith in Baba depend on what happens to him during the pandemic crisis? Or would his faith stay firm, irrespective of what happens?

He chose the latter.

So like many of us, he lost assignments and went through all sorts of turmoil. However, he remained steadfast in his faith in Baba.

I have received many emails which are reflective of the opposite scenario. People have lost faith in Baba because, for instance, they did not get the jobs they wanted. Life was too challenging, and things did not turn out the way they expected them to.

You see, this is the acid test for the sincere seeker, the sincere disciple, one who has total and absolute trust in Baba, knowing that

His will prevails at all times. But, in the case of the others who have a fluctuating faith, dependent on whether things turn out in their favour or not, it is understandable that it is only human to be like that.

However, the point is that life is unpredictable and challenging, especially in this scenario, and therefore all the more the reason for us to reaffirm our faith in Baba to take us across the ocean of existence, as it is said in the Satcharita.

My sincere request to all of you is to use Guru Purnima as an opportunity to express gratitude to Baba for all your experiences, even the tough ones, because we are all here to learn life's lessons and grow through them.

Nothing happens without a reason. So you would do well to express gratitude and reaffirm your faith that, no matter what comes next, you know that your life is in divine hands; you are ready to live life courageously and face whatever the next moment brings.

I hope this short message will serve to strengthen your bonds with your Sadguru, Sai Baba. May we support each other on this most beautiful journey called life. In an environment where the future is unknown, we need to hold each other's hands and move forward.

So here's wishing all of us an auspicious Guru Purnima 2021.

May Sai Baba's blessings be upon us through these challenging and unique times that we are facing.

All the very best to all of you. Thank you.

To view the corresponding video, scan the QR code.

22

Self-Knowledge—the True Wealth

Nikhil: A devotee particularly asked if we could get your input on the *Brahma Gyan* leela, which was imparted by Sai Baba to someone who had come to receive Brahma Gyan from Him in a big rush. What are the learnings and pointers one can take away from this vital leela that Baba has shown us?

Gautam: From what I recollect of this story, the concerned devotee was a wealthy man whose material needs were sufficiently fulfilled. He was in search of Brahma Gyan, which is the knowledge of Brahman, or the knowledge of Creation. He came to Sai Baba saying that he wanted to receive Brahma Gyan immediately and was very emphatic about it.

But then, as we all know, Sai Baba could see beyond appearances and, therefore, He played out the leela. In the presence of this wealthy man, Sai Baba asked one of His devotees to go and collect some money from someone else's house—five rupees or something. After ten or fifteen minutes, this devotee came back and said that the person was not at home, so he was not able to collect the money. And then Sai Baba told him, 'Never mind, you go to this other devotee's house.' And again the devotee came back saying that the person was not at home.

This scenario repeated itself a few times, and while this was happening, the wealthy man who was waiting for Brahma Gyan witnessed it all.

After repeating this leela a few times, Sai Baba told this wealthy man, 'In front of you, I sent someone to collect money from various devotees, and they were not at home. But despite being so wealthy, it did not even occur to you to part with that money after having so much of it in your pocket. Then what kind of Brahma Gyan are you looking for? If you are so attached to your money that it does not even strike you to put your hand in your pocket and offer some of it, then your getting Brahma Gyan is out of the question.'

Receiving the knowledge of Creation or the knowledge of the universe, or whatever you may call it, is impossible if one does not feel for others. So here was a wealthy man who had so much money, but the thought that Baba needed the money didn't arise in his mind. The motive was so egocentric and so rooted in the me that he was blind to everything else, even to this leela.

Baba obviously dispatched His devotee to various people's houses, knowing they would not be there.

N: Absolutely.

G: Otherwise, the leela would not have played out, you see. This is what He was pointing to: You may want what you want, but what is the intent behind it? If you truly don't consider yourself separate from others, then how can you, a rich man, be so miserly that the thought of offering some money does not even occur to you? How can you even dream of getting Brahma Gyan?

And so this, I think, is a big lesson for everyone because we all are not only materialistic but also me-centric. *What is in it for me? What will I get out of this situation? What will I get out of this relationship?*

And this was a classic example. Baba laid bare the ego of this wealthy man.

N: Generally speaking, all saints have said that money is something that should be shunned, not for the money itself but because it can inflate your ego. That is also one of the aspects.

G: I would not say that money has to be shunned, because in this day and age, we all know how crucial money is. Money is a means to an end; it is needed to buy things. But the problem is that we have made money itself the end. We have made it the object of our attention and desire. We hanker after money and go on collecting more and more of it.

Now the sage does not do that. The sage is generous with his money because he knows that to give money to others is to give money to himself. That is the sage's relationship with money, whereas our relationship has got corrupted. Not only do we go after money and hoard it, but we tend to do so even to the detriment of others.

I'll give you another classic example. I think it's in another story of Sai Baba's, or what He mentioned once. It was regarding a government official who came to Him, and He told the government official, 'If you are involved in taking bribes, you are not My devotee. So there's no point in coming and prostrating before Me. You take advantage of your job and harm people by taking bribes.'

So this is the maya of money, and it is more so in this day and age. That is why I think that these leelas of Baba's, especially to do with money, are most crucial. Our relationship with money must be a pure one.

N: Coming back to the Brahma Gyan leela, when you go to a master, you should present yourself with utmost humility, rather than make demands. In the wealthy man's case, I believe he even said, 'Baba, give it to me fast,' when Baba was sending a devotee to get five rupees and enacting this leela.

G: Yes, absolutely. But unfortunately, humility is not a quality that can be acquired as such. Humility happens when you see that you have so much to be humble for and that so much has been given to you by the Divine. Something as simple as our basic needs are met so easily. The thought of humility is bound to arise when we acknowledge that, but the fact is we've taken all that for granted, and we want more.

So humility is a prerequisite. If we don't have that when we approach a master, then our ego is going to be taught very harsh lessons. That is exactly the case with many stories in the Sai Satcharita, in which people who go with a puffed-up ego end up learning very hard lessons in humility. And if you don't learn that, then you can be quite sure that the Universe will send you umpteen lessons till you do so.

N: Baba had spoken about some prerequisites for Self-realization in the Sai Satcharita, in the chapter where the Brahma Gyan leela is mentioned. This is covered in detail.

Just to sum up the essence of it, could you talk about the purpose of human life in general because Baba has spoken of rnanubandhan in so many of His leelas? He says it is not necessary that everyone is granted a human life, and in one of your earlier podcasts, you mentioned that the special gift humans have is being aware of being aware, which is not possible in any other species.

So, in connection with that and knowing that our audience comprises aspirants and devotees of Baba's, could you speak a little bit about the seriousness of the spiritual path and not taking human life and birth for granted?

G: Yes, absolutely. Even Ramana Maharshi has said that the purpose of life is Self-realization. Or if you look at the Bhagavad Gita, it is all about spiritual illumination. So that is clearly the purpose of life.

But what should be the result of that? It should be the way our lives are lived as a result of that spiritual illumination. Are we living lives of awareness, or are we living lives steeped in ignorance?

And that is why we have the teachings and the spiritual scriptures—to illumine our daily living. They are not just to be read theoretically while considering day-to-day life to be something else altogether.

Man is the only species that is aware that it is aware. When this awareness is shining, then man has the ability to act out of compassion and not harm another being, and lead the quality of life which is laid down in, let's say, the Bhagavad Gita.

But most of us are, unfortunately, not doing that, because our lives are steeped in ignorance, in the 'me and my story', and my wants and my desires, to the detriment of others.

But everyone's journey is a journey of spiritual awakening. When it will happen and how it will happen differs. How much suffering has been allocated to each of us differs. We do not have control over that.

And that is why masters like Sai Baba have come to wake us up from this dream of daily living. A dream where we are perpetuating reaction after reaction through patterns and conditionings, and creating bundles of karma based on doership. They have come to show us the way out of that.

N: Someone listening to this certainly has to have a certain yearning, otherwise they would not be listening to this conversation.

Could you speak a little bit about intensifying this yearning or, rather, praying for the sort of intensity that could make the spiritual path their priority in life?

G: Mostly, but not always, it is a setback in life or a form of suffering, which brings us onto the path. When that happens, then you could say that that yearning itself is sincere. However, we tend to get distracted from it because of the travails of daily living, and that can lead to straying off the path.

I also had people come to me and say, 'We don't have time for spirituality, but we are happy to attend your talks once a month.' They have segmented spirituality from the rest of their lives.

It doesn't work that way. If, deep down, you know that your breath is not in your control, the blood flowing through your veins is not in your control, and you start understanding that there's so much which is not in your control and which is controlled by a Higher Power, then that would lead to more awareness in daily living.

Gratitude for being in a situation thanks to a number of forces, none of which are in your control, arises. Consequently, you start questioning the quality of your life and your engagement with it: *Am I aware of the harm I am doing to others or myself? Am I aware of the content of my thoughts during the day?*

That is spiritual awakening; that is the spiritual journey.

Now this should be happening naturally; if it is not, it means you are still mired in the game of life.

N: Yes.

G: So, to be honest, there is really nothing you can do as such to intensify the spiritual yearning but to allow it to happen because that is what will happen. However, we tend to delay it. We delay the inevitable.

Let's not forget that everyone's journey is the journey 'home'.

We are all going to a destination, which is the same place we came from. Our existence here is temporary and transient. If our spiritual fire burns brightly during the few years that we have been given, we are only doing ourselves a favour. That is something that has to be realized by us. No one else can do it for us.

N: In the Brahma Gyan leela chapter, Baba specifically talks about discernment and dispassion being vital. These qualities help us navigate daily life, choosing the right over the pleasant.

Could you talk about that aspect where, with awareness and by the grace of the guru, one can get dispassion and discernment?

G: It's a natural outcome of the process, you see. Supposing you know from your own life's experience that all your pleasures and pains have come and gone, then detachment develops automatically. Because if that detachment doesn't develop, then one is involved in the various pleasures and pains, and that leads to suffering. So detachment is a natural outcome of being on the spiritual journey because you know that your happiness does not rest on pleasures; you know that pleasures are fleeting. So this life does become a life of detachment in the sense that you are the witness of all that happens in your life. You don't tend to get involved in the events like you used to earlier.

And that results in discernment. If I know, based on my life's experience, that something is not good for me because it is going to, at some point or another, create suffering, either for myself or another, discernment arises.

These are two basic pegs on which we can stand: discernment and dispassion. Why would you get into something if your experience has shown you that it is going to harm you? Without these two, you keep going round and round on the wheel of karma. But when these two are introduced into the equation, that senseless turning of the wheel stops.

N: Some may attain this state of dispassion and discernment in a flash as if the sword of knowledge has cut through the ignorance of the past. With others, it could be an incremental process, where the intensity of their past desires and past patterns slowly abates. And if someone is in that boat, so to speak, and they notice that they are getting pulled by past patterns and desires, could you give some advice there?

G: In most cases, it happens incrementally. The sudden transformations are rare, and thank God for that because many of us would not be able to handle the sudden transformation, and nor would our families. So the incremental way, the gradual way, is the natural way.

There's really nothing to be done because once it kicks in, it's going to take its course. The problem is, we get in our way. That is why a friend of mine had a beautiful prayer, which he would say every morning: 'Today, I promise myself I will get out of my own way.' [Refer to talk 5.]

That's all that needs to be done.

N: Is there anything else you feel we can take away from this leela that I might not have asked you about?

G: There's one more point which I'd like to add: Take a look at your relationship with money because, let's not forget, that leela was about money. What is your relationship with money? How open are you to giving money away? How possessive are you of your money?

This leela mentioned in the Satcharita is addressing the miserly man in us wanting Brahma Gyan. So if we introspect on our relationship with money, we will be amazed as to the deep conditioning we carry behind it.

A Tibetan course which I studied decades ago said something very beautiful: 'What you truly possess is what you give away.' We think we are doing charity to other human beings but, actually, we are giving only to the one Divine Being which is operating through all beings. This is what it is pointing at. Therefore, we need to live that knowledge, live that understanding, that we are not getting diminished by giving our wealth away. In fact, we are enriching ourselves because it is an offering back to the Divine. After all, where did we get the wealth from? We got it from the Source, and we are giving it back to that Source.

N: To sidetrack a little bit, talking about money, currently with the Covid situation that many people are facing across the globe, their livelihoods might be challenged. Many people might have a lot of insecurity about their financial situation and their financial future because it's quite an unprecedented situation.

In that light, can you speak a few words about the fear of loss?

G: This is natural; this is bound to happen. But we create too much psychological suffering over this because, ultimately, all we can do is do our best and keep trying. Beyond that, things are not in our control.

Nevertheless, the thinking mind creates stories. *What will happen to me? Why did this happen to me? What has God done to me?* The 'me and my story' gets perpetuated thanks to fear.

So whenever these thoughts of fear arise, they need to be witnessed. The witnessing is what will take us very far in challenging times like this. But we tend to convert that witnessing into observing and, therefore, judging. Then we judge things as being 'good' and 'bad' and 'harmful to me', and then we can lay out at least fifty different possibilities of something 'bad' happening to us, which is what the ego does.

The mind of the enlightened one does not do that. It does not mean fear will not arise. Fear will arise as a natural biological reaction, even in the enlightened one, because we don't know the future. But that fear is not taken ownership of.

That is what we have to learn, that when fear arises, it is to be witnessed and, thereafter, surrendered to God's will.

I know this is not easy to follow, especially in a situation like this, but you will be amazed that when the psychological suffering of the fear is dropped, one feels a deep and immense sense of peace despite the gravity of the situation.

And that peace is nothing but what Baba says: 'Have faith in Me. Have faith in the Divine.' Because things happen according to Prarabdha. It is that faith which brings peace, which gives the strength to deal with situations like the present one.

N: Could we end with a prayer of surrender to Baba that devotees can have in their heart? Could you share something like that, which devotees could just pray to Baba?

G: It reminds me of what my spiritual teacher, Ramesh Balsekar, said: 'What is the most genuine prayer? The most genuine prayer is a prayer of gratitude.' So one could pray: *O Lord, You have given me so much that I trust that You will give me exactly what I need to take me further on life's journey, and that is why I am grateful to You.*

That is important because, otherwise, we tend to take it for granted. A prayer of gratitude which says, *I already have received so much from You that I have surrendered to You as a devotee, and I have surrendered because I know Thy will be done,* could do wonders.

To view the corresponding video, scan the QR code.

23

Spiritual Friendship and the Spiritual Ego

Nikhil: On the spiritual journey, aspirants come across fellow seekers with whom they have something in common—spiritual friends, I would say—and who introduce them to a particular guru, path or teaching. These relationships can be helpful but can also be tricky because ego dynamics can come in sometimes.

So, I felt it would be nice to talk to you about the various aspects of spiritual friendship.

Gautam: Sure.

The beautiful aspect of spiritual friendship is that there's something which binds the friendship more than what usually happens in the case of social friendships. It is a spiritual journey, a shared interest in looking for things in life that are deeper than the usual material desires. So, in that sense, spiritual bonds of friendship could be very strong. Let's take the example of the disciples of a particular master, *guru bandhus*, as they are called. They could be a tremendous support to each other on life's journey because of their spiritual inclination.

Seekers find that once they start the spiritual journey, their friendships change. Some of the old friends drop away because interests differ. If your interests are spiritual in nature, then you seek out these kinds of friendships, or you just attract them. Consequently, people do feel guilty that they are abandoning an old set of friends for a new one. But that is the way life is. The flow of life is going in a certain direction, and one goes along.

So, I would start by saying that it is beautiful because it is a pure friendship. The needs are not linked to our regular interdependent needs of wearing social masks and projecting ourselves in a certain way. I think it's a very big thing.

Also, a lot of people get isolated when they are on the spiritual journey. I'll give you an example.

I know someone in Delhi who is following a particular master who has passed away. The master was living in Mumbai. Now he yearns to have more friends in Delhi with whom he can discuss his master's teachings. But nobody he knows is interested.

So, here is someone who has lost interest in regular friendships. He has had enough of those. Now he is looking for a spiritual bond in friendships, but he is finding himself isolated because there is nobody around he can talk to about these matters. He likes to share the teachings and discuss them. Therefore, he goes on the internet to find groups and forums, but the fact is that he feels a vacuum within himself.

Many people are in this situation. They sometimes feel they are alienated from their own families, firstly, if they are the only ones on the journey. And it's the same scenario in their circle of friends. It is also unfortunate that society tends to look down upon people who are on the spiritual path because they are not considered normal.

So I would say that these are the various aspects of spiritual friendship.

There is this concept of, as I mentioned before, guru bandhus, where fellow disciples of the same guru have a very close-knit bond by way of karma or rnanubandhan.

Now you asked how this relationship can go awry. How can the spiritual ego come in the way of friendship? Because this does happen.

Let's say I introduce someone to a guru. After some time, I find that the guru is very fond of my friend, and I feel ignored. Then I start disliking my friend. This happens because the guru–disciple relationship is a cherished one.

I have seen it happen with my guru, that when someone new came into his circle, he would be very fond of that person. The guru does not differentiate. He is Consciousness. But the spiritual ego of the disciple kicks in. And that is one way it does so.

Then there is the most common form of spiritual ego when the person feels they know what is best for you.

N: In that respect, I like what Rameshji would say about not giving your opinion or advice unless it is asked for.

G: Yes, that is very important. But do you know why? Because that means that you feel you know best.

N: You know more than God.

G: Exactly. Because when you give advice you are already taking a higher position—*I know better than you.*

Now, of course, a teacher will advise their student, or a parent will advise their child, simply because they have many more years of experience. But here we are talking of friendships, you see. And we tend to do this; we tend to dish out free advice.

But if we really accept that everyone has come with their own destiny, we wouldn't do so. God knows everyone's destiny. Sai Baba knows the divine will. He doesn't need your interference in it for sure. Therefore, you could give what you think is great advice, but, in reality, it could be detrimental to that person's journey.

As Rameshji mentioned, if you only give advice when you are asked for it, it means the Universe has asked you for advice through that person. So if you are being asked to give it, then, by all means, give it. That way, you know that your ego has not come into the equation with a sense of doership that you know better.

So this is a very important point you have raised because, as they say in spiritual circles especially, the spiritual ego is even bigger than the normal ego.

N: It is. And also, sometimes, spiritual friends get over-enthusiastic about pushing someone onto the path they are following. If there is a devotee who is a beginner, or not that visibly committed to a teaching or a master, others can be very imposing in their behaviour with them.

G: Yes, at one level, there is an innocence to it because you have been impacted deeply by your master. So you want to share that with your friends. You want to introduce your master and the teachings to them.

That is beautiful. But the problem is that, despite resistance, you still try to force your will on the person to come and meet the master. There may be a little resistance from a friend who is not spiritually inclined, and it's okay if you try to influence him. But some people literally don't leave you until they have dragged you to their master. Not only do we force our master on someone whose master is someone else, or who doesn't have a master, but we start imposing on them the way we feel they should think about things. And whenever you exert too much of your own will, it means you're exerting too much doership into the equation. You're not allowing things to flow naturally. If it is someone's destiny to come to a particular master, they will come, sooner or later.

So, these are the classical traps of the ego that one can fall into on this journey, unfortunately. That is when the innocence gets lost because the doership has come in through the back door.

N: Correct.

If someone who is the 'perpetrator' of the imposition hears this conversation, they would definitely get pointers for being aware of this, and it may fall off. However, if one is the 'victim', could you give some pointers on how to deal with this in the most natural way if you're not comfortable? How do you distance yourself in an amicable way?

G: Yes. This will happen naturally when you have the requisite understanding. Let's say you are at the receiving end where someone is trying to aggressively enforce their teacher's views on you or pull you to their teacher. However, you have the understanding that this person is driven to do what he is driven to do. Their nature is to be pushy, so they are being pushy. You don't blame them for that, you don't hold them accountable for that, you don't condemn them for that. You let it go.

So once the blame and condemnation is out of the equation and you still feel deep in your heart that you don't want to go along with their viewpoint, you will tell the person, 'Look, I understand where you're coming from. I understand how deeply impacted you are by the teachings, but I'm really sorry; this is not the time for me to comply with your suggestion.'

You won't hesitate to say that, and at the same time, you are not acting in defence. You are not feeling threatened, as if someone's holding a gun to your head, even if it may appear like that. The understanding that they are doing precisely what they are designed to do acts as a cushion to the relationship, and you excuse yourself.

Now it could be that you are so timid that you get dragged along, even though you don't want to go. In that case, it is your destiny. You see, the whole point here is that the only thing to be looked at is one's attitude in the situation.

That is all. The outcome is not in our control.

N: This takes me to something. The unconscious reaction is to point a finger at the other person. However, I believe it was Lao Tzu who said that if there's anything you ever find negative, change it within yourself. There is nothing really on the outside; don't try to change another.

So in this situation, if you are at the receiving end, could you also see it in that light?

G: What we just discussed is actually the same thing that you're talking about because you are not trying to change the person who's being pushy. You are not telling him 'Why are you being pushy? Don't be pushy.' Because you don't want to change him. God knows best, as we said earlier. You understand that that's the way he has been designed.

The net result is that there's less involvement and drama in the situation. And when that happens, it means that there's more peace of mind.

N: Are there any other aspects to this that you would like to share that, maybe, I have not asked you about?

G: Regarding spiritual friendships?

N: Even the spiritual ego; both are so interlinked.

G: The spiritual ego is, as we said earlier, a very tricky thing. For instance, if you have read all the Vedas and Upanishads, and you have heard the discourses of twenty masters on YouTube, you may feel you have more knowledge.

On the other hand, you have friends who have not done all that. They have probably just read, let's say, only the Bhagavad Gita or visited one master.

Now there is only one measure which I keep reiterating, and that is the degree of peace you feel in your daily living. The whole point is that between you and your friend, who is the one who is more at peace? That is all that matters. The rest is irrelevant.

So the spiritual ego has to be careful because it loses sight of this—that the measure is peace of mind. If that awareness is there, the spiritual ego will always be on its guard. It will catch itself in the process of asserting itself. But by and large, that awareness is not there. Therefore, the spiritual ego becomes even trickier than the normal ego.

We've often seen in spiritual circles that in the case of masters who have thousands of followers, the latter feel that their master is the greatest.

I'll give you a relevant example; a real-life example.

I met someone who was the disciple of a master. The master was known, but not as well-known as the more prominent ones today. The disciple and I were having a conversation over tea with someone else. Suddenly, the topic changed to the auras of masters, and referring to one very big master who has thousands of followers, he said, 'By the way, I could see — — —'s aura and it extended just two feet beyond his body, whereas my guru's aura extends twelve feet.'

I responded, but not by way of retaliation as I don't have any allegiance to both these masters. I said, 'It is to *you* that one master's aura appeared as extending twelve feet beyond his body, and the other's, as two. It may not be the same for someone else.'

He didn't like what I said because his position was that since *he* saw it, it was the truth. This is the spiritual ego.

Supposing you have been gifted with the ability, as in this case, to see people's auras. Your ego then declares that your master's aura is bigger than another master's. You may not be wrong, but it is *your* truth. It is not *the* truth.

This is the point that people miss out on, and I'm so glad you raised it. The large number of sincere seekers following your channel need to introspect and delve into topics like the ones you have been raising in this podcast because I feel what you have raised here is one step ahead of the videos that we have done so far.

N: Yes. You see things as *you* are, not as the way *they* are.

G: Right. If you have the awareness and understanding that whatever your view in life is, it is based on your genetics and conditioning, then you know that you are only seeing things through your conditioning. It could be an event, a thought; it could be anything. With that understanding, you know that the other is viewing the same thing based on their filters. So there's no argument there. You may put forward your point of view, but the other may not agree with it, and that's okay.

N: In our relationship with Baba, when life events unfold, we may look at an event and see it through our viewpoint. And based on whether it is favourable or not favourable, we may go to Baba and say, 'Oh, why did this happen?'

But if one has no filter at all, then that is where saburi comes in. You let the event unfold with no interference, no judgement. And how one event links to the other, in other words, causality, can never truly be known. So that, I also feel, is an important aspect to remember at all times.

G: Very true but very hard to live by. I'll again give you a first-hand case of a friend of mine who is a devotee of Sai Baba's. He was trying to go abroad, and he had to go for a very good reason. There was an issue to sort out.

He kept getting messages, let's say, from the Universe, that Baba felt it was not the right time for him to go. But he was very keen on going and was wondering why obstacles were coming in the way. He kept telling me, 'What is wrong with my wanting to go? The intention is good; it's to sort things out.'

Little did he know that had he gone, he would have got stuck because of the Covid pandemic.

Now, to live with the faith that God knows best is the hard part. We question what is happening because of our limited vision.

So, maybe that's a topic for another day, but it's a good one you have raised. We've spoken about it before, but one can see these things from so many different angles.

N: Absolutely. It takes me back to Jawahar Ali's story with Baba. That leela is so important. We discussed this in an earlier episode: Baba demonstrated that if one truly minds their own business and plays their role without any criticism or judgement, they will sail through a lot of turbulence.

G: Yes, absolutely, because all the dramas we create are in our own heads. The Jawahar Ali story has many facets. It's a very unique story. I'm glad we discussed it earlier, and people should read that again and again in the Sai Satcharita because they will see how someone of Baba's stature handled the situation with humility. Then, with our limited viewpoint and preconceived notions, who are we in comparison?

To view the corresponding video, scan the QR code.

24

The Law of Attraction and True Surrender

Nikhil: Today we are going to talk about something very interesting: the Law of Attraction and true surrender to Sai Baba.

The other day, I had this feeling that we should cover this topic. I was thinking about it in the morning, and strangely enough, that very evening, I got an email from a devotee saying, 'I practice the Law of Attraction, and I'm very committed to Baba, but internally, I feel a conflict, and I wonder if I'm being true to Baba.'

Subsequently, I felt that we should cover this topic because it was no coincidence to have the thought before that email came.

So we would like your insights on this as these two teachings seem to be contrary to each other.

Gautam: I must admit, I am not an expert on the Law of Attraction. I have read about it here and there, but I do understand the principle behind it, which is based on affirmations, so, yes, it is worthy of exploration.

To begin with, I would like to say that the Law of Attraction is an ancient science. It is the science of vibration, and even the *Mahavakyas* in our scriptures, or the great sayings, such as '*Aham Brahmasmi*' and '*Tat Tvam Asi*', are affirmations. They mean 'I am not the limited body with a name but Consciousness.' So this is a very solid foundation of the principle.

Now let's take a very simple example.

Our thoughts throughout the day could either revolve around

wealth or poverty. These are one of the pairs of opposites in duality. By wealth, I do not mean just money in the form of coins and currency notes. One could live a wealthy life feeling richness and abundance all the time, not feeling lack. We human beings tend to focus on what we don't have, but if we shifted our focus to what we have, our vibration would be that of a wealthy person. So again, the Law of Attraction is a perfect science in that sense. Whereas if we focus on lack, it is called poverty consciousness, and the law of vibration says, 'Like attracts like'.

N: Correct.

G: So if you are vibrating with poverty consciousness, it's not going to help you. Whereas if you are grateful to God for what you have got, and you are vibrating with wealth consciousness, then you will exude that quality, that vibration.

Having said that, let's come to the Law of Attraction as one generally understands it. Let's say you have a material desire: that car which you've been admiring or the perfect house. You visualize it; you feel and act as if it's already in your possession, as if you are living in your dream house, driving your dream car, and so on and so forth.

Again, it is a science. There's nothing wrong with it. We don't want the audience to think that we are not in favour of the Law of Attraction.

However, there are two things that happen.

One, we lose sight of the present moment because we live in an imaginary future. So if someone is making too much effort, or there is too much doership, then they will always be living in their minds with these visuals based on a future scenario. The present moment would tend to get lost.

Two, if you do not get what you want, there is bound to be frustration.

So these things can sidetrack one's spiritual journey.

When we come to surrender to Baba, this does not need an explanation. But when we consider practising the Law of Attraction and surrendering to Baba, together, how do we deal with this paradox?

If you are enjoying practising the affirmations or the visualizations of the Law of Attraction, by all means, go ahead. But if you are struggling to do so, if it is a chore, if it's something you don't look forward to, then you have to consider dropping it. It's as simple as that.

However, if you are practising it, is it creating suffering for yourself or others? That is the next criterion. *Am I suffering? Am I questioning all the time? Is this suiting my temperament?* You have to ask yourself these questions. You have to be honest with yourself.

As long as something is enjoyed as a practice, so be it. But as Krishna has said in the Gita, put in all efforts, but know that the results are not in your control. If one has that understanding, then I would encourage everyone who's following the Law of Attraction to go ahead.

But, sometimes, one senses frustration. Where there's frustration, where there's anticipation, there's anxiety. Is your life becoming more anxious because of this?

N: I would like to probe one aspect of the Law of Attraction. Many people experience that they have a wish, and it gets fulfilled. But at some point, I think even you have said this before, that that wish itself becomes the cause of misery.

For example, they want a particular relationship, they get it, it appears that it is flowering and then, finally, it falls apart.

G: Exactly.

N: So, I see that in the Law of Attraction, the assumption is made by the person practising it that they know what is best for them.

G: Correct.

N: Whereas on Baba's path, you surrender your ego and your wishes to Baba, saying, *Baba, You know what is best for me.* If one is committed to Baba and, let's say they get more into Baba's Satcharita, they become devotion-oriented.

Here is where it could become slightly conflicting, till they make the transition to knowing that they are at Baba's feet, and regardless of what happens, it doesn't matter. Baba will give what is needed for them.

THE LAW OF ATTRACTION AND TRUE SURRENDER

So could you talk about that aspect of transition?

G: Well, that is true. As Nisargadatta Maharaj said, what comes unasked is what is meant for you. Because that comes from the Universe, without you operating your individual will. That indicates a high degree of surrender.

Now it's also a matter of age. When one is young, one has many desires. Let's say if someone hearing this podcast is fifty plus, then they've already been through a large part of that process of understanding that a lot of their needs were not met and their wishes didn't come true. Therefore, surrender is easier for them.

So, a large part of our life, if not all, is predestined. That is why they say surrender to the Source, surrender to Baba. If you can live like that, then that is the best way.

But if you do want to exert effort, and you feel drawn to the Law of Attraction, then make no mistake; do it if you feel like doing it but keeping in mind all these factors that we have just spoken about.

Sometimes, you may have surrendered to Baba, but the thought processes in your mind may be very life-negative. So an affirmation is needed to correct that. For instance, if someone with an agitated temperament recites the affirmation *I am peaceful, I am peaceful, peace, peace, peace* internally, with a lot of feeling, its vibration is bound to have an effect because the opposite has been going on all these years in their mind.

Affirmations are part of the Law of Attraction; so, in that sense, they are beautiful tools. But instead of looking at the science behind them, we expect material benefits from them. Most of us do that. Not only wealth. 'Material' even means a relationship.

I think, when it goes in that direction, there are pitfalls.

N: Correct. So if it is seen from the aspect of positive life-affirming affirmations, then it is healthy and fine. But when you try to steer life by how you feel is best for you, then, inevitably, I think, everyone will realize its limitations.

G: Yes. You may be one of the few chosen who practise the Law of Attraction, and you may get excellent results. If it comes easily, that means it was meant to, it was destined to. What we are discussing here is to ensure that the person does not suffer while they are performing this practice. Our intent is just to point out the pitfalls and the blind spots.

I will give you one example. This is going back, I think, fifteen years ago.

I met a doctor from Australia who was treating a cancer patient. The cancer was in quite an advanced stage, and the patient enrolled for one of the courses based on the Law of Attraction. He was assured he would see positive results soon. However, it did not improve his condition, so he was very distraught.

He went back to the institution that was teaching this course, and said, 'What do I do now? I have been following the practices diligently, but my end is nearing.'

And they told him, 'You didn't put your heart and soul into it, that's why you haven't improved.'

Subsequently, this patient told the doctor, 'If I don't put my heart and soul into it because my life depends on it, then who will put their heart and soul into it? After all, my life depends on it.'

N: True.

G: So what happened is that this young man died with the additional guilt that he was not good enough for the course, he didn't put his heart and soul into it and, therefore, he did not get the outcome he desired.

So this doctor was telling me that, as it is, his patient was having a rough journey towards the end, and then he got saddled with this guilt, which made it even rougher.

N: One has to be very aware and cautious of this limitation. Especially if someone young is practising it.

G: I read a lovely book called *The Dynamic Laws of Prosperity*. I think it's more than a hundred years old. It had such simple tools, which are only common sense, and they would fall under the Law of Attraction category.

For example, the author says that if someone owes you money, think of them as being prosperous. Don't think negatively about them and indulge in criticizing, blaming, and condemning them. Instead, think that they must be having a reason for not giving the money, which you don't know about, and you will get that money.

Now this approach makes so much sense to me because it's a science. We tend to always judge and condemn, and here it is saying exactly the opposite: if you want prosperity, which in this case means wanting the money that is owed to you, think prosperous thoughts. Simple.

N: Correct.

G: So, like I said, this book is more than a hundred years old, and, likewise, there are ancient texts that give very pragmatic advice. I recall reading something else. I don't know if it was in this book or another book, but it made so much sense. It said that if you want prosperity, you should see prosperous visuals, abundant visuals. They need not be just fancy neighbourhoods; you could see beautiful green fields and valleys full of flowers, which is the abundance of nature, and all that gets imprinted in your consciousness.

N: True.

G: So it is a simple science, but in this materialistic era we live in, it has attached itself to objects and relationships that the me wants and feels complete when it has those things.

N: Coming back to Baba, He has said that He will give us what we want in the hope that we will want what He wants to give us. I feel that Baba giving us what we want is also, in a way, the Law of Attraction, as He fulfils our desires. So there is something in common here.

G: Yes.

N: Baba is saying that, in the beginning, it is okay; we will ask for things and He will grant them. But ultimately, that stage has to be transcended.

So I think that is a big pointer as well for people practising the Law of Attraction. Desires have to be transcended for surrender to follow, where you go according to how Baba scripts your journey.

G: Yes. There are two points here.

One is that you can interpret 'I will give you what you want' at another level. You may yourself not truly know what you want. The inner truth, or what is truly required for your well-being, may not be what you think you want. So when Baba says, 'I will give you what you want,' I think He is addressing the want that He knows is best for you. We may still think in terms of our desires.

N: True.

G: The second point is that it's a pretty tricky statement that Baba has made. You feel that you'd want what Baba wants to give you rather than what you want. What I mean is that *your* wanting itself drops away on its own.

So He has tricked us with this sentence. [Laughter.] I mean, it's common sense: compared to what I want and what Baba wants to give me, which will I take?

N: Naturally, that which He is giving me. I do feel that if people can just contemplate this, there's a pointer hidden in this statement.

G: Yes, it's a very deep statement. I think it can be read at multiple levels, just like the Satcharita can be read at various levels.

I think the audience should ponder over this statement, especially those who are practising the Law of Attraction. They can consider all the aspects we have covered and then see how they feel about carrying on and what direction they want to take.

N: In that email that I had exchanged with the devotee I spoke about at the beginning of this discussion, I told her, 'If you look back at all the things you've had in your life, whether you've had them consciously as a desire or you were just happy to have had them, over time, either you've realized that the joy they gave you was temporal, or that joy turned into pain. And if you contemplate this sufficiently, then you will become ripe enough to want what Baba wants to give you.'

I felt that could be a bridge for someone practising the Law of Attraction; they shouldn't feel alienated from Baba's teaching or feel any guilt.

G: Yes.

The last thing I would like to state about desires is that you realize that fulfilling your desires is not going to give you true happiness, as you so rightly said. Now, as Rameshji would say, a desire can arise even in a sage, but the sage understands that whether or not the desire is fulfilled is God's will.

Secondly, when the desire arises in the sage, the sage merely witnesses the desire arising and sees the course it will take. Whereas we run after the desire to the detriment of others and ourselves. We start pursuing it, wanting more of it.

And that is why he would say that you can't kill desires by suppressing them or by fulfilling them all the time; witnessing them is all that is needed.

N: Earlier, when you spoke about the power of affirmations, it reminded me of something Ramakrishna Dev was emphatic about. He said that if you repeat to yourself, 'I am free, I am free,' you will actually become free. And if you say, 'I am a sinner, I am a sinner,' you will become a sinner.

And that is exactly the same thing you mentioned. So when he himself had said this, one's inner dialogue is something to be very vigilant about.

From this perspective, all our thoughts, in any case, are affirmations. So it is nice to have ones that are conducive to progressing on the journey.

To view the corresponding video, scan the QR code.

25

How to Know Baba's Will

Nikhil: How does a devotee know what is Baba's will in any particular situation? Could you speak a little bit about this and give us some pointers?

Gautam: Sure. Baba represents the Source. You could call it the Source, you could call it Consciousness or you could call it the Divine; you could give it any such name.

Whatever happens is perceived as either good or bad, and we think that only good can happen to us according to Baba's will. But He has never said that. He has clearly stated that we have to go through our Prarabdha, but He is there to mitigate the effect and to provide us the strength to go through it. So whatever happens, good or bad, is Baba's will.

There's this misconceived notion that Baba would not want anything bad to happen to me. You say that the Source only represents good because you are looking at it from an individual perspective of wanting only good to happen to you. That is a common mistake on the spiritual journey. Life is not only about pleasure. We all have seen that. In fact, we have more pain than pleasure in our lives.

So when we say that everything is Baba's will, what it means is that everything is the will of God, whether you like it or not. That must be understood by Sai Baba's sincere devotees. You yourself have interviewed luminaries on your channel who have been through tremendous hardships, such as Aai and Meena Kapur. Their thinking was not that none of this would have happened if it was Baba's will.

In fact, they are even more ardent devotees of Baba's than others who think so.

So this is a very important topic that you have raised because there is a lot of delusion around it.

'How can Baba take my job away from me? How can Baba take this relationship away from me?' I have received emails like that too. It is not Baba doing that. It is one's Prarabdha Karma. We have come here to settle our karmic accounts. And it is in times like this that we need faith in Baba instead of questioning how it can be His will. Most certainly, it is His will.

I'd like to add another point here. How to know, as you rightly asked, when it is Baba's will and when it is not? You can rest assured that when things are not going according to your will, it is Baba's will. That is another way of looking at it.

You have a limited perspective, so your wants and needs are based on what you think they should be. And when the Universe does not provide them, it means there is a higher will operating, which is not your will.

N: Can you give an example, just to simplify it a little?

G: Sure, we can take various examples. Let's take a very simple example of a boy wanting a girl in his life. He tries everything possible to woo her, but she is not interested. Now he could think that his will is to get this girl and Baba is not helping him achieve it, because he is seeing it from his perspective. But when he is not getting what he desires, despite his individual will and effort, he needs to accept it as Baba's will because, for all you know, he has been spared a relationship that was detrimental to his well-being.

N: Correct. He needs to trust that whatever is happening is happening for his best, although he may not know it.

This brings me to another point. A devotee should develop the deep faith that regardless of what happens according to his Prarabdha, his love and devotion to Baba is steadfast. It is not dependent on his life circumstances. Otherwise, he is going to have a conditional relationship with Baba.

So could you speak a little bit about that aspect as well?

G: The guru–disciple relationship depends on the faith the disciple has in the guru, no matter what happens in their life. That is true faith because it is that faith which can take you through some extreme situations, which you would, in any case, have to face, even without having a guru. You may not be able to face them; you may break down. But faith in the guru—the guru being the representation of the Absolute, which Sai Baba is—will see you through the darkest times.

As we started by saying, karma has to be lived. We have to go through it. But to keep us afloat despite whatever cards life deals us is the role of the guru. That is what Baba says He will do.

It is not a bed of roses. You can't assume that you will get the job of your dreams or marry the girl of your dreams or have a large bank account or go through the Covid crisis with no negative effects on you. Why? Because Baba is your guru? He never said that.

So let's get real. Let's see what Baba is. Baba represents Consciousness. Consciousness is all there is, including opposites of every conceivable kind. Pleasure and pain are the two polar opposites which we all face in life.

We create suffering for ourselves when we do not acknowledge and accept that the pain in our lives is also part of our destiny and the will of the Divine. God never said, 'I will only give you a life of pleasure.'

N: The problem with this is that it doesn't sit well with certain people. They cannot conceive that the will of the Divine includes pain. So then why don't we just rephrase it to say that the way manifestation works, things do break down. As Eckhart would say, the way the instruments of Consciousness function, they are designed to break down, and things don't always work out for you.

That is why the masters tell you to go through all of it so that you get out of the birth and death cycle. Till your Prarabdha is worked out, Baba is pointing you inward, to that space of freedom, so that you are released from the karmic cycle. But many people do not focus on this.

G: Yes. Unfortunately, what they don't realize is that they are prolonging their suffering by making this demand from Baba to not give them pain. They are living an illusion because the reality is altogether different.

So then why not wake up to that illusion, understand that this is the fact of life and be at peace with it, rather than avoid it, because when you avoid it, you are creating suffering for yourself.

N: Also, when one is in a challenging situation, one would do well to face it with saburi, with trust, and have the attitude of *'jhelna padta hai* [one has to bear it]*'* or a smiling, patient approach that this too will pass.

G: Yes, so what role does the guru play in this? To explain, let's use this lockdown example, where people are worried about their jobs.

The first step is that you accept this happened because it was meant to happen. So your mind is not full of *Why has this happened to me? I don't deserve this. I have done so many good things in my life.* All that dialogue is finished because you have accepted the will of the Divine, the Absolute, or Baba. This is the situation before you. The point is that you have not overlaid it with psychological suffering.

The next step is that you are concerned about your job. Questions will emerge, such as *Will I lose my job? How long will this go on for? Will my employers cut my salary?* These are all valid concerns. Even in a staunch devotee of Baba's, concern will arise because it's natural. But which of these concerns ultimately turn into reality? Only time will tell.

But because you have come to terms with the situation, there will be no blame and no condemnation of the situation, the virus or your employers. You will accept that this happened because it was destined to happen, and rather than rely on your puny little will, you will lean on the shoulders of your guru and his will to take you through this crisis.

So that concern, which is a valid concern, will not get translated into foreboding, depression, angst and undue worry, which spill over and make not only our lives miserable but also those of the people we are living with.

For a staunch devotee of Baba's, it will not happen because his faith will create that cushion. That is the difference between accepting everything as God's will and not accepting it.

N: What you just explained reminds me of an extreme example of the same. Osho spoke of a very advanced devotee who went through intense hunger, and his prayer of gratitude to God was 'God, thank You for my hunger. This was my need, and You satisfied it.'

Osho went on to say that with this attitude, the devotee was truly free. It was a very beautiful and deep pointer, that surrender and gratitude were possible in an extreme situation.

This takes me to another point where many people talk of free will and their will, but I personally feel that if you have absolute trust in your guru, or Baba, and He knows what is best for you, what is the value of having any free will or choice when you totally surrender to Baba?

G: Absolutely, because it is Baba's will which starts operating in your life. So what will happen in practical terms is that you will stop trying to control outcomes like you used to because your life has shown you that very little is in your control—you intend one thing and something else happens.

You work towards something and you may or may not get the rewards; that is your life's experience. At the same time, you know that your breathing happens without you doing anything or that your heart pumps without any effort on your part. So that little control that you thought you had over life, when you hand that also over to the higher will, you know that whatever is meant to happen is going to happen for the best. You stop interfering in the will of the Divine.

But unfortunately, you have such strong convictions in your mind that you develop tunnel vision. You lose the bigger picture, and this is true even in your dealings with others. You think you know what's best for them. That's the narrowness of your vision and your desire to control them.

Control is based on fear. You fear certain outcomes, so you try to control things obsessively. But when you allow things to happen, when you hand over the reins of your life to Baba, you accept situations more easily, and it makes your life simpler. You will still do what you have to do.

As I said, concerns will arise and the working mind will step in and figure out possible outcomes—which are better, which are not; what you should do, what you should not; and suchlike. That is the functioning of life. But there will be no room anymore for all the psychological rubbish that is heaped over it.

N: Can we run past a few more practical examples?

For instance, if someone finds resistance in carrying out certain decisions, they can take it as a given that the decision taken is contrary to Baba's will, because, as Nisargadatta Maharaj said, 'What comes unasked is meant for you.' [Refer to talk 24.]

So there is a lot to take away from that.

G: Absolutely, because the very fact that it has come to you unasked means your will was not there at all. You never know what the next moment brings. It could be pleasure or pain. That is also coming unasked.

But what we try to do is that we try to guarantee that all the next moments of our lives will only bring us pleasure. It is impossible.

We tend to keep exercising effort in a direction while the Universe is constantly showing us that it's yielding no result. So how much of our effort, based on our volition and doership, are we going to keep exercising? That is why, even in some ancient spiritual texts, it is said that whatever happens in your life with not too much effort or with least resistance is what is meant for you. Because then you know that it has happened by the will of the Divine.

There was a *jnani* from Gujarat, who was also referred to as Maharaj. I forget his name. Someone asked him about working hard and striving for money.

The jnani replied, 'Look, if you are destined to do that, you will. That does not mean you will get the money. Because whether you get it or not has already been decided according to your Prarabdha. And therefore, at a certain point, when the money comes to you, it is only because the seed in your astral body, which is meant to produce wealth, has sprouted.'

Now does that mean you sit back and do nothing? It does not. It means you do what you are naturally inclined to. If you are naturally inclined to work hard, by all means, work hard, knowing that the amount of money coming in is not in your control. That is the message of the Gita.

So one has to live like that; live according to one's nature.

Someone may tell a timid person 'Don't be timid. You have to be strong to survive in this cruel world.' But when it's not in their nature to be strong, by trying excessively to do so, they are creating suffering for themselves. Instead, they should accept that their nature is to be timid because God made them that way. So, when fear arises, they can witness it when it arises.

It is so much easier to accept one's God-given attributes, rather than create this problem of 'What should I be?' versus 'What I am'. That is where the suffering lies.

N: Unfortunately, in this world, extroversion is encouraged, and many introverts are forced to fit in against their will. So, in that sense also, many things according to society's perspective are imposed upon them.

G: That is very true. Yet, despite that, if one is comfortable with one's innate nature, they will lead a relatively peaceful life than if they struggle to go against it.

N: Another example I want to cite is that of Baba's param bhakta, Kakasaheb Dixit. After Baba left His body, sometimes, Kaka would have questions for Him. So he would make two chits, one with a 'Yes' written on it and the other with a 'No', and he would fold them. Then when he picked one of them and opened them, with absolute faith, he would know Baba's will by seeing the answer written on them.

So if some devotees have questions, they could try that, but then they have to have the absolute faith that Kaka had. Because, even here, I can see that someone may make up their mind that they want to do something and repeat the chit-opening process three times. Then that is cheating.

G: [Laughs.] That's true. It also happens with Tarot card readings. If you are not happy with the first reading, you tell the Tarot reader to deal the deck again because you want a particular outcome.

N: This is a very good example to show the workings of the mind and the personal will.

One has already made up their mind what the outcome should be. There's this assumption that what they desire will be good for them.

G: Yes. If you look at Kakasaheb's example, he used the chits as a tool when he was undecided about a certain thing. Hence, he needed a 'Yes' or a 'No'. He had full faith in the guru, and he took the answer of a 'Yes' or a 'No' to be the guru's word because he was confused. He followed the guru's decision, whether it was a 'Yes' or a 'No'. He was not invested in a 'Yes' outcome.

N: There's also this tendency to want an opinion to validate your own. So you discuss the issue on hand with a few people until someone says 'Yes, yes. This is good for you.'

So these are just tendencies of the mind that one can become aware of.

G: I use this common example. Let's say you see a movie, which you love, and you go and tell some friends, 'Hey guys, have you seen this movie? I loved it.' And someone says, 'Oh, did you? I didn't like it at all!' Now, are you willing to accept that that person's point of view is as valid as yours, or are you going to try to convince him by saying 'How can you say that? It's such a good movie.'

Most of us do that. When we face an opposing viewpoint, we think the other person is wrong, and then we try to rectify their point of view.

N: One of Baba's primary teachings was not to get into a confrontation, which is easily forgotten by many.

G: Yes, because you forget that the other opinion is also an opinion from the Divine Itself. You are not the only one, you see.

N: Right. It reminds me of a story where a certain guru's disciple was sitting in a forest, when an elephant started charging towards him. This elephant's *mahout* yelled out to him to get out of the way. But based on what he had heard from his guru about everything being God's will, he said, 'No, I'll just stay put.' And then the elephant ran over him.

The guru admonished his badly injured disciple the next day, saying, 'Even the mahout is God. So when he was shouting out to you, why did you not move, you fool?'

G: It was as if God was saying, 'I came to you as the mahout, telling you to get out of the way. But you were so confident that the elephant would not be able to harm you. That was all in your mind, and your mind was so closed.'

N: I also feel that if one truly realizes in all humility that they do not know anything at all about anything, and only Baba knows the big picture, then how does the question of wanting more arise? Even if you had the option of having free will, you would throw it away.

G: Yes. However, to reach the state you have mentioned may sound very simple, but very few have attained it, and those few are living a life of peace. Because if nothing really matters, which is the outcome of what you have just said, you will be at peace. So that is well said.

N: So, Thy will be done. Baba's will be done.

To view the corresponding video, scan the QR code.

26

Seekers, Disciples and Devotees

Nikhil: I feel today's topic of discussion could prove to be an important roadmap for many of Baba's aspiring devotees.

A few years ago, I came across a beautiful article by Robert Adams, the Advaita teacher, wherein he classified the types of spiritual aspirants that exist into three categories: the beginners, who are the seekers, followed by the disciples, and then, finally, the devotees. In some circles, the words 'devotee' and 'disciple' are used interchangeably, so we'll keep that in mind. Robert gave some characteristics of these three types, and I found it particularly helpful in my journey. If we could discuss this, hopefully, there will be some nice pointers for those who are on the spiritual path.

Gautam: Sure.

N: What Robert said was that the beginners, or the seekers, are those who are new to the spiritual dimension and are, perhaps, exploring different teachings.

G: Right.

N: Then comes the stage where a seeker becomes a disciple, where they will either come to one teaching or one master and stick to that path. So if it is bhakti, then it's only bhakti. They will not go from teacher to teacher or attend every spiritual talk in town.

Then the next stage is that of the devotee, where they are committed to the master. They are only interested in serving the master; they have no desire or will of their own—not even for Self-realization.

Their only happiness is in serving the master and being in the master's presence.

Robert gave a beautiful example of a devotee of Ramana Maharshi, who used to fan him for fifty years. He never spoke a word. He would just stand there next to him all day and fan him. And then one day, he dropped dead. And Sri Ramana said, 'He's not coming back.' [Refer to talk 8.]

I feel that these are some characteristics people can see in the devotees we have known through the channel, such as Aai—the ones who are intimately connected with Baba. And there's a lot to take away from this.

G: Yes.

Let's consider a seeker's journey with Baba and see what these three stages mean. Now, as you said, the seeking could be such that Baba is one of the masters the seeker is interested in and there are others as well.

Then what happens is that one focuses only on Baba's teaching because that appeals to them the most. So after the seeker has looked around and imbibed the messages of different masters, they follow only Baba.

Now comes the third stage of being a devotee. In this case, we know that Baba is not in form anymore. So how can one be a devotee? And what is it to be a devotee? If one is living and breathing the master's teaching, then one is a devotee, you see. So that deals with every aspect of your life. We recently covered the Law of Attraction, and that is a great example because it relates to this point.

Now, if you are anchored in Baba's words and teachings, and you are viewing everything in your life according to His teaching, morning to evening, and acting in harmony with it, then you are a devotee. For example, Baba tells us not to bark at anyone like a dog. If you are living that, you are a devotee. But if you have studied that, understood that, and it makes sense to you at an intellectual level, and yet you find yourself losing your temper and being rude to people, then you are still a disciple.

N: Correct.

G: So it is a very important leap from being a disciple to being a devotee. The devotee lives the teaching. The disciple has certainly absorbed the teaching. There is definitely an intent on the disciple's part because they have been drawn to it. They understand that what Baba says makes sense, but it has not yet sunk into the heart.

N: Yes.

G: And that is also natural. That's a process, you see, because we have years and years of conditioning behind us. It takes time for the old conditioning to be replaced by the new learning, which, in time, becomes fresh conditioning.

So it is a process. It's not like there's one batch of people who are disciples and one batch who are devotees. It's an internal process, which Robert is pointing to. One shouldn't get stuck on being a disciple, because the growth is from the disciple stage to the devotee stage.

With living masters, you will find that they have a group of volunteers who offer a large part of their time in seva because they have been impacted so much by the teachings. They want to offer something back in gratitude, in the spirit of love and service. They obviously cannot offer back spiritual wisdom because that is what they have received from the master. So what is the next best thing they can offer? The lifespan they have been given, the intellect they have been given, the abilities they have been given. The offering could be in terms of spreading the teaching or looking after the master, if he needs looking after; that is circumstantial.

The ancient masters of India have said that if you have a guru, then you have to treat everyone in the guru's family and everyone connected with the guru with the same level of respect and love that you give to the guru. That only happens when one is a true devotee because, at the disciple stage, this may still not be part of one's awareness.

So, according to me, this is what Robert Adams is trying to point out—the different stages.

N: I feel that the very awareness of this, once it seeps in, will give aspirants a clear road map for moving ahead in the right direction.

Talking of masters and being of service to them, there is one thing I have observed. In fact, even Robert had spoken about this in the 1990s—that there are masters at every corner. And that phenomenon is true to a larger extent today. Some of them are obviously not real masters, but he said it is important for the devotee to not just have a relationship with the master where they see him once a year at a retreat and in their minds think they've ticked the box *I have a master* in their mind. I mean, okay, that is fine, but the relationship Robert emphasized was one where there is a personal relationship. As you beautifully said earlier, the inner circle serves the master as they are impacted by his teachings. And if that is the sort of relationship one has, then they can say that they are devotees. The master knows exactly what is going on in their lives. It is not where they meet every six months and then they go back to their own lives. So could you talk about that aspect a little bit?

G: Well, that also is circumstantial. I'll give you an example in connection with my teacher, Rameshji. There was a lawyer from Sweden who was, perhaps, among the top ten lawyers there. He was quite wealthy; he had other businesses also. Despite being a busy man because of his work-related commitments, he would take time out to come to Mumbai, maybe once or twice a year, and be at the feet of his master, Rameshji. Now, beyond that, he could not do much because he could only come down for two or three days.

This lawyer liked a particular book of Rameshji's called *Sin and Guilt*; it was a small book. When he was in Sweden, he would devote some time to translating that book into Swedish as he felt that his fellow brothers and sisters would greatly benefit from the message in that book. So, although he was thousands of miles away, this is how he offered seva to his guru. He didn't care whether the book sold or not as he didn't need the money. He did what he thought he should do because his master's message impacted him and he wanted to share it.

So what I'm trying to say is that even if one can't physically be with the master for circumstantial reasons, it doesn't mean one can't offer seva.

N: Exactly.

G: The intent was there, and it arose naturally and sincerely. My teacher saw this, as was evident from the fact that when we published a book called *Peace and Harmony in Daily Living*, in 2003, he dedicated the book to this Swedish lawyer, Göran Ekdahl.

N: One other aspect I see, which is very close to this, is the settling down on one path. If it is a young aspirant, initially, when they're exploring different paths, they may come to Baba and they may also go to a few other teachers. For some time, that is fine, but ultimately, they should settle down on one path.

Many ask what the essence of Hema Ma's and Aai's devotion is, and I say that it is the love in their heart for Baba. Their whole existence is Baba. You can't ever imagine Aai being interested in reading books or having any other interests of that sort.

G: Yes, as Nisargadatta Maharaj said, to get water from the land, you don't dig shallow wells all over the land but one deep well. [Refer to talk 4.] Also, what tends to happen is that, initially, when we are exploring teachings, we start comparing them. I have experienced this myself. Many people write to me, asking me for my opinion on what a certain master said.

Now that is not fair—not fair to that person, not fair to me, and not fair to the seeker. If you are following one teaching, *you* decide what your views are on it based on your intellect. See whether it satisfies you and transforms your life. However, the mind tends to accumulate various concepts and teachings, pit one against the other and start judging them. That is the maya of the mind, you see.

I would like to add something here, which I have been feeling, specifically in relation to Baba. A large part of Sai Baba's teachings is pure Jnana Yoga.

N: Yes.

G: But, over time, it has largely been His chamatkars which have drawn people. I do feel that the time has now come when Baba's teachings will not only be known but will spread, based on His teachings of Jnana Yoga. If you look at chapter four of the Satcharita, on which we have done a short commentary, while I have focused on a story, the beginning section is all Jnana Yoga. That is why I keep emphasizing living the teachings rather than the miracles.

Now, someone like Hema Ma and Aai, particularly Aai, who is of a simple mindset, will live the teachings through her heart because she takes Baba's words as a command. But there may be a different set of people today, perhaps youngsters, perhaps those more inclined to the path of knowledge, who will now be exposed to Baba's words of wisdom. How they imbibe them and live them is also 'living the teachings'.

So all these options are placed before us by the same master, and they are not really two different paths, Jnana and Bhakti. Jnana is saying that nobody does anything; everyone is an instrument of the Divine. And what is Bhakti saying? Bhakti is telling us to see God in everyone. Are they any different? They are not. Their essence is the same, but some are inclined to Jnana, and others are inclined to Bhakti. The point is that it is 'living the teachings', either through Bhakti or Jnana. You have to look at those people who are shining examples of living the teachings.

N: Regardless of one's inclination, whether it is Jnana or Bhakti, the thing that the devotees have in common is that Baba is the top priority.

G: Right.

N: And essentially, that is what I see with all the intimate devotees. Despite their practices, their whole existence is Baba; they only want to serve Him. And I just keep coming back to one thing: the very remembrance of this fact can take one very far on their journey. For example, if one is a young seeker, a lot of energy may just be expelled, jumping from one path to another, and it could make someone, in fact, even more lost or restless. Or they could be reading a lot of books and sharpening the mind more, trying to gain more knowledge. But, in contrast, the devotees are pretty much empty because that is when they get what Baba is giving them.

G: Yes, but see, when one is young, it is the age of adventure and exploration, so I think that is not something that one can avoid. But what will happen is that, at a certain point in their journey, hopefully, they will reach a state where they will ask, 'So far, whatever I have imbibed, has it made a difference to my life? Out of the five masters I visited, is there one who has touched me more deeply than the others?' This is the stage where there can be a transformation from seeker to disciple, although it is not necessarily so.

Let's take for instance someone who has been following Baba's teachings among others. He should introspect whether His teachings have given him peace and solace. He may find that, obviously, they have, because he is drawn to them. Then he can go deeper into the teachings, read the Satcharita, and mark those sentences that impact him so that he can look at them again and live the teachings therein. That is the way to, as Maharaj said, dig deeper in one place. [Refer to talk 4.] The main thing is that when you are absorbed in one master's teachings, they become the content of your consciousness. Your entire consciousness, morning to evening, will be full of that vibration. That is being a devotee. If you think of your master all the time, you are a devotee.

N: So I hope that these are some helpful pointers that devotees can reflect on and that there's something for them to take away from them. Is there something else you would like to share?

G: I would like to use you as a case in point. Today, there is so much available in terms of social media and digital technology. These are great opportunities for seva. So I would like to say this, especially to your younger audience, that if they are moved by your channel or by any channel on Sai Baba, they can think about offering their services and their time. They will enjoy it and love what they are doing, and it will be a great contribution because they will be helping their fellow brothers and sisters discover what they have discovered. That's all I'd like to say.

N: Those who are inclined and those who've been impacted are welcome to get in touch with us as there is a lot of work that they could help with.

To view the corresponding video, scan the QR code.

27

Do We Really Treat Others as Equals?

Nikhil: The other day, one of my friends mentioned that he was washing his car for the first time in all these years. And that, somehow, made me wonder whether we really see everybody and treat them as equals—the security guards and people with jobs that are not very high profile— in cities where people live busy lives, especially in India, where it's easy to get household help. Or do we have a subtle complex about it?

Gautam: Right.

N: And I felt that has a lot to do with Baba's teachings if you look at them deeply because Baba emphasized absolute love for the other.
So could you talk a little bit about that?

G: Sure. In the context of India and Indians, what you have raised now is of specific significance, and there are two reasons for that.
A lot of us living in urban India are English-medium educated, whereas ninety-nine per cent of the population is either uneducated or has studied in regional languages. To start with, this has created a divide between those who are English-speaking and those who are not. Also, the first group has developed Western tastes. Everything—from their breakfast and dressing style to their whole demeanour—is different.
So, this happened as a result of conditioning. That is one aspect.
The second aspect is that, in India, we carry a heavy burden: the caste system. Even though it is not visible so much in the urban

areas now, subconsciously, the collective conditioning has created a prejudice about what lower caste and higher caste people are capable of doing.

Therefore, what Baba mentions on this front becomes more pertinent. In the West, you could be affluent and educated, and you would still share a meal with your chauffeur at the same table. I have seen that when I have travelled abroad; the ones who work for others are not treated any differently by the latter.

I had the same experience in Goa about fifteen years ago, let alone the West. I got very friendly with a couple from Ireland. One day, they picked me up to join them for lunch, and to my utter surprise, they also invited their driver, who they had hired during their stay in Goa. I was taken aback because we, in India, are not used to that. As you mentioned, we look at the people who wash the cars or the drivers differently.

And then I realized that this is something which comes so naturally to people overseas, which I have seen across various countries. But with Indians, this is not so.

N: Correct.

G: Also, when I was with my spiritual teacher, I met so many foreigners at his satsangs. We would go for tea after the sessions, and I would find myself sitting, for example, with either a bricklayer at a construction site or a lady who cleaned people's houses [both foreigners]. And you would have no idea about this because they speak your language, have the same tastes as you do and engage in the same topics of discussion.

I realized that these boundaries don't come up when we are with people from the Western world, because that has been our conditioning. But with our own people, they come up because we have this kind of default setting, as mentioned earlier.

This is a mistake that we make. Everyone is designed differently and comes with their own destinies, both economic and geographical.

Baba's teaching becomes pertinent because it is an equalizer. If it is the same Consciousness functioning through everyone, then aren't we all equal?

So, I wanted to lay the ground for this discussion in the Indian context first.

Then there is another thing which we miss, and now I am talking on behalf of all of humanity. Sri Aurobindo said something very beautiful: 'It is irrelevant what work you are doing. But how you are doing that work, the sense of the Divine Presence while you are working, the Godhead behind the work, that is of utmost significance,' which means your driver could be completely in the present moment driving the car, which you have never felt at work; yet you feel you are above him.

N: You know, simple folk have a deeper sense of contentment or joy. I have personally found that they sleep better, have less anxiety and are happier with the little things in life. Even though they may not have much, they will share whatever they do have.

Talking about default settings, there was an incident that happened about a year ago. My driver had lost his child, so, naturally, he was quite dejected. I happened to be talking to him about it, when one neighbour came and just barged into our conversation, expecting me to drop it and talk to her instead.

So I just told her, 'Right now, I am speaking with him. I will get back to you soon.'

I could tell by her body language that she took offence because I did not speak with her, and she walked away. It didn't bother me, and I didn't meet her later. However, it made me think about why one assumes that they should be given preference over someone else just because he happens to be a driver. And it's not that he is devoid of emotion. As you just said very beautifully, he could be more present than someone else; maybe he is enlightened, for all you know.

G: Yes, exactly. In our building, we have a new liftman [elevator operator]. The consistency and sweetness with which he says 'Namaste', hasn't changed in the last three months. It's such a beautiful namaste, and he greets everyone like that.

It is quite likely that when we have a bad day, our namaste will go out of the window or we'll forget about it or say it in a curt tone.

So everyone in our life is there to teach us something, and it is the simple people, as you said, who have simple needs and are living simple lives who often do so. I re-emphasize the fact that we, in India, need to learn this lesson more than people abroad.

N: That is why I brought it up. When I heard my friend say that he was washing his car for the first time, it just hit me that this is something that many take for granted. But the present situation [Covid lockdown] has now become an opportunity to look at this aspect of our lives, where we make certain assumptions.

G: It is a turning point. I have seen videos on Facebook where, for the first time, garbage cleaners are being applauded as they go about their daily chores. It is because of this unprecedented situation that we have seen their worth, and we are applauding it. Now, after this situation is over, we have to see whether we go back to our conditioning or whether we have learnt from it and become transformed by it, so that from this point on, we are well aware that there are people who are doing the dirty work of collecting garbage, which we shun, and live with that awareness.

But, unfortunately, human memory is very short-lived.

Yet, situations like this lockdown occur, and they could be transformational. You are raising such pertinent points, so hopefully, the sincere spiritual seeker will grab these opportunities, these insights, which are coming their way, to live the teachings.

I will keep hammering this point because my teacher used to say that the shell of the ego has become so hard that it needs constant hammering to break it open.

So, back to that point: Are you living the teachings of Sai?

N: Baba would emphatically repeat that poverty is much higher than kingship; much higher. Aai has spoken about this too.

G: Yes, and Baba would ask people to go around with a begging bowl because there are lessons to be learnt from it.

N: Another aspect, since we both have spent time with Eckhart Tolle's teachings, is that this could even be applied to a child–parent relationship, or any relationship for that matter, where one may have an unconscious superiority complex. Maybe someone is physically stronger or someone thinks they are more intelligent, but then, in the realm of Being, that outlook takes you far away from the truth.

G: Exactly. That is the whole point because we have started wearing a mask, which creates a sense of separation from others. We put on different masks with different people: with our driver, we are one person; with our colleague at work, we are another; and with our family, we are yet another.

The spiritual journey means dropping these masks to reveal our true identity—who we truly are.

N: Yes. It reminds me of a story about a Zen master from Japan. One day, the king came to meet him, and this master looked down to see that his palms were sweating. So, in all honesty, he told his students to stop revering him as their teacher because he had not yet realized the Ultimate. His palms started sweating in front of the king, which meant that he saw some difference between him and other people.

I felt it was a deep story because when we see that all beings are equal, we will not have a difference in our behaviour or put on a mask, depending on whether we perceive someone as big or small.

G: Yes.

N: Even Dharamdas Baba would ask you to introspect on whether you see a change in your behaviour when you talk to the rich and talk to the poor.

G: Also, wherever there's a monetary transaction where the employer is paying their employee, it tends to get converted into the right to behave in a certain way because the employer is paying the money. They feel they have purchased that relationship, so they can behave however they like.

N: Yes, that is very wrong.

G: This is a common pitfall on the path. If you were to truly follow Baba's teachings, and if everyone is an aspect of the Divine, then you are conducting a transaction with the Divine for Divine services rendered, maybe in the form of a housemaid, a driver, or whatever. So your transaction, ultimately, is with the Divine only, but we lose sight of that. We still think of people as individuals, you see.

I read somewhere that Sai Baba had once told somebody that whenever he looks at anyone, he should imagine Baba's face on that person. That brings in a sense of equality because then you see Baba in everyone. Baba has said, 'See Me in all beings.'

N: Yes, and Baba has pulled up many devotees regarding this aspect. Once, a lady came asking for alms at Nanasaheb Chandorkar's residence, and they gave her something. Then when she continued to ask for more, they shooed her away in a rather harsh way.

Later Baba caught hold of Nanasaheb and spoke to him about the incident, after which he transformed over time.

I do feel that this is an important aspect of Baba's teachings. On one hand, you may do bhajans and worship mechanically, but, on the other, if this aspect is lived, I feel that Baba will be much more pleased with it.

G: Yes, because this is true devotion to God. If you are respecting all your relationships, if you are devoted to them in all possible ways, then this is living bhakti. It is not just between you and a murti of Sai Baba's. It's all about living it.

I would like to end by bringing up something that we all tend to forget. We all are going to die but we act as if we are going to live forever. And the other thing is that when we die, the cremation ground does not distinguish between an employer and an employee.

So, you see, we are shown all the time what the reality is. Our bodies are going to turn to dust. But when we are living, we forget that.

If our brothers and sisters who are Sai Baba's devotees delve into not only these podcasts but all the content on your website, it can take them very far on their journey to the Divine.

To view the corresponding video, scan the QR code.

28

Surrender—the True Prayer (Gautam's Talk)

Namaste, everyone.

There is something I would like to share with you. It is a reflection based on the various emails I have received from Sai Baba's devotees, especially those who are experiencing pain and suffering of some form in their life and are unable to accept it.

Why is this happening to me? Why is Baba not giving me this job? Why has He taken my loved one away? Why is He not giving me the relationship I desire? Why is Baba holding back? And so on.

The psychological suffering gets enhanced by such questions.

And then there are others who have accepted the divine will and ask Baba for strength to deal with the situation they are placed in. In their case, while the pain is still there as that is a part of life, its duration is not extended in the form of psychological suffering.

The Buddha said that samsara is dukkha, nirvana is Shanti. Life, or the world, is sorrow and suffering. Nirvana, or enlightenment, is peace. He didn't say nirvana is joy. He did not say it is happiness which depends on an outcome. It is Shanti.

I would like to share with you all, the words of Joel Goldsmith, a Western mystic. He was a healer, and he had a very specific teaching.

In the passages that I am about to read out, you may replace the word 'God' with 'Sai Baba'. Because, after all, if Sai Baba is considered a ray of the Absolute, then Sai Baba too is omnipresent, omniscient and omnipotent—all-pervading, all-knowing and all-powerful. He is everywhere; there is nowhere that He is not.

So please go along with me on this very short journey of listening to Goldsmith's words because they address this point in particular.

To bring ourselves as an empty vessel to God and let God fill that vessel is the highest form of prayer. Let us not take our finite views of what is good and what is bad to God, nor take our human hopes and ambitions to Him. But let us go to God as if we really trusted Him more than we would trust our own mother. Trusted Him as the Divine Love and the Divine Wisdom of this world, which, in truth, He is.

So Goldsmith lays this foundation to start with: one of trust, of being an empty vessel, rather than being filled with all our hopes, fears, desires, ambitions, etc.

When we do that, we are children of God. But so long as we are doing all the talking, telling, asking, pleading, beseeching and advising God, we are mortals, and our prayer does not reach God. Our prayers reach God only when we permit ourselves to be empty vessels, when our full faith and trust is 'Thy will be done in me, Thy grace, Thy peace,' and then wait in silence, completely empty, as the Word of God comes to us and fills us, fulfils itself and its plans in us.

You see, this is a very important point because we feel that our plan is the right plan. God doesn't know what's good for us as well as we do. And our plan is based on our thought processes, which, in turn, are based on our life experiences. In other words, our conditioning. That is how limited our planning is.

But when we open ourselves to a higher dimension, we realize there is a plan far more elaborate and intricate than what we can perceive through our limited conditioning. That would be called being open to Baba's grace. So that is the trust which Goldsmith is talking about.

Let's take Baba's words: 'shraddha' and 'saburi'. Goldsmith's words explain the deeper meaning of these two words. Shraddha and saburi do not mean that I have a specific want based on my desires and my needs, and so I'm going to wait with faith and patience to get only that outcome which I desire. That is truly limiting in our approach to Baba.

And so it is, that if we are among those who are fulfilling some niche in life, into which we have been thrown through circumstances beyond our control, or in which we have placed ourselves through ignorance, certainly, we need the prayer of fulfilment, which is the prayer of emptiness. We need to learn how to release the whole situation into God, willingly admitting, 'Look here, I certainly have messed up this life of mine so far. Let me give up, and You take over.'

This is what true surrender is. Giving up this obsessive control over life, trying to control outcomes all the time, trying to control people all the time. It's all domination and control that the ego engages in. And here is an invitation to give up trying to dominate and control people and situations.

At the risk of repetition, in my previous dialogues and talks, I have said, 'How much is truly in our control? The Earth is spinning at a certain rate and revolving around the Sun at the same time, which is not in our control. Gravity, not in our control. Breathing, not in our control. Blood coursing through our veins, not in our control. What happens the next moment, whether it brings us pleasure or pain, not in our control. Our conditioning from the time we were born, our geographical location, the religion we were born into, the parents under whose umbrella we grew up, the school we went to, the college, etc., not in our control.'

Yet, the ego is trying to micromanage and control everything in life. And the beauty is that we all know that even deep sleep is not in our control. We cannot choose to go into deep sleep. It just happens. And the fact is that deep sleep is so peaceful. That is why one wakes up and says, 'I slept so well.' The absence of the ego with its sense of doership is deep sleep.

So let's go on a bit.

There is no other way to pray. When we pray in that way, we are praying to the Infinite Wisdom of the Universe, trusting Divine Love to fulfil Itself in us. As long as we are advising, suggesting or outlining to God, or even hoping that God will act according to our personal wisdom, we are not praying to God but to our own mind. This is no way to pray. Rather, we should surrender ourselves to God, so that God's will for us may fulfil itself, that whatever it was for which we were born (and we were all born for a purpose; otherwise, we would not be here) may be fulfilled.

This is the true prayer.

I had a friend who had this most beautiful prayer. I've mentioned this before. He said to me, 'Every morning, I stand before my altar and pray, "Today, I promise to get out of my own way."' Because unknowingly, through ignorance, we put so many obstacles in our path: *Things should be this way and not that way. He should not have said this to me. I should not have said that to her.* Besides, we are second-guessing all the time. And our mind is creating such a muddle that we are unable to see what *is* because it has got overlaid by what we feel *should be*. What is God's will, the will of the Divine, is overlaid by the filter of what we feel should be or should not be.

So, if we can step aside and trust that just as this intelligence makes the planet spin at a certain speed, the Sun shine, our heart beat and our blood course through the body, so also, it governs our life without needing our input all the time. So acceptance of the divine will, or acceptance of Baba's will, naturally leads to surrender. Not 'surrender' as in 'giving up', but surrender to whatever arises in the moment and then dealing with it, the way we feel and think we should deal with it, without any drama invested in the situation. The drama of blaming Baba, or others, or circumstances, or situations.

A life without blame, condemnation, hatred, malice, jealousy, envy, pride and arrogance is a life of peace and harmony in daily living. When this garbage is no longer there in the thinking mind, our mind is at peace. Sukh-Shanti. The peace that surpasses all understanding. This means it is no longer a mental process. If we accept Baba's will, God's will, and surrender as a result of that, we are at peace.

And finally . . .

I am not entering the presence of God in order to enlighten God.
I am not going to God to present my views to Him, hoping to tell Him more than He already knows or to tell Him what is good

for me to have. I do not expect through this period of prayer and communion to influence God on my behalf.

In my childhood, I faced many challenges. We used to go regularly to Shirdi, and I remember when I was in school, the question would arise: *Baba, if we are visiting You often, how can You do this to us?*

We assume that Baba is an individual doing things to various devotees. But we should know that whatever challenges we go through are given to us for our evolution. That is why we have been manifested in this body of flesh and bone.

But there is something called grace. There is a Higher Power, of which masters, such as Baba, are representatives. Their Presence through their Being, their words and their teachings give us the strength to go through life's vicissitudes.

So, to pray to Baba telling Him what He should do is not the right way to go about it. Instead, you could pray, *You are all there is. You obviously know what I am going through. I don't need to tell you that.*

A spontaneous prayer may arise in a challenging situation, such as, *Please help me.* That is fine. But the incessant thinking process which we are mired in, when that goes out of the window, then we have this direct knowing that no matter what we are going through in life, whatever we are facing, there is That which is giving us the strength to face it. That Presence is always with us, behind us, on the side of us, ahead of us. That awareness is there, and that is what is giving us the courage to live life.

Then we find that the focus on the 'poor me' turns away, towards this acceptance, as Goldsmith says, of 'the Divine Love and the Divine Wisdom', which, you will agree with me, describes Sai Baba.

Thank you.

To view the corresponding video, scan the QR code.

29

How Baba Instilled Humility in His Devotees

Nikhil: I feel that for any spiritual devotee, it is important to have humility. In the Satcharita, there are so many instances where Baba has indirectly taught humility. There are also some outstanding examples of it in connection with Baba's intimate devotees.

Gautam: It's an excellent topic for discussion because there's a lot of misconception about this word 'humility', which we can go into.

N: I'll tell you how it came up as a topic for me. I was reading the Satcharita the other day, and in chapter fourteen, I read the story of this very rich devotee called Ratanji, who had come to meet Baba. He was quite a well-to-do man, and he had come to Baba with a desire to have a son.

Baba told Ratanji, 'Give me dakshina.' He made him empty his pockets, but despite that, the amount was not sufficient. So then Baba instructed him, 'Go get it from others, but give me the dakshina I ask for.'

Hemadpantji, the author of the Sai Satcharita, has commented on this, saying that Baba would often get people to go and ask for money from others. He would even get millionaires to go to poor devotees' houses asking for money as an exercise in humility. That is when I realized that it would be a worthwhile topic to cover with you.

So could you talk about this thing that Baba would do and also about humility in general?

G: I would like to start by saying that those who are truly humble do not know that they are humble because they are not being so consciously. The following incident will illustrate the point I am trying to make.

Years ago, on the front page of Bombay Times, which is all about Bollywood masala and gossip, a caption carried what one of the biggest Bollywood stars of India said in a statement: 'Basically, I am a very humble man.'

Now this sort of humility is nothing but inverted pride because you want to tell others that you are humble. Whereas, if we look at examples of humility, let's say the ones you have come across in people whom you have interviewed on your channel, I am quite sure that none of them would ever make such a claim. In the first case, it is the ego talking. The truly humble ones would have no need to do so. They are not doing anything to be humble; it is their very nature.

This point is very important. So when someone says, 'I am humble,' it is nothing but the ego coming in through the back door, and now it has become identified with the attitude of 'Look at me; I am such a humble man.'

If we look at Baba's basic message—which is very simple, nothing complex—as I have been saying repeatedly in so many podcasts, He says, 'See Me in all beings.' Now if you practise that, humility is bound to arise because if you see Baba in a beggar, or the CEO of a firm or a stranger on the road, you will have the same feeling towards everyone. So humility naturally arises if the teaching is lived.

It is so directly connected to living the teaching. You can't have someone who is practising Baba's teaching and is not humble. I mean, I am talking about a devotee of Baba's. There are others also who would be humble, of course.

Here we are saying that humility is a good measure of the teaching being followed in its true essence, as it is a natural outcome.

N: Baba would also empty the devotees of their pride.

In a story that we covered earlier, Baba did so with a rich man who came to Him, asking for Brahma Gyan in a big rush. [Refer to talk 22.] So, Baba and many masters have their ways of stripping away the pride of the devotees.

LIVING WITH FAITH AND PATIENCE

Could you talk a little bit about this aspect of Baba's, where he would, as in the case of Ratanji, ask someone to go and get dakshina because that was symbolic of something?

G: It was meant to teach him a lesson in humility because he had to go around with a begging bowl, asking others for money. The doorway to humility was being opened up for this man. Sometimes the ego is so encrusted, especially in the case of rich people who are very attached to their wealth and belongings. That encrusted ego is very hard to break through. But, by His grace, this man landed up at Baba's feet. He had to go around with a begging bowl, asking for dakshina, which, otherwise, he would never have dreamt of doing in his life.

It is a very beautiful method which we come across on innumerable occasions in the Satcharita: Baba sending people off to ask for money. Baba, in his mischievous way, would even send them to people who didn't have the money to give, so they had to keep going to others to get it. [Laughter.]

N: True.

G: Coincidentally, when you messaged me this morning about the subject of humility, I came across this paragraph written by Siddharameshwar Maharaj, which I find most pertinent:

> By humility, we can have a place in everyone's heart. By humility, one is always unassuming and becomes more pure and blemish-free. In this way, our unselfish life can permeate all beings. Humility is a great virtue. There lies great strength in being humble. It requires great bravery to remain humble. In humility, all is Brahman, and even the thought *I am Brahman* disappears. Where the sense of yours, others and mine has been swallowed up, all similes and comparisons disappear into one Unity.

You see, this is exactly what I have been saying. If you are living Baba's teachings, you see that everyone is Brahman.

You treat everyone equally, and not depending on your role-playing, as Eckhart Tolle so beautifully says in his book *A New Earth*.

All the time, we are playing roles, such as that of a parent or a child, or a boss or an employee. All these things go on—dramas of the ego.

But if you see Baba in everyone, or as Siddharameshwarji says, if you see Brahman in everyone, humility will arise as a virtue. As simple as that.

It is everyone's life experience that so little is in our control. We do something with a certain expectation, but something else happens. That should automatically lead to humility. Because you know that your power is quite limited and that the will of the Higher Power is what prevails. So it is a natural outcome of life's experiences.

But people think that they are the doers, and it's their actions that are responsible for where they are in society. Hence, they develop this pride, which is basically the absence of humility.

So that is what tends to happen. But generally, I have seen that those who are on the spiritual path have had a sense of suffering or loss in their life. That is why they are drawn to the spiritual path and also possess humility.

The flip side is that you have even spiritual egos that are very proud of their spiritual pursuits. Some are very proud that they have had experiences, let's say, of Baba, and they feel that they are special.

My teacher, Rameshji, was asked, 'How do I know whether a sage is truly a sage?'

He replied, 'I cannot answer that, but I can tell you when a sage is not a sage. If there is an absence of humility, you can rest assured that person is not a sage.'

So I would say that it is something that one has to recognize.

Let's take an example of someone on your YouTube channel. You have such beautiful people like Aai. Her life itself is an example of humility. I think she doesn't have to say anything to prove that she is humble. Her actions prove it. Her words prove it.

N: I often talk about all those devotees that Baba pulled towards Him. As He always said, 'It is Me who pulls My devotees, not the other way round.'

One outstanding example is Baba's param bhakta, Butiji, who was a multimillionaire. He gave up everything, came to serve Baba and was so humble. His reverence for Baba was so much that he would never speak to Baba directly. He always communicated through Mhalsapati and others, and even if Baba was communicating with Him, he would only look at Baba's feet.

Now that, to me, is the highest level of humility that any of Baba's bhaktas have shown. It was because of Butiji that Buti Wada and the Samadhi Mandir were built after Baba entrusted him with the responsibility of constructing them. But Butiji never made any mention of it, and to have that sheer reverence for your guru, where you only looked at His feet, is symbolic of probably the highest relationship one could have with their master.

G: This man was living the teaching that the guru is God in human form. What you have given is a clear example of considering your guru, in this case, Sai Baba, the highest of the high.

So that is what I was referring to. Their actions alone speak about their humility. You don't need someone to say that they are humble. Simple things, like looking down at the master's feet, show humility. It's a beautiful example that you have given.

N: People commonly ask, 'If everything is Baba's will, why is it so? What about us? Our free will?'

My reply to them is that if they are truly seeing Aai and Hema Ma and the other devotees as examples that they are following, especially as Baba's devotees, of what value is their free will when their whole objective is to surrender to Baba? This means they should leave their will, thoughts and everything at His feet, knowing that what He gives them and wants for them, only He knows best.

G: Yes.

N: You need to ask yourself if it isn't your mind coming up with all these questions. And if you are truly humble and surrender, following the example of the param bhaktas, then such intellectual pursuits will be put aside, and you will leave everything to Baba and accept with grace whatever He gives you, trusting it.

G: Absolutely. The ego does not like to be told it doesn't have free will, but its own experience has been that its free will is very limited.

There is so much that is not in your control, yet the ego still feels that its free will is so precious.

Once, while addressing a gathering, Sri Ramana Maharshi said, 'There is no such thing as free will.'

One man in the audience put up his hand and said, 'I beg your pardon, but my putting up my hand is my free will.'

To which Bhagavan replied, 'No, sir. If I had not said that there is no such thing as free will, you would not have put up your hand.'

N: True. [Laughter.]

G: So you see, everything is interconnected, and that is why we say, when you surrender to a Higher Power, or Baba, you are surrendering to a will that is far bigger than yours.

N: Maybe it would be more apt to call it 'apparent free will.'

G: Yes, exactly. Or as Rameshji would say, 'We have to act *as if* we have free will but knowing that the outcome is God's will.'

N: You have to know fully that the outcome, which even you say, is not in your hands. However, your intention should be pure and of the highest order. Rameshji would emphasize having the right attitude.

Maybe that truly is the only thing you can have. Based on their Prarabdha, two people have the same destiny outwardly, but it's their attitude to life which would really make a difference.

To view the corresponding video, scan the QR code.

30

Attitude and Free Will

Nikhil: Our attitude to life and its events could benefit us devotees if we just ponder over it. To elaborate, there could be one particular situation that is experienced by two devotees who have a very similar karmic pattern, but their attitude to it could be entirely different, which, in turn, influences their experience of that event.

Could you give us a deeper understanding of that, please?

Gautam: Of course.

Dayananda Saraswati was once asked, 'Is there such a thing as free will?'

Swamiji gave the example of a goat tied to a rope, which, in turn, is tied to a peg in the ground. Now the goat can roam around but only as far as the length of the rope would allow it. It cannot go beyond that. But within that length, the goat can graze around, go nearer to the peg, go furthest away, but not beyond.

Swamiji said, 'This is the extent of our free will because the circumstances have already been determined for us.'

Considering the scenario today, you've asked this question at the right time.

It is everyone's experience now, with the coronavirus situation, that we are forced not only to live indoors but that the way we work is also going to change, and none of this has been in our control; it has been forced upon us. So even those people who felt that they were in control of their life, now see things differently after learning the lesson life has taught them.

This is what Dayananda Saraswati was pointing to, that within your circumstances, which have already been determined by the Divine, you can exercise your free will, which primarily means your attitude to life.

N: Yes.

G: Because that is where the difference lies—in our approach.

As you said, if there are two people with similar karmic patterns, what reduces the load for one compared with the other is the psychological attitude.

Let's say there's suffering in one's life. There is more pain than pleasure. Not only do we live through the suffering or pain that is destined for us, but we also add additional layers of psychological suffering when we ask questions such as *Why did God do this to me? I have not done anything cruel to anyone.* This creates a lot of anxiety and mental disturbance.

This is the focal point of our discussion. Our attitude to life determines whether we suffer this extra load of the ego with its drama and antics. This is very important because, at the end of the day, we all know we have a fixed number of breaths given to us in this lifetime. This is already predetermined.

Now how are we going to spend those breaths?

Are we going to spend them in hatred, malice, condemnation, jealousy, envy and blame? Or is our mind going to be free of psychological suffering, and are we living moment to moment, meeting our destiny with the strength and conviction of grace behind us? Grace in this sense would be the blessings of the master.

N: Yes.

This takes me to something we had discussed in one of our earlier talks: that only the master sees the big picture. Then that feeling of *Why has life been unfair to me?* or *Why have I not got something that I asked for?* completely falls away because you leave that to Baba, saying, *Baba knows what is best. Only He knows my past and what is going to happen, so why not leave the situation at Baba's feet?*

G: Yes, In fact, my spiritual teacher gave a very beautiful example of a huge painting hanging in a museum. [Refer to talk 3.] Who is the painter? God. Baba. He knows the painting. It's His Creation. You, as an individual, have such a narrow vision that you see just a little bit of that painting, and then you start assuming things.

This is what we do, you see. And that is why Rameshji put it very simply. Some people might find it pessimistic, but it is the truth.

Rameshji says that all of us are limited in life to the form of our bodies and this limitation is like imprisonment. [Refer to talk 2.] Consciousness, which is who we really are, is limited to form. He would call it simple imprisonment because, with this form, we are further limited by our conditioning since childhood, over which we have very little control.

We human beings, by doing what we do, complicate this simple imprisonment so much that we convert it into rigorous imprisonment. We make life not only hell for ourselves but also for those around us. That is what psychological suffering does.

And we are mentioning this because of that magic word 'attitude'. What is my attitude to life? Do I accept that things are happening the way they are meant to happen? I may or may not like them. I'm not saying that we have to just lie down and do nothing. But as Eckhart Tolle says, first, we have to accept the 'isness' of the situation because it is there before us.

Let's say there's a challenge at work or there's a health issue. First, accept that the challenge is there because it is in front of you. Then, by all means, do exactly that which you think and feel you should do. So the difference is that this time, with that acceptance, the mind is calmer. The mind is not in a reactive, resistance-driven mode right from the start. *This should not be happening. Why is God doing this?* All that dialogue—which, otherwise, would embroil us in ill will, spite, jealousy, envy, condemnation, pride, arrogance, guilt, shame and so on—is finished. And when that happens, our mind becomes open. We are able to make better decisions. We respond rather than react. We weigh the pros and cons, and we deal with what life brings.

Isn't that what Baba has also said?

N: Absolutely.

I would like to share a very touching story that I witnessed in Dwarkamai, when I visited it one night, at about 1.30 a.m. I think it was in December 2019. Devotees can go and sit there; it's open all through the night. While they were cleaning the place, they asked devotees to step out for twenty minutes.

I saw a gentleman there, who was physically handicapped. He had one arm and one leg amputated, and I saw him go towards Baba and bow down. He squatted on one knee and did a full *sashtanga namaskara* to Baba. Then he got up and hobbled towards a corner of Dwarkamai, picked up a bucket and a mop, hobbled his way to the other corner, went down on one knee, and started mopping the ground there as a form of seva.

I was standing outside, looking at him and saying to myself, *Wow! Look at this man!* The smile on his face, when he did the namaskar to Baba, was out of this world—full of gratitude to be alive, to be there. You could see that shine in his eyes.

If this gentleman, who has every reason to complain that he's been treated unfairly, comes to his guru's door and has such reverence for life, then I think that there is no excuse for pretty much anybody to be otherwise. That's probably the hardest it can get, right?

G: Yes, but we lose sight of that because we are so used to our comforts and how things should be for us. Something like this should not only shock us but also transform us.

N: It's like that story we hear in school where there was a man who complained that he lost his shoes till he met a man who had no feet.

G: Exactly.

N: Nobody offered to help this man, so it seemed like he did this seva regularly. I wanted to go and just greet him, but I could not because they had barricaded the entry at the time.

G: Yes, in such situations, one can just send a quiet blessing that person's way.

You mentioned Dwarkamai and, somehow, I thought of the fire there—the dhuni. The dhuni is very sacred for the Nath Yogis who belong to the Navnath Sampradaya. They have a relationship with the fire, and the fire talks back to them.

And as we know, Sai Nath was also a Nath, among all his various attributes. So that fire, especially as it has been burning since the time it came into being, is very powerful.

If we go to an astrologer or a tarot card reader, they will say that ninety-five per cent of the questions people ask fall into one of three categories: health, money and relationships. All three are transient. Everything comes and goes in life. Money comes and goes, relationships come and go and even your family relationships, your parents, will pass on. Regarding friendships too, you lose some and you gain some. The same with lovers. Regarding health also, it's our experience that there are good years and not-so-good years.

Now the whole point is that when we are presenting ourselves in front of the dhuni, is our mind full of thoughts such as *Baba, give me this, Baba, give me that; give me success in my relationship; give me lots of money*? Or do we say, *Baba give me what You want to give me; give me what You feel is best for me; give me the strength to deal with whatever comes my way; give me the courage to live life by following Your teachings*?

These are not thoughts that come up spontaneously because we are too stuck in the mundane issues of life.

What is fire? It comes from the Sun. And what is the Sun? Nothing but purity. In fact, in our scriptures, the Sun is called 'visible Brahman', the only God who is visible. Why does fire rise upwards? To go and meet the Sun. You see, it's symbolic.

So the dhuni is a very auspicious fire. That's the point I'm trying to make. You may say it's got nothing to do with attitude, but since the Dwarkamai scenario came up, I just thought of mentioning that whoever goes to Dwarkamai must present themselves before the fire and ask the fire to purify them. Let the fire do the job. That would be the right attitude.

N: So, if you have any other pointers on attitude that you would like to share . . . ?

G: To sum up, I think attitude refers to the attitude to people in our lives, the attitude to events we are called upon to face in our lives and the attitude to our thoughts. This is actually a spiritual practice.

One can keep asking oneself, *What is my attitude?* During the course of the day, when I encounter events or people, or the thoughts in my mind, are they life-negative thoughts? Are they negative reactions to people? Are they negative reactions to events?

And you know, the surprising thing is that one just has to be a witness. Just witness your attitude; you don't even have to make a change. The change will happen. The first step is whether you are aware of your attitude. Because most of us are not. Most of us are battling with life—psychologically, you see. So this witnessing element makes you aware of thoughts such as *My God! I'm actually thinking all the time: fear-based thoughts, life-negative thoughts; I'm thinking ill of people: I don't want this guy to succeed; I don't like this girl's nature.*

Look at your attitude. Be aware of it. Do not judge it, because, after all, we all have been conditioned by our circumstances. But that witnessing is what brings about a transformation in the attitude. It will happen.

To view the corresponding video, scan the QR code.

31

Serving Baba—the Highest Sadhana

Nikhil: Service to the guru is not something that many people give due consideration to. I feel that many of Baba's devotees, unfortunately, have the feeling that since Baba left His body in 1918, there is no way that they could be of service to Him.

In the truest sense, of course, Baba does not need anything from us, and we can't give Baba anything. But I felt that if one has that feeling in their heart that they want to serve Baba, it can make a very big shift in their attitude internally and open doors on their spiritual journey.

Could you speak about that a little?

Gautam: Yes, this is again a beautiful subject you have chosen to discuss.

To start with, it appears we are serving an individual, but the guru is God in human form. The guru is Consciousness. So we are serving God, Consciousness, the Higher Self. You can call it by any name. In this case, we are serving Baba.

Now, generally, there are two ways to serve the guru: One way is to offer dakshina if you are affluent enough. You can offer money for fulfilling the needs of the guru. The other way is to offer seva.

Seva can take various forms. You can be physically present for the guru and run his errands. Or you could do seva by spreading the guru's teachings.

Now, obviously, in Baba's case, you can't serve Him physically as He is not here in physical form. But you can do seva to propagate the teachings in either Shirdi or any Sai Baba temple next to you. Or you could do it even by living the teaching and sharing it consciously with people as part of your day-to-day living.

I can't even say it is a *rahasya*, a secret, but it is seen and validated that those devotees who have offered themselves to their master have taken leaps and strides on the spiritual journey. There are innumerable accounts of that, which we don't need to go into.

Siddharameshwar Maharaj said that even the wind which passes through a guru's house should be worshipped. If the guru has a dog in his house, the dog should also be venerated. [Refer to talk 31.] That should be the degree of worship. And that is possible only when the devotee has surrendered to the guru principle, to the force of the guru, totally.

N: When devotees go to Shirdi, there may be a common tendency among them to complain about the *Sansthan* not doing things that they feel it should be doing.

But I would like to mention what happened in my case. The last time I went to Shirdi, I noticed there were a lot of dogs getting injured by the *palkis* that were coming in. So I discussed this matter with Vinny Ma, some people from the Sansthan and a few locals to hear their side of the story. Then I shared this information with Mohanji and his organization, and they very kindly put into place something with the aid of an NGO to help the animals, calling them Baba's dogs.

G: Right.

N: I feel if one goes with the attitude that they can try and help, in whatever way they can, isn't that a far better approach than complaining about things not getting done?

G: Yes, you see, historically, there is an issue here if we look at India specifically and a temple town like Shirdi. India was not prepared for Shirdi to become what it became. When I went as a youngster, there was no queue. One could just walk into the main temple. But now, with the population explosion, coupled with the lack of a sense of discipline, there is chaos when the pilgrims throng Shirdi.

If you visit pilgrimage sites in Europe, you see the orderliness, you see the cleanliness. Take, for example, Lourdes, which I have been to. It is a holy site dedicated to the Divine Mother. You feel that people are there with their hearts wide open. And why do you feel that? When they make you take a dip in the holy water, they have four men assisting you. Each of them speaks different languages, and they ask you which language you would like to be spoken in. So that is the care and sensitivity of the people who volunteer there.

You raise this point: What can we do in Shirdi? We can make it a better place for sure, to the degree we can. Beyond that, it's not in our control. Each individual, taking not only their skill sets but also what is in their hearts, can attempt to contribute. You see, that's all we can do. The results are not in our hands.

But today, awareness levels are high; people are more conscious than ever before. We have advanced technology, so there are platforms, such as social media, which allow like-minded people to come together. Yours is one such platform. And we know the strength of a group versus an individual.

Now, for example, you can find out who are the right people in Shirdi to connect with as far as the Sansthan is concerned, and people can come together, give their suggestions, offer their services there or just go there themselves as individuals and do whatever they feel they should.

N: Correct.

G: There are various ways to approach it, but I do feel that it would be a sign of selflessness if that starts happening, and that's why I feel you again raised a very pertinent point. Most of us just go there and are concerned with our darshan and how long we have to stand in the queue. Then we get out and go to our hotel room, you see. That is what we are all programmed, you can say, to do.

But yes, of course, I'm sure many opportunities would be available to lend a helping hand.

N: Yes. You know, Vinny Ma would say a very beautiful thing when she would take people on a walking tour of Shirdi: 'I do not charge anybody anything, but you take Baba's history from me and go share it with five other people.'

G: Beautiful.

N: Now that becomes seva.

So, if people do visit Shirdi often, they can take up a task like that. Some can offer to clean up Dwarkamai, some can volunteer as tour guides for free, talk about Baba and Baba's teachings and take visitors to places of significance in Shirdi.

One could also help collectively, and I'm pretty certain that the Sansthan would not say no if one approached them with a proposal to offer help.

Talking about that reminds me of the time we went together to a guru's ashram in the North when we recently went to Delhi and Gurgaon. Everything about the place was so well-organized. It was quite a beautiful experience we shared.

G: You know, I was very touched because, if I remember correctly, we were picked up from the main road by volunteers in their own cars. They picked us up—there was total silence in the car—and dropped us at the point outside the ashram. It was their way of doing seva.

And that was quite touching because not only are they giving money in terms of using their own fuel, considering they could be coming from various places in Delhi, but they are also giving their time to their guru, although he is no longer in the body.

N: Yes.

G: That was very beautiful to see, and at each step, I remember the person offering us a bottle of water, making us queue up for darshan and taking us to the hall where they feed you. Everything is done in a very gentle and systematic manner.

It shows that they are living the teachings of their guru.

N: Correct. We need not limit it only to Shirdi. There could be devotees all around the globe; I'm sure there are Sai Baba temples all over.

G: Yes.

N: One could start doing *annadaan* in their localities or spread Baba's teachings in different forms. Because Baba taught the path of Karma Yoga, it would be very apt for one to help others.
Could you talk about service in general to mankind?

G: Normally, this happens on its own because when you follow the teachings of a guru like Baba, then qualities like compassion do develop. It should not be that we come across as being preachy by telling people what to do and what not to do.
But as you rightly pointed out in the beginning, the difference here is that Baba is no longer in form. So, sometimes, we tend not to make that extra effort to do seva.
As you said, seva could be done anywhere. For example, you may be a businessman in a town in the US, and you may think of ideas to do seva for your staff. For instance, in India, sometimes we pay for the driver's or maid's child's education. That is also seva to Baba and a sign of your generosity increasing, which is the opposite of being miserly and hoarding. By following the teachings, the heart opens, you see.
So you have to constantly keep asking yourself where you could give as you have been blessed with enough to share. That should become the mantra.

N: That would be really beautiful.

G: Also, I must add a word of caution here, and I will explain this by narrating an incident.
In my guru's last days, the sense of seva to the guru was more evident because everyone knew that he didn't have much time left.
A lady who had been coming for years to attend his talks saw that others were giving envelopes as dakshina because our guru was more prone to falling ill at that time. One day, right towards the end, after everyone had given their envelopes, she got up, walked up to him and placed an envelope at his feet.
Guruji looked at her and told her, 'This is not coming from the heart. This is coming as an obligation because you have seen others doing it.'

She was taken aback to hear his words. This comment must have hurt her. But, you see, you can't hide anything from the guru. The guru sees and knows all.

This is not a trade-off. You know, like people say, 'Give ten per cent of your income to charity, and you will keep earning money.' Your relationship with the guru does not work that way.

So one should not feel, *I must do seva, then Baba will love me more.*

N: Absolutely.

G: The seva is for you, not for Baba, because you are helping yourself. This point is sometimes missed.

N: Correct.

On a slightly different note, doing seva on the outside is wonderful. And as you said, it must come from a genuine feeling that arises from within, not as a compulsion or some sort of obligation.

Then, on the individual level, where you spend time with Baba's teachings and do meditation or dhyana on Baba, that also, in a way, is living the teachings. Could you talk about that aspect?

G: Well, that is a sadhana, a spiritual practice, you see. If that is not happening, then you are not a devotee. That must happen in some way. Otherwise, you are just imbibing the knowledge intellectually, which is still not a bad start.

But let's be clear that if the idea is to transform your life, then you have to live the teachings. I gave the example of a government officer, who was Sai Baba's bhakta, and yet he was taking bribes. I have read—I don't know if it's in the Satcharita or another book on Baba—that Baba has clearly said, 'Do not take a bribe if you are in a government position.' [Refer to talk 22.]

Now is there any point in being Baba's bhakta and taking a bribe at the same time?

So that's it. That is seva to oneself. Are you living the teaching? As simple as that.

N: Gautam, in today's day and age, as you said earlier, we have the luxury of social media and ways to communicate, which were not possible before.

Also, a whole new community is forming around Baba's devotees, where they can get together and do things in common, keeping Baba's teachings in mind.

Could you speak a little bit on that aspect? How can devotees have that support?

G: Well, my understanding is that it's a different world today, as we know, compared to when Baba was there in the body. His devotees are all over the world. And now, with social media, they are connected. So, to have a community like that is a very powerful force.

In fact, such a community can make a positive shift by not only spreading awareness about Baba and His teachings but in Consciousness as a whole, if they are living the teachings.

So I do foresee a big role for devotees to play in this, and I think it is the right time to start the ball rolling by their coming together.

N: Yes.

G: And talking about what a collective can do as a group reminds me of the time when Maharishi Mahesh Yogi experimented with group meditation in a certain city. Statistics showed that the crime rate dropped in that city as a result of the group meditation. That is the impact which a group can have.

So the time has come, and the platforms are available. People no longer need to fly down; they can be helpful from wherever they are. As long as there's common ground, much can be achieved.

N: Yes. One last question before we end today's podcast.

Baba symbolized the coming together of different communities, religions, and cultures. He didn't discriminate between people from different backgrounds. In fact, He was taking us to a place beyond our conditioned self.

Now, with the pandemic, unfortunately, people are being discriminated against across the world. Could you speak a little bit about that aspect? What can a devotee do as an individual to live and spread Baba's message or live the teachings?

G: I really don't think there's much that anyone should do except be a living example of the teachings. That is why Nisargadatta Maharaj would tell people involved in social service to first take care of their affairs and see that they are sorted out as individuals. Because, if everyone did that, then there would be no one left to sort out.

To reiterate, I think the first step and the main step to take is to live the teachings.

Sri Ramakrishna said something beautiful: 'So what if the world is covered with thorns? Wear sandals and walk all over them. And those sandals are the knowledge that God alone exists.'

This means that, in Baba's context, if you see Baba in everyone, you will understand that nobody truly does anything. It is Baba functioning through all of manifestation.

Then you will start living that teaching and will wear the sandals that Sri Ramakrishna was talking about.

To view the corresponding video, scan the QR code.

32

Baba's Explanation of Rnanubandhan

Nikhil: We recently posted a leela, not mentioned in the Satcharita, that Vinny Ma had narrated, and it is related to the concept of rnanubandhan. [Refer to Glossary.] I feel that the whole crux of Baba's teachings is in this one story. Anybody familiar with Baba's life and teachings knows that this concept occurs again and again in them.

So, for today's episode, I would like to discuss rnanubandhan, something that Baba emphasized a lot and mentioned in the Satcharita.

Gautam: Sure. I have seen this video.

Very little is spoken about rnanubandhan traditionally in the scriptures. But what I love about Baba is that He has explained it very clearly. So, yes, we will go into that.

N: This particular story is so amazing. A lady took care of her younger siblings when their parents passed away and fulfilled all their needs. But now, in her hour of need, when she was ill, none of them came to her help. She felt abandoned thinking that after all the sacrifices that she had made for them, they were kith and kin only in name.

It is then that Baba appeared to her. Not only did He heal and comfort her but He also explained to her that what was happening with her was due to her rnanubandhan with her siblings. By taking care of them, she had repaid her debt from a previous life wherein they had done the same for her.

I felt that for those feeling let down or dissatisfied with their relationships, this story could create a massive transformation in their outlook towards life.

G: Right.

What Baba has made very clear is that all our relationships are on account of rnanubandhan. The family one is born in, the friends one has, the enemies one has and the people one doesn't like are all on account of rnanubandhan.

Baba had this uncanny ability to tell for how many lives He had known someone, for instance, His closest disciples. He could see the rnanubandhan in these relationships. Similarly, He would reveal to people who came to Him that they and someone else had known each other for a particular number of lifetimes. He could see that because, after all, He is all-seeing, all-pervading. He is the Source.

I really want to emphasize to our audience that everyone in your life is there because of rnanubandhan.

Now, in this beautiful story, which is not in the Satcharita, but which you made a podcast of, Baba explains to the lady that her relationships with her siblings are on account of rnanubandhan.

Expectation is a different story. If you are doing something for someone, it is because of the debt you owe that person. You may not know it consciously, but it would only happen because the *rna* is still pending.

N: Yes.

G: It does not mean that the other person has to reciprocate, because, for the other person, there may not be any rna left in the relationship. It is *your* turn to give this time and not take anything in return.

In life, we want to give and take, you see. That is how the thinking mind functions: *I have done this for so-and-so, therefore so-and-so should do this for me.* It doesn't work like that. Therefore, we end up frustrated because our expectations of how people should behave with us are not fulfilled.

So what Baba tells this woman is that it was her duty to take care of her siblings in this life, which she fulfilled very well. And the rna ended there; the bondage finished there because they did not have any debt left to repay her in this life. Baba advised her to let go of her expectations and drop the drama that they had abandoned her. However, He also assured her not to worry as He was there to take care of her.

Now we all have to see one very important point here. The biggest mistake which Baba pointed out that this woman was making was her harbouring the feeling *I did this for them.* This doership is the problem. You think you do something and therefore you must be repaid.

This is what Baba would constantly bring up in all His teachings —the point about doership. That is where pride and arrogance come in.

In this lady's case, it was the rna that operated and made her take care of her siblings. But she had this sense of doership and the consequent expectations, and rightfully so, in the sense that the mind works like that. *If I have taken care of so-and-so, then so-and-so will take care of me.* That has to be seen as the nature of the mind. It is not about right and wrong.

So Baba shows us two things here: One, 'Are you carrying this sense of doership in your relationships?' And two, 'Do not have expectations, because if the rna is over, you will not get back what you would like in return.'

What is the result of coming to this awareness? Peace, calm, and an acceptance of God's will. Accepting that no one truly does anything.

In the woman's case, it meant that she had to accept that her siblings' not coming to her help was unintentional. She had to accept that it was her destiny as well as theirs. After accepting that it was God's leela, Baba's leela, the sense of doership got eliminated, and consequently, there was no blame and condemnation.

In her special case, Baba came to this lady, that too in His kafni and not disguised as someone else, sat with her, and explained to her that her siblings were not doing anything to her; the rnanubandhan was completed. And that she would get a man called so-and-so coming into her life, who would take care of her. What does that mean? That means her rnanubandhan was with that man, and he would be coming into her life because he had to give back to her this time by taking care of her.

So, you see, these expectations of people from their relationships are unjustified. That is what Baba is showing us. You have an expectation, hence you are setting yourself up for a big fall; that is what most of us do.

It's a beautiful story. When you listen to it, do listen to it with one eye on your own relationships because Baba is always talking to you. The story is the medium of communication. You don't want to hear it and then keep it aside just thinking of it as a wonderful story. Please look at all your relationships: family, friends, colleagues at work or even strangers you meet on the road, bus, train or wherever. These are all forms of rnanubandhan. Please look at them in the light that rnanubandhan is something whereby your accounts get squared and that nobody truly does anything. Don't hold people guilty of not giving back what you think they should give back in the relationship. This is a beautiful spiritual exercise.

N: Yes. I would like to talk to you about a particular aspect I found in the story that all of us can take as a pointer. This lady had been given an assurance by Baba that she would be taken care of. The story very nicely illustrates how, when one surrenders to Baba, He takes over your responsibilities.

Most people have certain expectations from people or tend to depend on them as well as on certain things in their lives. I felt it would be wonderful if every devotee, in their life, in their own way, were to depend on Baba for everything. Aai is a prime example. It doesn't matter to her if family members, friends or other people are there for her or not. She has no expectations from them. Baba is everything to her.

I felt this is a very nice example because, in a way, everyone is going to abandon you as it is the very nature of life. Loved ones pass away and a lot of things change constantly. But the Source, that is Baba, is eternal.

G: Yes. It's the same thing that Baba Himself said, that if you see Him in everybody, then whatever happens, you will no longer accuse individuals of doing anything because it is Baba who is doing it.

Now, someone like Aai is already living this teaching. So, for example, if she is encountering a difficult relationship, she knows that it cannot happen without Baba's will.

N: Yes.

G: That is the degree of surrender because she is aware that Baba knows everything. So that itself gives comfort to the devotee because they know that this difficulty would not be placed before them unless it was Baba's will. The fact that the other person in the relationship is not the doer is already accepted. The fact that she sees Baba in that person's form is already happening. Therefore, the rna is not perpetuating. You see, when there is conflict in a relationship, we perpetuate the rnanubandhan.

Let's take for example a couple who starts fighting after two or three years of marriage. Like a tennis match, their verbal accusations keep going back and forth: 'No, you said this', 'No, I didn't' and so on. This is the rnanubandhan being perpetuated because we are blaming each other, we are condemning each other.

So, to get out of this deadlock, to snap this bond, if there is an acceptance that nobody does anything, if one sees Baba in every form, this action-reaction loop breaks. This action-reaction loop is what keeps us reincarnating. Reincarnating even in the same situation. Let's say we have a point of view which someone doesn't agree with, and we keep defending it, arguing about it and fighting over it endlessly. We are reincarnating into the same story again and again because we've held our point of view. We don't like what the other is doing. This action-reaction loop is going on and on. This rnanubandhan is not going to break.

But when you accept that someone else's point of view is as valid as yours, you don't have to prove your point. You put it forth once or twice and then let it go. You stop playing the tennis match. So, there is no reaction anymore. Then you become the witnessing presence, or you walk away. So, you don't perpetuate the rnanubandhan, you see.

Most of us in our lives are perpetuating this bond with hatred, malice, ill will, spite, jealousy, envy, blame, condemnation, pride, and arrogance. Once you see that nobody is the doer, all this baggage drops. This is what Baba is showing us.

N: Yes.

G: I'm glad you mentioned this story because if the audience went and saw people such as Aai in action in their daily living, they would realize that shining examples like her are not blaming or condemning others; they have accepted them for who they are. And like you said, Aai has left everything to Baba.

N: This Rnanubandhan leela is such a beautiful example of Baba's word, what His promises mean to His devotees, and how, even after His Mahasamadhi, every day, millions of devotees experience His promise.

I feel this would be a major motivation for a devotee to read the Satcharita and the leelas therein in this light and live their lives with faith. Then Baba's grace would be equally accessible to all.

Also, there is a beautiful chant of 'Sai, Sai', which Jyoti has done recently. Baba has promised in the Satcharita that if one repeats His name—Sai, Sai—repeatedly, then it is His responsibility to take them even across the seven seas.

This particular japa is so simple. I feel if any devotee hears it morning and night or just meditates on it, it is going to have a profound influence on them. I mean, it could not be simpler than just chanting Baba's name internally all day, hearing it and meditating on it, because this is Baba's promise. This was my takeaway from the Rnanubandhan leela, and I'm so happy we've got this by Baba's grace—this chant by Jyoti.

G: Yes, the thing with chanting is that when you constantly hear it or recite it yourself, then the japa becomes *ajapa japa*. It means that it keeps repeating itself without you consciously doing so.

So, since the recording is uploaded now, it's a beautiful idea to play it in our intimate space all the time.

To view the corresponding video, scan the QR code.

33

Have You Already Made up Your Mind?

Nikhil: In this episode, I felt it would be a good idea to delve into how some devotees make up their mind beforehand when they look to Baba for guidance. Here we are talking about those devotees who have questions or are in a situation in life where they feel they want Baba's guidance, intending to act according to Baba's will.

And in that connection, I am reminded of a saying: 'Let life flow, and let events take their own course without offering resistance.'

Gautam: Right.

N: One thing I've observed, going back to my past, is a tendency to take up a position according to my preference and to want to steer life in that direction before giving myself a chance to find out what life is offering me.

Regarding Baba and His devotees, maybe there's something they don't know; something that Baba is offering them for their greater good, but they need to be patient.

So could you give us your views on this, please?

G: Sure. Perhaps we have covered this before, but I think it warrants delving a bit deeper into this subject.

I will give you a real-life example, about a close friend of mine who is Sai Baba's devotee. He wanted to take his son to the UK for studies. The plan was set in his mind. His friends in the UK had worked out the schools to visit as well as the admission procedures, and his lawyers gave him the options if they had to relocate to the UK. So everything was on track, beautifully, you see. What's more, he thought it was all Baba's doing, that everything was working according to what he had in mind.

But whenever my friend laid down chits, which many Baba devotees do to get clear answers, the answer was a 'No'. So he was baffled because all other things, as we have seen, were pointing in the opposite direction. He just could not come to terms with the fact that Baba was indicating a 'No'. He thought to himself, *It doesn't make sense, because this is the right thing, the right time* and so on.

My friend was supposed to go one week before the lockdown, and ultimately, he could not go at that time due to the prevailing circumstances. That is when it dawned on him why the chits were saying 'No'; it would have been futile to go to the UK when the entire world would be in a lockdown situation. Four months of lockdown have happened so far.

So this illustrates your point quite perfectly, that we not only make up our minds but feel that Baba can have no problem with this position of ours because everyone is benefiting and it's the right thing to do. We get confused when we get intuitive answers, which are contrary to what we want to hear, and then we start doubting and questioning. This is what happens when the mind is fixed.

If one has full faith in the chits and goes by what they indicate because they have always guided them in the past, then the questioning would not happen. Perhaps bewilderment, yes, but questioning, no.

Another example I often give in my talks is about a large painting in a museum, which you can see only partly by the light of a torch in darkness; you cannot see the whole picture. [Refer to talk 3.]

Likewise, there is something beyond what your mind and intellect can see and understand. That bigger picture is what you can surrender to the Divine, to Baba.

But this is what we don't do. We just stay limited to what our eyes can see and what our mind can think; that's it.

N: So, perhaps, we can reflect on our past experience, for example, in a relationship, and see how making up our minds in advance had not worked out in our interest.

G: Yes.

N: When that understanding seeps in, you could probably ask yourself what are the things today that you have already either made up your mind about or have certain preferences for or expectations about, which will make you conditionally happy.

G: Right.

N: And if those things are seen in this light, then do you feel that it would be like surrendering those things to Baba?

G: Yes, absolutely, that would be true surrender. True surrender is the surrender of the mind.

The thinking mind is offered to Baba, saying, *Look, I know my thinking mind and its limitations. Therefore, I offer it at Your feet because You know best.*

The main thing here is that when we have something in mind and it doesn't turn out the way we want it to, no doubt, we feel disappointed. But therein lies the learning. We all learn through suffering. When we don't get what we want, we are suffering. And there's a reason for the suffering: we have all incarnated on this plane of existence to learn life's lessons.

So, when someone who has seen enough setbacks in life realizes from their own experience that things didn't work out the way they would have liked them to, the more they will reflect on it and the more the surrender will happen.

N: Yes.

G: It reminds me of J Krishnamurti, the great Indian philosopher, who said very succinctly, 'Do you all want to know my secret? My secret is that I don't mind what happens.'

In this case, the mind makes up no stories about what happens. No judgements are passed about situations. In effect, Krishnamurti was saying that his thinking mind does not get embroiled in what happens in life.

N: This is such an important point because some devotees may probably have not gone down this path of reflection so deeply, in which case the tendency to have things their way may still be alive.

However, it is one thing to think, *I want this for certain*, and quite another, to have a small wish, which you might present to Baba, saying, *Baba, I would like to have this experience. It would be great if You wish it too and could give it to me. If not, I'm absolutely fine with whatever You decide.*

Then, to start with, that puts you in a space where you request Baba with a lot of humility and reverence, and without demanding something from Him.

G: Right.

N: Furthermore, you are in a place where you are in total acceptance that it may or may not happen and that it will not affect your happiness.

I'll give you an example from my own life. Five or six years ago, before we moved to our new home, there was no concept of Airbnb. It was a very quiet neighbourhood. Then, all of a sudden, Airbnb arrived on the scene, and things changed. So, occasionally, when there is a bit of a hullabaloo in my surroundings, I just joke with Baba, saying, *Hey, Baba, you know what? I have a slight preference for silence. Whenever You wish, I'm happy to go wherever You want.*

Now, that keeps me in a free space. I am not complaining to Baba, *Oh, this is a problem. The situation should be different from what it is. How can You keep me here in this noisy place?* You know the stories the mind gets into.

So, could you cite a few examples or give some more insights about it being perfectly fine to have a preference but not make any demands?

G: Yes. What you have spoken about is the ideal scenario, which you are practising. For many people, to make a wish and not be attached to the outcome, although there is a preference, is not what they are striving for because, for them, the wish they make is based on a need. This is why the Mother of Pondicherry kept saying that most of your prayers to God are all need-based, based on the needs of the 'me and mine', or 'my life story'. That is not the true prayer.

So, as you said, if the wish is made knowing whether or not it is fulfilled is God's will, then the wish carries with it a lightness.

As the saying goes, 'Be careful what you wish for because you might just get it.' Because you think you know what is best for you. For instance, you may wish for a relationship with someone, but after you are together, all hell may break loose. And then you will repent, wondering what you got yourself into.

God knows what is best for you. Your view is limited. Your view is limited by the light of the torchlight on that large painting. So please be careful what you wish for.

N: Yes, the best wish is no wish.

G: Exactly. The best wish is to accept, or rather, to put it another way, ask God to give us a frame of mind where we are completely surrendered to Him. That is the best wish.

Now, I am reminded of another example of a rigid mind, which works on past conditioning—set patterns, set thought processes—which we are hardwired with, making us rigid.

In medieval times, when armies were engaged in battle, they all had specific formations. For instance, the Romans had a particular formation for the cavalry, the archers and the infantry, and they would be trained to carry out these formations. These formations were planned; they were rigid.

Now the generals of the army knew that the problem with this is that the mind is conditioned. Supposing that in this whole approach to battle, something happens which is unplanned—maybe the enemy does something, or something just happens in their own ranks which is unforeseen—the soldiers would be thrown off guard because they were set by what their formation dictated.

So, to break their conditioning, unbeknown to them, the generals would assign twenty soldiers called 'clown soldiers' to do the most ridiculous things on the battlefield. When the army was in formation, suddenly, they would ride backwards or start doing funny things.

The generals were breaking the soldiers' conditioning by making them alert to the unexpected. And these were their own soldiers, luckily. In the process, the rigidity got broken; the soldiers became more alert because they saw the clown soldiers doing something which they were not prepared for. That brought their attention to the present moment and broke the hardwired conditioning.

I am saying this because this is what happens to us. We can get overcome by the enemy because we are stuck in our rigidity, and in our case, the enemy is the thinking mind. Something surprising may happen, and we'll be caught off guard because we've been trained or conditioned in a certain way.

Rigidity can be broken, and broken internally, with the acceptance, *Look, something may happen which I am not comfortable with, and if I do not accept it as the will of the Universe, of the Source, or God, it is going to disturb my peace of mind.*

This is a very important point. Break the rigidity; break it before it breaks you. And that is where the grace of the guru comes in. That is where surrender comes in. So, to repeat myself, surrender this rigidity of the thinking mind at the feet of the guru.

N: The example you just shared was very beautiful. It reminds me of something the great master Gurdjieff would do. He would get his disciples to dig a pit in the ground, the whole day long, and then he would tell them to go fill it up again, just to break their conditioning

In different ways, different masters do the same thing. Essentially, they empty you.

To view the corresponding video, scan the QR code.

34

The Thinking Mind and the Working Mind

Nikhil: Today we will be talking about something that you have brought up earlier—the working mind and the thinking mind. So could you tell us briefly about the difference between the two, please?

Gautam: Yes, this is something I would love to share with the audience because it will make the understanding very simple.

The thinking mind is the mind which is always going into the dead past or an imaginary future. And most of us know that our minds are doing that.

We are either always reminiscing about happy memories, saying, *Oh, I wish things were like that once again!* Or we are always thinking of painful memories and lamenting, *This happened to me, that happened to me; poor me!*

Similarly, we are projecting into the future: *I'm not happy where I am right now. I want to be in a space where everything is ideal. Only then will I be happy.* This is an imaginary future. Or we project a fear, based on the past, into the future: *This happened to me in the past, so I better be careful. Otherwise, it could happen to me again in the future.*

This is the thinking mind. It is always thinking of the past or the future. And we find that so much of our mind content is made up of this activity of the thinking mind. And what happens when this thinking mind is in the past or future? We are no longer in the present moment. But life is lived *now*, in the present moment.

So, in that sense, look at the disrespect given to the present moment, which is so sacred because we are here right now. But when we go into this dead past and the imaginary future, we lose the moment, we lose the presence, we lose the joy of being here right now. So that is what the thinking mind does.

Now we come to the working mind. The working mind is that which is engaged in work. Let's take an example: You could be at your office, sitting at your desk, doing whatever work you are doing, and focused on your work. The attention is brought to the present moment.

So, in that sense, a working mind is a meditative mind because it's not running all over the place. This distinction is very important because it helps us see in our everyday day life whether we are mostly in the thinking mind mode or the working mind mode.

I hope the difference between these two concepts is clearly understood now.

N: Yes.

Could you further elaborate by giving a few examples so that people can see how these concepts could be applied in their lives?

G: I have already mentioned the example of a surgeon performing a surgery, which explains the concepts of 'thinking mind' and 'working mind'. [Refer to talk 2.]

N: This reminds me a little bit about what Eckhart Tolle would say, and I'm going to go into the aspect of spiritual practice here and how important the role is of spiritual sadhana for every devotee.

Eckhart gave a very beautiful example. He said that many people engage in dangerous activities or extreme sports, such as mountain climbing or driving a bike at super-high speeds. In such moments, their mind is forced into concentrating on something because it's a do-or-die situation for them. Consequently, they feel really peaceful when they are engaging in that particular activity. But when they come out of it, their mind starts worrying them again.

I feel this is a very important concept that Rameshji has highlighted for us. Its application would be very useful for, let's say, someone who has lost their job and is sitting at home. For example, such a person can volunteer for seva instead of sitting all day and worrying about their future.

Is that right?

G: Yes.

So, coming back to Eckhart's point, what is happening with racing-car drivers, tightrope walkers or mountain climbers is that there is no room for their thinking mind to operate because if it does, they are dead. They have to be in the present moment, which is the working mind in operation.

N: But, you see, Eckhart said this from a negative standpoint, where people who have unstable minds and are not grounded tend to engage in these dangerous activities as they [these activities] are probably their only means of finding peace.

G: Yes, I'm coming to that point. They need to indulge in that extreme activity for their working mind to become engaged. Now the problem is that you can't be mountain-climbing all the time. You can't be driving a racing car all the time to keep the working mind engaged. Why? It's not natural, you see. The point here is, Who am I without my working mind and my thinking mind? That question has not been asked, so we are incessantly engaged in activity. We cannot sit still.

Now let's take something very simple. Forget mountain climbing and all that.

A girl who had come to my talks confessed, 'I can't sit still, so even when I have nothing to do, I am looking at my messages repeatedly and checking out everyone's DPs on WhatsApp.'

I asked her, 'What will happen if you sit still? What will go wrong?' She said, 'I can't bear it. It's unbearable.'

What is unbearable? We are afraid to ask, Who am I without my mind being engaged? That is how identified we are with mental activity.

Another incident I remember happened at one of Rameshji's satsangs. A lady who had come there used to be a fashion model in her younger days. She was about sixty years old, and she told Rameshji that, earlier, she used to be the centre of attention. The world used to look at her—even people who didn't know her. When she would cross the road, heads would turn. And now that she was old, nobody recognized her. She was not married, and she was alone. Nobody gave her any attention. Thus, she went into a depression for many years.

My teacher told her that if it was making her miserable—which it was, that's why she had come there—then, to start with, she should consider that an idle mind is the devil's workshop. He said that if her career was finished and if she was not doing anything, then her mind was going into the dead past where she was noticed by everyone. The first thing was to take care of that. Therefore, he suggested that if she was lonely, she could find others who were lonely also and spend time with them.

She objected to that, saying that it was not possible for her to go around looking for lonely people.

Rameshji told her, 'Look, it's very simple. I hope you are listening to me. Find others who are lonely.'

Then he suggested, as an example of what he meant, that she could go to an orphanage taking gifts with her for the kids there as she had earned a lot of money in her younger days. Spending time with them would help engage her mind. Something productive would be happening, and at least she would have taken the first step away from this obsession with who she was in the past.

So, you see, that step needs to be taken.

It reminds me of another incident, perhaps, in the year 1999, when I was twenty-nine. I was in Hong Kong and Eckhart Tolle, who at that time was not very well-known, had come there to give a talk. I happened to be on holiday, and a friend of mine who was in the police force was with me.

While we were at the dinner table, my sister invited him for Eckhart's private talk the next morning at a friend's house. So this friend who was a police officer asked my sister what Eckhart spoke about in his talks. She said that Eckhart talked about being in the present moment.

The police officer replied that he didn't need to listen to such a talk, because when he was facing a gangster, he was always in the present moment. Where else would he be? If he was not in the present, he would be dead. So, the talk was not for him.

He is right on one level: it is on his job that he is in the present moment. But what about the rest of the day when he is not facing a gangster? You see, this is a very important point.

To give you an instance, a boy once told me that he had attained so much clarity and peace after listening to me talk about the thinking mind and the working mind that he was sure he was no longer lost in the thinking mind. Earlier, he was lost in the thinking mind, and subsequently, the teachings had shown him the burden of being in its grip. After that, he was in the working mind mode all the time.

I asked him how he kept himself in the working mind mode all the time. Was he engaged in a job from morning to night?

He replied that he kept himself busy playing video games all day long.

You see? Now isn't that exhausting? What is behind this? We are afraid of the mind being still and quiet.

N: Yes.

G: This is what the wisdom teachings point to. You don't have to be active all the time. You don't have to be engaged all the time. You don't have to be identified all the time. Just sit, be still and witness the thoughts arising. Witness the events in your own life.

This is the journey to Self-realization, and all wisdom teachings, including Sai Baba's, are always pointing to it.

What Baba's teachings are doing is that they are stilling the mind. When He says, 'I am in everyone, I am in the dog' and so on, He's trying to show you the unity and connectedness of the Divine Force operating through everyone. If you accept that and you live that teaching, your mind will be still. And how will it be still? You won't blame and condemn people. You won't hate yourself. You won't hate others. When all these qualities drop away, you are left with a still mind—the still mind which is a mind at peace.

Many of us don't really follow these teachings. We think we do. We think we are living these teachings, but actually, we aren't, because the measure of living them is the degree of peace and true happiness we feel within.

And it takes courage to admit to yourself, *No, deep down, I am not at peace.* We tend to fool ourselves.

N: So it would be a journey of understanding the difference between the thinking mind and the working mind, and then, ultimately, transcending the mind, if not completely, at least as much as possible. That means being equanimous, peaceful, feeling joy within and not necessarily having to be engaged in constant activity internally or externally all the time.

G: Yes, now having said that, the main culprit here is the thinking mind because that is what keeps us identified with our story and the blame game of life: *He did this to me; she did that to me; God did this to me.* That is all the garbage of the thinking mind.

With this understanding, the first step is that all that dialogue is finished, which automatically results in peace, equanimity and calmness. As a result, the working mind will be engaged when there is a need for it to be engaged and not as a means of escape from the present moment. And when the working mind is not engaged, we are happy to either go for a walk by the beach or in the park, or sit at home, just looking out the window.

There's no anxiety that we are feeling within: *My God, I can't be still!* That struggle is over.

N: Yes, and there are typical escape routes as well to avoid the thinking mind altogether, which kind of numb the ego: meaningless conversations with people, drinking and all sorts of other activities. Eckhart pointed out that the idea was to go above the level of thinking and that such things submerge you and take you into a vegetative state.

G: Yes, because all these are need-based. Being very social, for example, is fun to a point, but we become dependent on it. Because we wear masks, we derive our sense of identity from what others think of us, and all these subtle games are played by the ego.

N: So it would be beneficial to become aware of these things, such as name-dropping, or typical escape routes. It might be too much to cover all of these in this podcast, but would you be happy to talk about it in another one?

G: Sure. Since you mentioned name-dropping, let's just see how it operates. 'I know so-and-so.' 'I know this Bollywood star.' Or 'I've taken a photo with him or her.' Right?

We feel that by knowing a Bollywood star and telling people about it, we will elevate our status in their eyes. So, we have derived our sense of worth from an identification with the Bollywood star, an identification with something external. *This is who I am. I know a Bollywood star. Look at me.* You see, that 'look at me' is the ego seeking attention.

Whereas with a sage, it makes no difference to him whether it's a Bollywood star or an ordinary person in front of him.

There was a world-famous singer called Leonard Cohen, who is no more. He used to attend Rameshji's satsangs. Cohen was a humble man, very simply dressed; you would not recognize any greatness in this man. He used to sit on the floor, near Rameshji's feet, and did not get any special treatment from him during the satsang.

Sometimes, after the satsang, Rameshji would say something about him: 'Have you heard Leonard's music? It is so deep and meaningful.' But that was all. Everyone in that room was treated equally.

The sage does not derive his sense of self from this kind of identification, you see. It does not mean that pleasure does not arise. If someone told Rameshji that a particular celebrity was coming for his satsang, he would say, 'Oh, I look forward to it.' But there is no sense of self derived from that.

What we tend to do is build our identities by trying to associate with people who are recognized in society; that is how this name-dropping game starts.

N: In Baba's community as well, one thing I feel devotees have to be particularly aware of, which maybe we can discuss in detail in the next podcast, is the tendency to get stuck in experiences and identify with them. If someone says that they have had a particular experience, another person is eagerly waiting for the first one to finish so that they too can brag about a similar experience

G: It's the same thing—that feeling of being special.

N: Correct. That is a very dangerous one.

G: It is. It's a pitfall, you see. It's the biggest pitfall for the devotee.

N: Yes. Once we had gone from Rishikesh to Uttarkashi with a Swamiji who had to attend a discourse there. And I remember that one of the masters on the stage said that in the spiritual tradition, amid the *sadhu* community, the minute somebody starts talking of their experiences, it's like blowing your own trumpet, and then one knows that that is their downfall. Internally, I was laughing because it's, you know, easier to see it in someone else than in yourself.

G: True.

N: So, to sum up this important topic, it would be the first priority, as Rameshji said, to take a few steps initially to get out of the thinking mind into the working mind, in a healthy and balanced way, through your job or maybe some volunteering or whatever it is. But this should be done keeping in mind at all times that it does not become a substitute for your spiritual practice or practising awareness. As Baba's devotees, maybe it can be your sadhana, or maybe if it's someone who's following Eckhart Tolle, then it could be practising stillness.

Whatever your practice is, given the crazy working hours nowadays, you shouldn't over-engage in your work in an abusive way, thinking, *Hey, I'm always in the working mind*, like in the police officer example.

So, thank you for sharing these examples as they have made it a lot simpler to understand the subject matter. I hope devotees who hear this can take away a lot from it because it's certainly, I would say, one of those foundational principles that one can be aware of at all times.

G: If you feel your thinking mind is overworking, make a switch to the working mind, if possible, and if not possible, witness how the thinking mind operates because it will reveal a lot to you. It will reveal to you your identification with the thinking mind. That itself, after all, is the journey within.

To view the corresponding video, scan the QR code.

35

The Middle Path (Gautam's Talk)

We have to understand a basic fact: this world is the realm of duality—duality of every conceivable kind, as my spiritual teacher would say.

Joel Goldsmith said something very beautiful. The tenet of his teachings was to give up the belief in good and evil; to give up the belief in two powers.

What was he pointing at?

That, if everything is God, there is nothing which is not God. This is very important to understand because it is the tenet of Advaita as well. All there is, is Consciousness. Everything is God's will. If there is something that we feel is not God's will, that means we have given something else power over God. Something so powerful that God has no role to play in it.

This is what happens. We create this split.

So it is very important to understand that duality is the framework of life and living. However, what happens is that the basic duality of life, of me and the other, becomes me *versus* the other. We create this conflict by fighting with people or by not accepting situations and events that happen in our life, and we thus give it power.

Nisargadatta Maharaj said that we are already imprisoned in this body. Consciousness, which is so vast, has become imprisoned in this limited form.

When we accept that, in life, everything has its polar opposite, because that is the nature of life, we no longer swing towards the extremes of these polar opposites. If you hold a pendulum at one end, it swings wildly to the other end. We find ourselves swinging from pleasure to pain and vice versa. As Maharaj said, between every two pains is a pleasure, you see. [Refer to talk 2.] No one has a life of pleasure, pleasure and pleasure. It is everyone's life experience that one moment, life is pleasure, and the next moment, it is pain. The important point here is that the pendulum is still when it is not swinging wildly between these polar opposites—this dance of duality.

That is why the wisdom teachings are there for us. When we live these teachings, we are no longer swayed by what happens in life, like we were earlier.

I am reminded of a beautiful story about a prince. I think I read it in one of Osho's books. I might have got the story a bit wrong, but this is the essence of it.

This prince had all the luxuries of life. In fact, he lived a life of excess. One day, he suddenly thought to himself, *What is this mayajaal I am stuck in?* and took to the other extreme: a life of austerity. He stopped meeting people and even started shrinking because of his newly adopted minimalist lifestyle.

In desperation, his parents took him to the Buddha, hoping that He would make better sense prevail in their son.

Now the prince happened to be fond of playing a stringed musical instrument. So the Buddha arranged for this instrument to be brought to him. He loosened its strings and then told the prince that He would like him to play some music on the instrument. But the prince replied that, of course, he could not do so as the strings were not tuned optimally.

Then the Buddha tightened all the strings severely and repeated His request. Again, the prince replied that he could not play any music as the strings were so tight that they would hardly move when he plucked them.

Subsequently, the Buddha explained to the prince the analogy He was drawing here: Life is the middle path; not these extremes, too tight or too loose. The middle path.

So when we find that this is the basic structure of duality, we are no longer swayed by it, choosing one extreme over the other. Accepting this as the design of life, we find that we are walking the middle path. We are less judgemental and less critical. We start condemning less and blaming less. We have less pride and less arrogance. We find that this framework of duality is honoured and understood for what it is, and the mind, which is no longer swinging wildly like a pendulum, is a mind at peace.

Perhaps, if it interests you, you could read the first article I wrote on Sai Baba's teachings: *Sai Baba and the Hidden Jewel of Advaita*. [Refer to Appendix.] It is about Baba's Advaitic sayings, and if you reflect on it, you will find the essence of what I have been talking about. Baba asks us to remove the barrier that separates us from Him—that of being mired in duality.

If you see everyone as Baba's Creation, you are no longer going to swing like a pendulum, hating some people and loving others. You start developing a sense of neutrality, accepting God's Creation the way He made it and not the way you think it should have been made.

This example of the pendulum reminds me of the first chapter of the Satcharita, about the grinding of the wheat. You could look at the wheat as our life being ground between the stones of duality. But the centre is the still point. It doesn't move, so the grain that lies therein does not get ground. It remains safe, so to speak. That is what I was referring to when I spoke about the pendulum being at rest. We find such an important lesson right at the beginning of the Satcharita.

That is the beauty of it. The Satcharita operates at so many levels. We may read a story once and derive some teaching from it. However, when we read it another time, we gain another understanding of it. Each point in any story in that book has so much meaning to it. After all, it is the Satcharita. '*Sat*' is 'Truth'.

To view the corresponding video, scan the QR code.

36

Baba's Teaching on Non-doership

Nikhil: One of the leelas in the Satcharita is connected to Baba's teaching on non-doership. I'll just recount the story in brief, after which I request you to share your insights on this important topic for devotees to ponder over.

Gautam: Sure.

N: In chapter fifty-one of the Satcharita, there is a beautiful story about a devotee called Pundalikrao meeting a swami while travelling somewhere with his friends. The swami mentions that Sai Baba is his brother and hands over a coconut to the devotee, requesting him to give it to Baba on his return to Shirdi. But this devotee and his friends, forgetting that the coconut was meant for Baba, had it as part of their meal.

Later, realizing his mistake and filled with remorse, Pundalikrao approached Baba, who asked him what the swami had sent for Him. Then, Baba instructed him because he was full of remorse and was being very hard on himself for his negligence.

In this story, I found something about non-doership, which I feel could be very insightful because it is simple and yet quite tricky. There are two sides to it, which I would like to discuss with you.

G: Sure. It is very important to discuss this story because, as often, the focus is on the miracle and not on the teaching.

Now the miracle in this case is that Baba asked Pundalikrao what his brother had sent for Him. This meant that Baba already knew that the swami had sent a coconut for Him. He had seen it through His vision. Now, this is just a small part of this story. The whole story, especially what Baba speaks about non-doership, carries the teaching.

N: Yes.

I would like to read out a bit from the book.

'After listening to what happened, Baba said with a smile, "Why should one take the coconut in hand at all, if one cannot safeguard it properly? Feeling certain that you would give Me My thing, My brother placed full trust in your words. But should it result in this? Is this all your trustworthiness? My brother's wish was not fulfilled. Is this the way you work? The value of that fruit can never be equalled, even if you bring many others. But now, what had to happen has happened. Why feel sad for it needlessly?"'

G: Here I would like to take a pause. Baba told Pundalikrao that he was entrusted with the coconut by the swami. What Baba means here is that if he had this errand to carry out of giving Him the coconut, he should have been aware of this.

N: Yes.

G: When Pundalikrao and his friends were on their journey back to Shirdi, they were feeling hungry and thirsty. One of them, we don't know which one, saw the coconut and mixed the coconut with whatever they were eating. This means that this act was done in unawareness.

Baba brings into question the extent of Pundalikrao's trustworthiness. Because if he was entrusted with the coconut, he should have taken care that it was delivered to Him. It means he should have been aware at all times.

So let us make no mistake that this is the first lesson that Baba imparts. Now we can go on to what comes next.

N: Yes.

[Continues reading.] 'So when Swami gave you the coconut, it was by My wish, and it is only by My wish that the fruit was broken. Then why regard yourself as the doer unnecessarily?'

G: Yes. This is a very important line because this applies to all of us.

It is not that this group of friends intentionally ate the coconut, which they knew was meant for Baba. Obviously, they would not do that. It was just a matter of circumstances. They were hungry, they were tired, one of them didn't realize the importance of the coconut reaching its destination and it was all done unintentionally. But once Pundalikrao realized the mistake, he felt guilty.

Baba clearly says that it was Him giving the coconut to Himself. He was the swami giving the coconut. He was also the one who broke the coconut as well as the one who ate the coconut. So why was Pundalikrao taking this burden of being the doer?

Now this is the second lesson. So, first, Baba establishes that it was an act committed in unawareness. But now that the act had happened, what Baba is showing is that it was destined to happen. Because Baba, as God, as the Source, as Consciousness, was behind the whole leela. But the individual took the action upon himself.

N: Yes.

[Continues reading.] 'You harbour an egoistic attitude and hence regard yourself as the offender. But just adopt this attitude of being a non-doer, and all your troubles can be avoided.'

G: Now what is 'all your troubles can be avoided' referring to?

It means the trouble created by the thinking mind, which leads to all the shame and guilt, and the resultant emotions, which clog your system. In other words, if the understanding is clear that it is Consciousness that acts, and that He, as an embodiment of the Source, is behind this entire episode, then you will not take this burden on your shoulders. You have to place this burden at His feet.

N: Correct.

[Continues reading.] 'Why do people own their meritorious deeds alone and not their sins? After all, the power of both is the same, so act without ego.'

G: Yes. Baba is reaffirming what He has said. Any action, regardless of whether it results in praise, recognition or an award, or alternatively, in condemnation, blame or punishment, is not your doing.

Baba is pointing out that if He, as God, as Baba, is behind an act, then an emotion such as pride has no place here. However, pleasure may arise. Let's say you do something and someone praises you by saying, 'You know, what you have said has really moved me.' It would be natural to feel pleasure on hearing that what you have said has made a difference to someone's life, but that pleasure will not turn into pride and arrogance. That load of pride and arrogance, which we call *ghamand*, will not be there when you know that this could not have happened without the grace of God.

Similarly, if something goes wrong, regret may arise: 'Oh dear, it's disappointing that this has happened.' But that regret will not turn into guilt and shame.

In the story, Baba is telling Pundalikrao not to take the burden of guilt and shame because, after all, He was behind the whole episode.

N: Yes.

So had this incident happened slightly differently, we would get to see another side to this story. Had Pundalikrao managed to deliver the coconut to Baba as requested by the swami, he could have felt that he was blessed to have been entrusted with such a task by a swami, which he was able to successfully carry out.

So, in both instances, is there ownership?

G: Yes, but only if that feeling of being blessed turns into pride that, of all people, he was the one chosen by the swami to fulfil the task.

N: So that is the feeling to look for in our everyday living.

G: That is what brings us down. And I must say that this story is so beautiful because of a couple of reasons.

First, my feeling is that this leela of Baba's was meant only for us readers because, as you said, Pundalikrao could have delivered the coconut. If the coconut was delivered, the story would not find its way into the Satcharita. So this story is meant for all of us.

N: Yes, this is what I felt too.

G: Second, and even more importantly, what is the gift being offered by the swami to Baba? A coconut. The coconut is the ego. The coconut which we offer in the havan is symbolic of us offering our ego. And the swami told Pundalikrao to offer the coconut at Baba's feet. Which means offering the ego at Baba's feet.

So what Baba is telling Pundalikrao and his friends is that if they offer their ego at His feet, then where is the question of guilt and shame coming into the picture?

You see, it's so beautiful that even the gift—a coconut—was wisely chosen to convey the message through this story. It could have been something else.

N: Correct.

G: But it was a coconut. And I feel this is important because this story is directly connected to the Bhagavad Gita, where Krishna says, 'The self, deluded by egoism, thinketh, *I am the doer*.'

I think that anyone will understand the message in this story once they look at it with this understanding.

N: Yes. So coming back to Pundalikrao bringing the coconut to Baba, if he does not have a sense of pride about it then it is just a spontaneous happening, and he will not even have a trace of doership. Is that right?

G: Yes, pleasure will arise, like I said. He will feel happy. It is human nature, but that happiness will not convert into pride and arrogance.

N: So either, the pleasure or the regret, would not have been stretched in time had Pundalikrao not taken ownership of the incident. He would have just told Baba that he made this mistake, for which he was sorry, and that he would take care not to repeat it in the future. But he would not have beat himself up over it.

G: Yes, because the incident is already in the past; it's gone. But the mind is stretching it into the present moment, and successive present moments, because now it's living in the past by being overly remorseful.

N: [Continues reading.] Then the next line is, 'The coconut fell in the hollow of your palms only because I wished that you should come to meet Me. This is the whole truth.'

G: Exactly. The whole incident may appear to be about a swami giving a coconut to Baba, but what Baba is saying is that everyone in this story plays an important part. What is equally important is that Pundalikrao had to meet Baba, for which he had to be given the coconut.

N: [Continues reading.] 'You are also My children. The fruit that fell in your mouth has itself been offered to Me. Regard it as having reached Me, most certainly.'

G: Yes. This is also very beautiful. What does this mean, that the food which they had, had reached Him?

Traditionally and ritualistically, before eating your food, you offer it to your chosen deity, or Baba, and then have it. Why is that done? To bring a sense of presence and respect to the act of eating. To understand that I, the ego, am not the one eating, but I, as the presence of God, the Consciousness of God, am eating it. And if I am a Baba follower, Baba is the form of God. The food is being offered to that Presence and not to me as the ego. That is the symbolism here.

So, again, this is what Baba is pointing to.

N: Sometimes, people have this attitude: *Since, in any case, I am not the doer, then whatever I do is okay. What does it matter?* Now, that is obviously the ego abusing a very important teaching.

So I feel it might be nice if you could talk about this as well because this is typically one of the tricks that the ego plays.

G: Yes. When the ego hears 'I am not the doer,' it then thinks, *Oh, then that means I can do whatever I like.* When it feels threatened, it comes up with these defences.

Now, when my spiritual teacher would say something about non-doership, someone would respond by saying, 'Oh, that means I can do whatever I like because I am not the doer.'

Rameshji would then explain thus: 'Look, supposing I give you a gun in your hands, will you shoot someone with it? First of all, is it your nature to do it or not? You will only do what is in your nature to do.

'If it is not in your nature, you won't be able to harm someone.

Secondly, and more importantly, this does not absolve you of the consequences of your act. You may have the full understanding that you are not the doer, but you are responsible for all your actions, and society will judge you.'

So nobody said you have a free licence to do whatever you want. Certainly not Baba. You have to be a responsible citizen if you are living in a society. If you're alone out there in a remote cave somewhere in the Himalayas, then you may not be concerned with society. We don't know.

N: But the karmic repercussions of your actions, regardless of where you live, are there.

G: Exactly. So like I said, it does not absolve you of the consequences of your action.

The whole point here is that if you lived with the understanding that nobody is the doer, you would not have thoughts of hatred, malice, jealousy, envy and suchlike. Because you would know that the other person is not the doer, right? Similarly, you yourself would not have thoughts of pride and arrogance or guilt and shame as you know that you also are not the doer.

Now, can you imagine a mind which is free of all this? That is the pure mind. Otherwise, we are, throughout the day, harbouring all these thoughts, feelings and emotions, which are like dark clouds across our consciousness, you see.

So which mind would you prefer?

N: It's wonderful talking with you because one may not have pondered over this leela and Baba's words, and realized that they are so impregnated with meaning.

And if we could also discuss other stories from the Satcharita, it could help give us some insights into them too. I would be most happy if we could do a small series: Reflections on the Sai Satcharita.

G: Sure.

To reiterate, if you really understood the essence of this story, then you would start looking at those people in your own life whom you have been blaming and condemning so far. It could be a family member, a friend or a business associate. But if you now look at them in the light of this story, and if you truly accept Baba as your master, then Baba is telling you, 'I am the one operating through them.'

N: Yes.

G: Now, do you have the courage to see what's behind this story, which also pertains to your own life, or are you just going to leave it in the Satcharita, which lies by your bedside, and continue with your relationships the way you have been doing so far? That is the test of the true devotee.

N: Many devotees are very sincere and do the reading very religiously, but I do feel these conversations with you will influence their lives and help them live Baba's teachings because Baba's words sometimes might sound very simple, but they are not very easy to live by.

G: Yes, it is all about living the teachings. Otherwise, it is mere theory. Even if you read the story every day for the rest of your life, it can still be just a story you are reading.

'Living the teachings' is the mantra.

To view the corresponding video, scan the QR code.

37

Sai Baba's Prophetic Words: A Wake-up Call

Eighty to ninety years from now, there will be a population explosion, and unusual diseases will spread throughout the world. Massive numbers of people will succumb to these diseases. There will be new diseases in different continents of the world, and a cure will be difficult to find.

Human beings will lose empathy and sympathy towards others, and people will be recognized only by the amount of wealth they possess.

This is going to be the dismal future of mankind.

—Sai Baba

Nikhil: Namaste. We have published a podcast of Vinny Ma's, named the 'Dismal Future of Mankind.' It is about what Baba communicated to one of his most intimate devotees. Baba prophesied mankind's future about eighty to ninety years ahead. And it has come true, as with everything else that Baba has said.

What struck me as most important is that Baba said man will lose empathy and sympathy for another man, and man will only be known for the amount of wealth he possesses. That is what we are seeing in this *Kali Yuga*. And especially during the pandemic, this prophecy has been validated.

I feel this would be a good topic to discuss with you as it would serve to reiterate Baba's teachings for the devotees and help them live the path of compassion He has shown us.

Gautam: Yes.

As we have been saying all along, Baba's life itself is an example of the absence of separation. He lived with both the largest communities, the Hindus and the Muslims. His way of living as well as his teachings embraced the outlook of both communities, which showed them that He was a living example of acceptance. That was His uniqueness.

Now it is all the more relevant, as the sense of separation today is so strong. One would have thought that if the teachings of all great masters were imbibed in our daily living, we would be a closely-knit society.

A collectively difficult situation, the pandemic, has made us aware and provided us with the opportunity to be closer to one another. Normally, when one is suffering, it is borne alone, and others take pity on the sufferer and express their sympathy. But now it is collective. So the opportunity is being given to wake up collectively from this dream of separation and help others as if they are our own. The whole of the Sai Satcharita lays this out for us.

So I do believe that while the sense of separation is strong now, and Baba has predicted that it will get worse, the teachings are already in place. The guidance is already there.

The fact that this book is available even today means that it is meant to help us see these times through.

N: From a devotee's perspective, one thing I felt is that Baba has shown us the path of service through His acts of kindness: He would feed people, animals and other beings. Baba is the epitome of compassion.

Can you give some pointers that devotees can adopt as a sadhana to add to their day-to-day practices?

One can start small, for example, by planting some trees or by feeding someone poor; in short, just getting involved in some way or the other in service.

G: There are two things here.

One is that the primary seva, if you ask me, is living the teachings. If the teaching says, 'Do not harm another,' then following it becomes a sadhana in itself. Because we harm people by what we say. We may use the sweetest words, but the way we say them is harmful because of the malicious intention behind them. Let's say we are judging someone or passing an opinion without knowing the full picture.

So the first seva is not to harm another being. Even Nisargadatta Maharaj told his devotees, 'Live your lives without hurting anybody. Harmlessness is the most powerful form of yoga, and it will take you speedily to your goal. This is what I call *"Nisarga Yoga"*, the natural yoga. It is the art of living in peace and harmony, in friendliness and love. The fruit of it is happiness, uncaused and endless.'

Why? Because if you truly realized that everything is Brahman, that all there is, is Consciousness, then could Consciousness harm Itself?

So, this is the primary seva. Why primary? Because you may do annadaan, you may do various practices, but you are still living a life of separation. You are still harming others by your thoughts, words and deeds.

Very interestingly, someone mentioned to me that they had taken up a new job where the boss happened to be a Parsi. Now some Parsis are notorious for using foul language. So this person was uncomfortable about it and told the boss that he wanted to leave the job.

I asked him why. I said, 'You know that by nature some Parsis are like that. What is the intent behind the foul language? Please tell me.'

The person replied, 'No, there is no intent, really; it's just part of his nature.'

So then I told him, 'Isn't it better to have a boss who uses foul language as part of his nature or conditioning, which has no harmful intention behind it, rather than someone who is plotting and scheming, and in that sense, abusing you in a subtle way? Which is better?'

We all know that Sai Baba Himself used unpleasant language at times. It arose in the moment, and that was perhaps the best thing meant for the person He was addressing. You see, it may be needed to shake someone out of the dream.

So the Satcharita is not to be read just as a manual of miracles, but we have to understand what is behind the storytelling. We have to ask ourselves at what level we are relating to it and how we are living the teachings.

That is the first seva.

Thereafter, as a practice, as a sadhana, what appeals to me?

Supposing I have money, and I don't have the time. So I donate money, not because I am going to get something in return but because I feel for those who don't have what I have financially. That way, my sense of separation will start dissolving.

I donate, knowing that I am donating to Consciousness—to an expression of Consciousness just like me; Consciousness donating to Consciousness—and not with the intent of earning brownie points with Sai Baba.

Talking about annadaan, I may be very good at mobilizing a force to feed people, but even collectively, we may not have the money to do so. Let's say someone gives us the money. Now, we make the most of our strength at the grassroots level by helping to cook food and distribute it to the poor.

Everyone can figure out for themselves what their innate strength is in terms of seva and sadhana.

You gave the example of planting trees. Some are geared towards that. I have friends who are very environmentally conscious; they know so much about trees and earth and nature. So this is an aspect of giving. Giving based on what one is gifted with.

A very important thing takes place here. In any of these forms of seva, the focus shifts from the me to the other. Usually, our focus is me-centric: me and my story; *I am the hero of my story*. The minute you do seva, the spotlight turns on the other. *What can I do for the other?* And the me diminishes.

It's just like what happens with bhakti. The spotlight shifts from the me to the deity or the guru. So these are all very subtle movements away from the me towards someone else, whoever it may be.

But the truth is that there's nothing apart from you. It is just a misconception. Nevertheless, it's a stubborn misconception. So these sevas and sadhanas are like tools to shift the focus away from the me, to make the me less relevant.

The problem is when the me comes back and says, 'I did this seva.'

N: True. As they say, if one hand gives, the other should not even know about it.

G: Yes. That is again a pitfall to be wary of for the devotee.

To view the corresponding video, scan the QR code.

38

How to Reflect on the Sai Satcharita

Nikhil: Could you share your views on how to approach the Sai Satcharita and give some pointers to devotees on how to read it as a sadhana, just like they do their *parayana* regularly?

Gautam: Sure.

I would like to begin by saying that it is called the Sai Satcharita. It is not called the Sai Charita. 'Sat' means 'Truth'. It even translates as 'Being'. And *'charita'* means 'life story'.

So this is not the life story of a man called Sai Baba. It is not the life story of a master called Sai Baba. It is the life story of the Truth which was embodied in Sai Baba. If we are reading this sacred book, viewing Him as an individual doing chamatkars and leelas, we are not doing justice to it. It is alright to be impressed by a leela. But the book will only benefit us if we read each chapter and ask ourselves, *What is in this for me? What is the leela showing me? How can I apply it in my daily living? What can I learn from it?*

If you recall, chapter ten of the Sai Satcharita makes it very clear that Sai Baba's intent for the true devotee was Self-realization. Jnana Yoga. Understanding. Knowledge being lived and not knowledge as theory. He did not want it just to be a book full of His miracles. That would be reading it at a very basic level. But He wanted us involved in the story. He wanted us to understand, to think, *What is this about?*

And we have explored so many of these stories.

I have always felt that Baba's hidden teachings were meant to be understood at a deeper level. Why hidden? Because, so far, the focus was only on the miracles and not on knowing what the stories hold for us. Now that understanding is emerging. Some people already had it, but many didn't. What is the Truth behind these stories? The Truth, the Sat, you see? They pertain to us. It is not just about the characters in the Satcharita. It is about us. Each character is us. Each villain in this book is us. That needs to be understood because we have all their traits.

I'm glad you brought up this discussion because I have kept myself armed with chapter ten, from which I would like to read a couple of passages.

'Sai is a mine of Self-knowledge.' This is what Hemadpant says: 'a mine of Self-knowledge'. He is not saying 'a mine of miracles'. That we know.

'Cling to Him for protection instantly to be able to cross the ocean of worldly life.' From birth to death.

'The most constant, undifferentiated Supreme Spirit personified in Baba is boundless and infinite, and fills this entire universe from Brahma right down to a tiny shrub.'

So, Hemadpant is very clear that these are teachings of Self-knowledge.

And chapter ten ends most beautifully.

'He who knew how illusory this worldly life is and was constantly engaged in blissful Self-absorption, before Him I prostrate in obeisance.' He is referring to Sai Baba.

Now why is he saying this? He is saying it for us. He is not saying that Sai Baba knew how illusory the worldly life is. That is at one level. But he is trying to tell us readers how illusory all this is. How illusory the sense of separation we are living with is.

What is the Sat? What is the Sat in Satcharita? You see, I keep pointing back to that. That is what this book is about.

And the last passage: 'He who gives Brahma Jnana, or Supreme Knowledge, by applying the collyrium of knowledge into the eye, to that great Sai, I bow in obeisance.' He who gives Supreme Knowledge.

So this kind of validates the work which we are doing, of telling people and devotees that this is a way of living. The Satcharita is a manual for living. Just keeping it by your bedside and reading a story because one is meant to read it is of no use. Or reading it and saying,

'Oh, Baba did this, Baba did that.' No use. But reading it, absorbing it and seeing how you relate to it in your life is its purpose. What does it show you by way of example? That is called living the Satcharita. Living the Truth.

Otherwise, the Truth will become a pillow. [Laughs.]

N: Talking of which reminds me that Vinny Ma shared a beautiful leela in a video titled 'My Charita Isn't a Pillow'.

So, in the next episode, I would like to talk to you about it.

To view the corresponding video, scan the QR code.

39

The Satcharita Isn't a Pillow

Nikhil: To continue with where we ended the earlier episode, there was this leela that Vinny Ma shared of Baba's, titled 'My Charita Isn't a Pillow'. It is published on the channel for those who would like to watch it.

To explain the story in brief, Baba appeared to a devotee's husband who was critically ill and healed him. That man was given a copy of the Satcharita by a friend to read, but as he was not Baba's devotee, he just put it below his pillow and slept over it.

When Baba appeared to this man before he was healed, He told him: 'My Charita is given to you, not to be used as a pillow; it has to be read and understood.'

Gautam: That is it. I'm glad you mentioned these words because Baba Himself has said them. So forget that I am saying them. [Laughs.] You may think, *Who's this joker saying, 'You have to understand and live by Baba's words,'* but now you're saying Baba Himself has said these words. 'Read and understood' means 'lived by'.

That is so important.

And this pillow business . . . we all do it. We have our favourite books, right? Let's say you are following another master, and you have your master's book by the bedside. You open it, you read a page, you close it. It could be *The Gospel of Sri Ramakrishna*, it could be anything.

But this 'read and understood' indicates that, after reading it, we should keep the book down and contemplate it. An important pointer here is that, as many masters say, you should tune your mind to something spiritual before going to sleep. And many people follow this practice. It's very important because what you have read filters into the subconscious before going to sleep. The subconscious is absorbing it; it is imbibing the Knowledge—with a capital K. There are hours when the conscious mind is not functioning in deep sleep.

So you should pay attention to what thoughts you are going to sleep with. It is a very beautiful practice because, though we are not aware in deep sleep, the teachings still operate. In fact, it is not interrupted by the conscious mind, and so it blossoms in sleep.

N: As people start reading the Satcharita and imbibing it through this series with you, one of the possibilities could be that they start becoming aware that they are not living the teachings.

G: Very true.

N: So could you talk a bit about that?

G: I think that's most beautiful because it means that earlier, they were unconscious of it. Now they are conscious that they are not living by the book. It is a very big step, you see.

Let's take a common example. Someone meditating feels that they had a lot of thoughts during their meditation and so it was a very bad meditation.

But I say to them, 'No, it was very good because now you know that there were many thoughts. Earlier, you were running after all the thoughts when you sat for meditation. Now you know that there were many thoughts.' Now the awareness has set in. Again, a big step on the spiritual journey.

So, coming back to what you mentioned about people knowing they are not living the teachings, let's say, earlier, they were functioning on autopilot. Now Baba has gifted them the awareness that they are not living the teachings.

That itself will do wonders. It will make us increasingly aware that we are not living the teachings. That is how it works. The opportunity is now manifest to allow the teachings to be imbibed more and more.

So it is not a negative thing. To say that I am not living the teachings takes courage. Many people are in denial.

N: I realize, for example, that in my case, the teachings are not very easy to live by.

I will just share this story. I was walking in the building complex, and someone honked outside the gate. They wanted to come in, and since the guard was not there, I opened the gate for them and continued walking. They just drove past, got out of the car, and walked away.

Within me, I said, *They did not even have the courtesy to smile and acknowledge me*, because if someone did the same for me, at least I would smile or say a thank you.

Now that was an expectation on my part, and I realized that the teachings are not easy to live by. However subtle it was, it was an expectation. I said to myself that although it is not easy to live the teachings, maybe the awareness that I am not living them is a pointer.

G: Yes, but in this example that you used, it is natural to expect. If a courteous gesture is made, it is usually acknowledged. But that is still not the issue. The issue is, it didn't happen.

The expectation, no matter how subtle, was not met, but with Baba's understanding, by living the teachings, you did not bear a grudge against that person for not acknowledging your help. That involvement was cut off because you accepted that it was meant to be this way, according to Baba's will. So, no individual was targeted anymore, you see. That is the difference.

And let's not forget that we have years and years of conditioning behind us. As my teacher, Rameshji, would say, the crust around the ego is very hard, and it takes constant hammering for it to crack. With some people, the crust is not so hard, and it just takes a few hits of the hammer. That is why Ramana Maharshi said that some people wake up to the spiritual journey after the first one or two blows early in life. But for others, it may take five or six blows, and eventually, you get the blows, and the blows are what make you take to the spiritual journey.

So it is certainly not easy to live the teachings, but when one is aware that they are not living the teachings, it shows that the intention is there to live the teachings. And then, the force of Baba's teachings, of Consciousness, will work to support the person because the person has, like I said, been courageous enough to acknowledge that the teachings are not being lived by them.

To view the corresponding video, scan the QR code.

40

Climbing the Ladder of Consciousness

Nikhil: I would like to discuss a leela of Baba's with you, mentioned in chapter nineteen of the Satcharita, in which Baba climbs up a ladder to the roof of Radhakrishna Ma's house. Surprisingly, this happened when He was very frail, a little before His Mahasamadhi. He could walk only with the help of others.

Baba came to Ma's house and asked for a ladder to be brought. Ma also happened to be unwell then. He climbed to the roof by Himself, without any support, walked to the other side with the ladder and came down. He then gave two rupees to the person who brought the ladder, saying that one should always pay for services rendered.

So, I felt many aspects of this story were not that easy to understand. I used to keep contemplating this for years, and, one day, when I was reading *The Gospel of Sri Ramakrishna*, there was a paragraph that just stood out for me. I can't say that it was pointing exactly to this, but it was so similar. I'll just read that out and then ask you for your views on this leela.

In chapter twelve of the Gospel, Ramakrishna Dev says, 'A man should reach the *Nithya*, that is, the Absolute, by following the trail of the leela, the relative. It is like reaching the roof by the stairs. After realizing the Absolute, he should come down to the relative and live on that plane in the company of devotees, charging his mind with the love of God. This is my final and most mature opinion.'

Gautam: Most beautiful.

So, I felt Baba's whole life was symbolic. He would not say anything; He would convey messages through His leelas. I felt there was so much more to this one. And when I read what Ramakrishna Dev says in the Gospel, something surfaced within me, although I am not saying for certain that it directly connects to this leela.

G: Yes, there are two things here. One is that when Baba climbed the ladder to the roof and came down, there was an audience who saw it; otherwise, it would not be recorded. So, He didn't do it for Himself. He did it as a demonstration, one could say. And as you said, He did it when He was unwell, before His Mahasamadhi, and not when He was young, fit and strong, right? So all the more the reason for us to treat it as attention-worthy.

Now what you just read out from the Gospel is, in fact, the perfect overlap. You see, the ladder is a phenomenon that people have seen in their spiritual visions. It is the ladder of Consciousness, the climb up to the Divine. It represents everyone's potential.

The ladder itself is a very significant symbol. The rungs of the ladder are levels of understanding. They are like the seven chakras of the body, or rather, the six chakras, the seventh being the *Sahasrar*, which is not a chakra but a centre. From the base level of survival and living, to the higher levels. From the *Muladhar*, *Swadhisthan* and Manipur, which is living from the gut, to the *Anahat*, the heart, the *Vishuddhi*, and then the Ajna, the eye of singularity, not the eyes of duality. These are the rungs of the ladder culminating in the Sahasrar, merging with the Divine. Now, once that journey, that potential, is fulfilled when the ladder is climbed, one has to come back to Earth to live the spiritual life.

So, in simple terms, supposing our spiritual journey takes us to this understanding that all there is, is Brahman. Everyone is an aspect of the Divine. After having that understanding, that all is one, now it has to be lived. We have to climb down the ladder, back to Earth, to live it.

How would we live it? If I live my life without condemnation, blame, conflict, jealousy, envy, hatred and malice, then that Divine Knowledge is brought down to Earth to live the teaching, to live the Divinity.

And that is what Baba has shown us by climbing up onto the roof and coming down the other side. So, sages among us live a life of enlightened living. It's very significant.

N: I think, at the beginning of the Satcharita, Hemadpant points out that there are many kinds of siddhas and saints. A few come for their own elevation, born to reach the Absolute, and depart. But masters like Baba come, get into maya—as Baba would say, although He is the Absolute—and take on the sufferings of others to elevate them.

Masters like these are very rare. Total compassion incarnate.

G: Yes. Otherwise, who would want to come back? I mean, once you merge with the Divine Light, you have no interest in descending back to Earth. So it is only compassion which does it. Only a compassionate heart, such as Baba's, can subject itself to all this.

N: Also, there's another aspect. Ramakrishna Dev says that if by chance, an ordinary *jiva* gets elevated and attains samadhi, in twenty-one days, the body will drop. It is only an incarnation of God that can come back and stay in the plane of relative existence after having realized the Absolute.

Based on what Ramakrishna Dev says, the fact that Baba has come down to live amongst us mortals shows that He is an incarnation. I cannot say for certain that this is the only meaning of what Ramakrishna Dev says, but this is what I am seeing at this point in time.

G: Very true. That is why it is said that for many people, the moment of enlightenment is the moment of death. Because it's like an explosion; a normal body-mind organism cannot take the impact. So to come back, only a high-level master can do that.

N: It also makes me reflect on Hemadpant's commentary in the initial chapters, where he emphasizes again and again that Baba's compassion and that of masters like Him is for the elevation of mankind. He said that, otherwise, many who have reached this elevated state live in the mountains.

Something to make us reflect on their compassion and grace.

G: Yes. It reminds me of the folklore, or myth you could say, about the Buddha reaching the Gates of Heaven. The Gatekeeper said to Him, 'Master, we are rejoicing that now You're finally with us. Do come in.'

And the Buddha said, 'No.'

The Gatekeeper persisted and said, 'But we have waited for millennia for You to enter these Gates. We are all lined up for You in celebration and festivity and joy.'

But still, the Buddha replied, 'No.'

'But why?' asked the Gatekeeper, taken aback at the Buddha's refusal to enter the Gates.

The Buddha laid a condition: 'Not unless those who are following Me are allowed to enter before Me.'

Compassion. Compassion.

N: This reminds me of Swami Vivekananda, who was a disciple of Ramakrishna Dev. He had mentioned something beautiful as well. He said that Shiva is pleased with those who put everyone else in the line to worship Him first and themselves go last because, otherwise, it is selfish to think of only me and my elevation, and let everyone else be.

G: Yes. As Ramana Maharshi said, 'There are no others.' [Refer to talk 3.]

So, compassion is the natural outcome of the awakening, one could say. If compassion has not happened, awakening has not happened. Then it's still the me and the mine; my awakening. It won't work, because it is the me that is the problem, you see.

To view the corresponding video, scan the QR code.

41

Sai Baba's Emphasis on Reading the Pothis

Nikhil: *Pothi*-reading is a form of sadhana. In the Sai Satcharita, you see many instances where Baba would give devotees religious scriptures to read, not just to give them access to information but for the express purpose of reading them repeatedly. And there were many instances where He would send one devotee to another who was reading a particular scripture, to get answers to questions that they would initially approach Him with. He would also pull up devotees if they neglected their sadhana time to visit Him at Dwarkamai. So Baba laid great emphasis on discipline, on a fixed routine, as we can see in the Satcharita.

In Vinny Ma's commentary on chapter nineteen of the Satcharita, she's made a list of pothis read by each devotee.

Aai has been religiously doing her pothi-reading sadhana from 9.30 a.m. to 12.30 p.m. for years. Come what may, she never breaks that routine.

Baba would ask devotees to read certain books. For example, one of the scriptures very dear to Baba and His devotees was the *Vishnu Sahasranama*.

So I would like you to speak about reading these books, as well as the Sai Satcharita, regularly, as a sadhana for devotees.

Gautam: You see, this works at various levels.

Let's keep aside the fact that these are religious or spiritual texts. When there is discipline to be maintained, it means that priority over the mundane should be given to the practice. What tends to happen is that we give priority to the mundane and relegate the reading as secondary. Now the mundane, the material, is fleeting; it's transient. What is important today is no longer important tomorrow. So, are we going to focus our lives on just this mundane stuff or the Truth?

When the masters insist on a practice at a particular time allotted for that activity, they are ensuring that you prioritize it over the mundane. It is very important to understand this because we all tend to do the opposite. You may choose to meet a friend or take a phone call, and your practice is pushed into the background.

The first thing is to bring it into the foreground. Out of twenty-four hours, at least one or two hours, or half an hour, or at least ten minutes, should be given to this most important practice.

Secondly, it is a vibration. These books may appear as words, but they are sacred as they carry vibrations. To elaborate, research has shown that chants and mantras in Sanskrit create new grooves in the brain.

So the pothi is a vibration. You are immersed in its vibration while you are reading it. It is not just about reading and understanding. It becomes the content of one's consciousness. Your vibration gets affected by it. So this, again, is of extreme significance.

With this kind of commitment, you will find that the rest of your day is permeated with this vibration. That is its importance. It is not to be seen as a routine prescribed by a guru. What is the point of that? Do understand that reading is keeping holy company. It is not just the practice of reading. We are in the company of Truth when we are reading. Especially, when we don't have a master sitting in front of us, the book becomes the master. The Guru Granth Sahib, the Book of Knowledge, kept in the Golden Temple in Amritsar, is venerated and revered as the master.

So, when we read, are we thinking that it is a burden to repeatedly read the same book or are we—with reverence—feeling, knowing and understanding that the master is present as the book?

The vibrations are being absorbed, and your consciousness is being impacted by this process. It is very significant. Otherwise, tell me, why would Baba emphasize it? The fact was that, as you said, He told different people to read different books. Why would He do that?

So people need to look at the deeper significance of pothi-reading. What does it do on various levels? Thereafter, the sincere practice of reading will yield results. It is bound to.

N: I feel stories are very much a part of the human psyche. We remember and process them. If you read stories of faith or, for that matter, even the Gita, there may be instances or trying moments in your life when your mind begins to waver, and instantly, a line will just sort of come up and bring you back to the centre.

G: Yes.

N: But that happens once there is repeated reading with reverence.

In today's age, when you are bombarded with an influx of information, you will not watch the same news or a repeat telecast even one hour later, because its value is short-lived. But you will read a religious scripture written five thousand years ago repeatedly all your life. *That* is the value of the scripture.

How long do programmes on TV and even the things you purchase give you joy or value? They are so transient.

G: That's where we started, by saying that the focus is on the material and the transient while keeping the practice aside.

Now look at the Hanuman Chalisa. Do you know what happens when you keep reciting it? Hanuman is *Pawan Putra*, and so the Chalisa deals with the breath. It is structured to regulate your breathing while you chant it. Now the average person doesn't know this. Look at the ingenuity of the Hanuman Chalisa. It is meant to help you breathe a certain way. Look at the science behind all this. It is not just pothi-reading, which we started off by saying. It is a valuable science.

Therefore, someone like Sai Baba put so much emphasis on it. That *He* has recommended it as a practice, in itself should be enough for us.

N: Baba was a strict master. A great devotee of His, Kakasaheb Dixit, was put in a room in the wada by Him for nine months to do his sadhana. He was not allowed to leave it for that period, even to come to meet Baba. So that is the emphasis given by Baba to discipline regarding one's sadhana. Obviously, when Kakasaheb was in there for nine months, he was doing his reading. And Vinny Ma has made references to the books he would read regularly.

When we watch the TV series and read all the stories about Baba's close devotees, it all sounds very nice. But the kind of penance and service they have done for Baba is unparalleled. It is not for no reason that they are called param bhaktas. So if people look at what the day-to-day lives of these staunch devotees were like, then there are certain cues to be found there.

G: Yes. But those were different times. Today, there is so much fragmentation with technology, social media, etc. Needless to say, it's a bit harder now than before. But that is why the examples these devotees have set become all the more important.

You gave this example where Kakasaheb was doing nine months of sadhana. It reminds me of something. It is said that when the Buddha was passing away, His devotees came running to be near Him. He told them that He would have been happier had they continued with their practice instead of coming there to impress Him. You see, the emphasis is on sadhana.

Whatever the circumstances may be today, because these are very different times from then, give time to your practice, but give it totally and not as a compromise. Nothing is being imposed on you. So give it with all your heart and all your mind, as an offering to the Divine. Take a time you feel you can manage, but at least start, and stick to it for your relationship with the Divine. Nothing else should interfere.

N: In my own case, there's something I call 'following the joy'. When you practise for some time consistently, you begin to feel a certain joy, a radiance of peace and bliss inside, whether it is through your meditation, japa, bhajan, reading or whatever. Now, naturally, when you begin to experience that, wouldn't you want more of that?

G: Not only that. That joy of Being, as I call it, which does not depend on circumstances or things happening, just that simple peace of Being, stays with you despite whatever you may face during the day. You rest in it more and more.

To view the corresponding video, scan the QR code.

42

Missing the Point (Gautam's Talk)

I remember a history lesson in school, which was about a war that took place in the 17th century, and in the same chapter, there were two different years given about the war, which was obviously a typographical error. I think, in one place it was 1661, and in another place it was 1666, or something like that, and one student asked the teacher which of them was the correct date.

Now we are talking about the pre-internet days when you couldn't google for whatever information you needed, whenever you needed it. And so this whole thing became quite an issue: Which of the two was the correct date? A suggestion to go to the Asiatic Library in Mumbai and look up different encyclopaedias and papers was put forth by some.

The war was finished; it was part of the dead past. What lesson there was for us, what we could learn from that chapter, was in the here and now. This is the risk of being immersed, not only in history but anything to do with the past. If what I learnt from that event stays as the focal point, then the value of the lesson is throbbing, alive and present right now.

Let's take spiritual masters—Sai Baba, Ramana Maharshi, Sri Aurobindo, Ramakrishna and others—and their lives, which have been catalogued so well for us because each event in their lives had a very deep significance. So it is important that the history concerning these events has been maintained accurately. But again, as time goes by, we have different versions of the same event, in various books, competing with each other. And then we get stuck in this: 'Which is the right version? Which one should I follow?' You see, all that has got to do with the mind.

So we have to be careful—especially those who are on a spiritual journey, like all of us participating here—that, if we are immersed only in the historical aspect of a master, it remains an intellectual stimulation, consigned to memory. Knowing the year in which a certain event happened and that you are right about it has limited value.

How can I bring a historical event to the here and now to benefit from it?

For instance, let's take the beginning of the Satcharita, where Hemadpant had an argument with another person, and Baba disapproved of it. That was a historical event. Now I may say that it occurred at a particular time of the day, and another person may specify another time. But when I bring that story to my life now, what is Baba showing me through this story? It is about arguing, holding one's position rigidly and assuming that one is right. Now I have made history relevant to my life. I have brought it to this moment. If that does not happen, we can find that the teaching is just at a mental, historical level, which surely is not its purpose.

Recently, I read a book about Sri Ramana Maharshi and his closest devotees who were with him. It is a historical account. But it is so enjoyable because it talks about how Ramana Maharshi was with different devotees, and their thoughts and feelings . . . just like the Sai Satcharita, you see. Because we can relate to it and bring it into our own life.

So don't let the historical aspect of even a sage's story become so important that your focus is just on the historical details and not on how the story can permeate your daily living.

I am reminded of a friend's daughter who could rattle off anything from memory. It surely was a gift. She'd remember people's birthdays, telephone numbers, etc., even if she met them once or twice. God had given her a fantastic memory. But every discussion with her was about peoples' phone numbers, licence plate numbers and suchlike. The data kept coming up. That is how the mind operates. I can't even say she did it consciously; it was who she was.

Now the point is that our mental faculties are vast, and we can get stuck in streams of knowledge and data; in words, to put it simply.

As they say, reading a very beautiful recipe is not the same as tasting the food. When it comes to a teaching, when it comes to even a sage's history, reading it is not the same as tasting it. What does tasting it mean? It means living the teaching.

For example, I read a story where Baba says, 'Don't get into arguments with people.' I know that story line by line, I know all its details, but if I find that I'm still arguing like never before, then it has not impacted me. So this does not mean that the knowledge in the story has no value. It means I have limited the value of that knowledge because I have not been open enough to draw the essence of the story, contemplate it, and allow it to express itself through me.

So we have to be careful because the thinking mind, or the ego, can make us feel very good about knowing all the tiny details of the story. We should let it translate to our life and our relationships with others, and make it *our* story.

To view the corresponding video, scan the QR code.

43

Am I Receptive to Sai Baba's Teachings?

Nikhil: I feel it would be interesting to explore how devotees can be receptive to Baba's teachings.

Baba would often say that numerous people who came to Him had their *ghada* [pitcher] upside down, and as a result, they would never absorb the teaching. In connection with this, can we discuss the story of the *Ramdasi* in chapter twenty-seven of the Sai Satcharita?

Gautam: Sure.

I think the Ramdasi is tested by Baba to see if the teaching has impacted his daily living. And that is the acid test. Are we living the teachings of the master, or is it just a convenience-based model we have adopted, with no direct impact on our daily living?

N: This aspect is brought out forcefully in the story. The Ramdasi was in the habit of sitting in front of Baba and reading some sacred texts. One day, he picked up a quarrel with Shama, an intimate devotee of Baba's, merely because Baba gave a pothi belonging to him to the latter.

In response to the Ramdasi's fit of anger, Baba said to him: 'You are straining your every nerve to admonish him. Why be so sad without a reason to make an exhibition of your temper to the whole world? How can you be so quarrelsome? You read the pothis all the time, and yet your heart is still impure. Every day you read the Ramayana, you repeat the Sahasranama, but you have not given up the wild wilfulness, and yet you call yourself a Ramdasi. What kind of a Ramdasi are you? You ought to be detached and desireless in every sense of the word, but here you are not being able to give up your attachment to that pothi. What can one say of this behaviour of yours?'

G: Right. Very sharp words and to the point because, to put it in context, we have a situation here where this man has been reading the holy books for a long time, and when he finds that someone has got hold of his copy, he erupts like a volcano.

Now Baba set this whole thing up just to test the Ramdasi; He Himself had given the pothi to Shama.

This story points to something very important. Anger can arise in anyone. It can arise even in the Ramdasi as a spontaneous reaction, but in this case, he indulged in it to such an extent that he even threatened to bash Shama's head. So that *involvement* in the anger is the poison, which is exactly what Sai Baba's words are expressing.

There's a disconnect between daily living and what we think we are doing on the spiritual journey, and this is the most beautiful example of it. Trust Baba to take someone who's immersed in the scriptures and make an example out of him for us. These chapters are there because they speak to us.

What Baba was showing the Ramdasi was that he thought he was beyond attachment. But, in reality, he was attached to a book, that too a book which he knew by heart; a book which a fellow guru bandhu had been given by Baba to read and whom he was blaming unjustly.

And so the Ramdasi is actually us. We get involved in situations where we blame people and condemn them, ranting on and losing sight of what has really happened. This is a lesson for all of us who are reading the Satcharita.

Once again, I marvel at the Satcharita because it picks the perfect examples to show us where we are straying from the path.

N: This is so true. Besides, this particular leela has so many dimensions to it. Baba explains the significance of the Vishnu Sahasranama to Shama and the importance of reading each name [of Vishnu] daily.

And as we all know, every word of Baba's is impregnated with deep meaning. So while reading the pothis, one has to contemplate these leelas to get the most out of them.

G: Yes, most certainly, because we tend to read these as stories, a story every night before sleeping, and then put the book away. And that is why I reiterate, perhaps to the point of boredom, that each story has to impact your daily living and your relationship with the people in your life—family members, friends, strangers, colleagues—whomsoever it may be.

N: Could you give us some specific pointers for our daily living so that we could become more receptive to Baba's teachings?

G: This story is the perfect example. Now are we receptive to this story or is our ghada upside down? If we read it just as a story about the Ramdasi, our ghada is upside down. Whereas, if we realize that Baba is talking to us, then our ghada is upright and open.

It reminds me of a story in which a seeker went to meet a Zen master. After climbing a very high mountain, he finally reached the master's cave. The Zen master offered him some tea to refresh him after his long and arduous journey.

But the student, displaying frustration, told the master, 'I've climbed this mountain. I want the Truth. I've been searching for you for years. I have no time for tea. Don't waste my time.'

Nevertheless, the Zen master poured some tea for him and continued pouring it till it started spilling over the cup and out onto the floor. And then he told the seeker, 'You know, you are already so full of your own concepts, your own searching and seeking. You are just not open. So whatever I pour into you is going to pour out of the cup. It's going to pour out of you because that receptivity is not there.

'Here I am. You've taken me as your master, and I'm offering you tea, but you are so impatient, so impertinent, that you are very clear that it's a waste of your time. That means you know better.'

So, about the ghada being upside down, I think we are all guilty of it in some way.

So let's say you shout at someone, which is understandable; it can happen. But when we get involved in that shouting and make life hell for the other person and ourselves, then our ghada is upside down, you see.

N: So I think awareness would be the key whereby we reflect on our day-to-day life in relation to the leelas we read.

G: Absolutely.

N: Do you have any other pointers that can help accelerate the process of absorption?

G: I feel that anyone who's on this journey is, in a way, receptive, but we are blind to our faults. And the minute we realize we are accusing, blaming or judging others, we need to just pause a bit and ponder, *Hey, what exactly is going on here? Why is this happening?*

So this self-awareness needs to kick in during the day with whomever we come across. I would truly recommend this as a possible practice: If you really want to live Sai Baba's teachings, don't resort to just reading the Satcharita. Look at your relationships. At the end of your working day, think back on whom you encountered and what you spoke to them about. Were you critical? Were you judgemental? This process of reflection will take you very far.

N: One other aspect of the story was the emphasis that Baba laid on discipline and the reading of the pothis as a sadhana. He would reprimand devotees if they swayed from the particular sadhana they had committed to. We see many instances of it throughout the Satcharita.

Recently, a friend of mine mentioned that she reads the Hanuman Chalisa and does Baba's aartis, but sometimes she loses momentum.

So I told her, 'See, it's very nice that you do it, but do you know the meaning of the aartis? Do you know the meaning of the Hanuman Chalisa? There are translations available. If you just take the time to read them and then do your sadhana, you may feel more zealous about it because it will also work as an affirmation.'

A few weeks later, she enthusiastically informed me that it had made a tremendous difference to her sadhana.

G: The point of discipline is a very important one because you used the word 'committed'. How committed are we to the practice? That is the key.

Joel Goldsmith used to say that if you really wanted something and someone told you to meet them at three o'clock to receive that thing, you should ask them to specify whether they meant a.m. or p.m., keeping in mind that that person worked at all sorts of odd hours. You should be willing to go at any time and not at your convenience. You should want it that badly.

But, honestly, many of us have a convenient approach to spiritual matters.

N: This is a beautiful example that you have shared because, in this very chapter [chapter twenty-seven], there is a story about Baba's intimate devotee Megha. He was a shining example of guru bhakti. For him, it didn't matter whether it was a.m. or p.m. He would walk miles just to bring the sacred water to give Baba a bath on a particular day. He is one of the devotees who got the most out of his association with Baba. When he left his body, Baba wept for him.

N: I had a few questions, which I've asked you. If you would be happy to take some more questions today, could some devotees ask you a few?

G: Sure. More than happy.

Questioner #1: I have a doubt that I would like to clarify. Whenever I am confused I go to Baba and I lay chits, with a yes or no, and then whatever He gives me, I take.

This is not only with me; I have seen it with most of the Sai Baba devotees. But those who are not Baba's devotees ask me, 'Why do you want to do that? Why don't you ask for God to give you the strength to help you through whatever you choose? Why do you want to ask Him if it is a yes or a no and be confused again?'

So could you please guide me on this? Am I doing it right or wrong?

G: We all must do exactly that which we think and feel we should do. Yes, we can listen to others, and we can factor in their opinions; that is fine. But for you, if this method of laying chits works, by all means, please use it. You see, some of us are not able to take decisions easily, whereas others are able to do so. We are all made differently.

I too have a very dear friend who's a Sai Baba devotee, and I'm familiar with what you say because he also puts chits when he's confused.

I will tell you something very interesting. I had taken a German lady with her two daughters to a shop in Mumbai. They wanted to buy gifts to take back home. Now the elder daughter was very clear about what she wanted. She ran from shelf to shelf, picked up whatever she wanted, put it in the shopping basket, and her shopping was done.

But the younger daughter was finding it difficult to decide. She would put an item in her basket, have second thoughts and put it back on the shelf. She was getting frustrated, and their mother, seeing this, thought that my time was being wasted. So I told the mother, 'Look, don't worry about me. Your younger daughter is confused. It's her nature. So why don't you go and help her decide?'

So, one daughter could take decisions, but the other daughter could not. We are all made that way. Nobody is to blame for such things. In such situations, if you need a tool, such as the laying of chits, and if it works for you, why not? There's no harm in it at all.

Q #1: I go to Baba and get a 'yes' chit, and I'm still confused. So I don't comply with what the chit says and do exactly the opposite. In that case, it would not make sense, right?

G: Yes. That is because you are looking for a certain outcome to begin with. That is what happens, you see. That is a very big problem.

I've already spoken about this friend of mine who wanted to go to the UK with his son to admit him to college and he kept getting a 'No', the reason for which he could understand only in retrospect. [Refer to talk 33.]

Your second question shows how the ego is trying to push for an outcome that it is not getting. So, you have to be careful about that.

Questioner #2: I've been listening to Rameshji's teachings lately and a question has popped up. It is about 'Thy will be done.' Everything is done by God, and I am not the doer. How can I truly understand the concept of non-doership? Because if something bad happens, I really can't come to terms with it. I ask myself, *How can this happen to me? Why would God want this to happen to me?*

G: These are words from the Bible, which mean, 'Not my will, O Lord, but Yours be done.' Let's explore this.

Whatever we decide to do is based on two factors: our genetics and our conditioning. The parents we were born to, the income group they were born in, the geographical area they were born in, the religion they were born into and so on and so forth.

Now, who created our conditioning? We didn't create it. The environment created it. God created it. It was beyond our control. So, what we think is our decision, deep down, truly depends on factors which are not in our control and which God made.

When you say that I am not the doer of my actions, it means that there's so much vastness: so many factors come together and make me the person I am, and therefore, I am truly not the doer of my actions.

Now, more importantly, I may do what I like, but the results are never in my control, you see. Sometimes, I get what I want, and many times, I don't. Then, in whose control are the results? Once again, the answer is God.

We have to understand what this means in daily living. Supposing someone upsets you—your sibling or your friend—and you understand that this person is coming from their own blueprint, the way God has made them, you accept that they were meant to hurt you. It doesn't mean you become someone people will walk over, but you accept that, okay, this person is acting based on their conditioning, their belief systems, which God created for them.

You don't start finger-pointing, hating, blaming and condemning people like you used to. This understanding is there. So when you put your point of view across to the other person, it is from a position of response and not reaction. That is how the teaching of non-doership percolates into daily living.

I just gave this brief example so that everyone can fully accept that all the people in their life, especially the ones they don't like—the people who push their buttons, who trigger them—are acting out their script based on their destiny. They will be gentler towards them and more compassionate, and they will still express their point of view, but there will be no venom, no spite and no hatred in their words. Their words will have a different vibration when they speak to them.

I'm glad you're exploring this because these are concepts that impact daily living and have the potential to transform your relationships with people.

Questioner #3: We all experience the ebb and flow of life, and it is something very normal. Even our spiritual life is not different in this respect.

So how do we maintain the same level of zeal and enthusiasm in our spiritual life? Because there are days when, although we are connected to Baba, we do not feel like praying with that much reverence or devotion.

G: Could you explain that further? Why are there days when you feel that the zeal is not there?

Q #3: For me, I think it's very natural that there are days when you are so engrossed in your daily life or your work, or something is going on with you, that you do not feel like praying, the way you regularly do or the way you are supposed to pray. You just don't feel like you are *that* connected on those days.

So how do you maintain the same level of enthusiasm in your spiritual life?

G: I would like to put it across to you in a very different way. As the phrase goes, work is worship, right? Now, while being engaged in work, if you are being mindful of how you are with people, how you are with yourself and how dedicated you are to the work you are doing, isn't that also being engaged with Baba's words and teachings?

So remembering Baba does not mean just praying to Him and having the zeal to do so. In whatever action you are performing during the day, if the awareness is there, if the master's grace is upon you and if you are giving your hundred per cent to the people you encounter and the work you are doing, then that is the teaching in action, which is as important as remembering Baba. In fact, I would say it is even more important because then we know that the teaching has translated into daily living.

The zeal you're mentioning doesn't need to refer to a practice; that is just one aspect. But if you started viewing your entire day at work in the light of Baba's teachings, I would say the zeal will be multiplied even more. So don't compartmentalize and separate worship from daily living.

I'll give you an example to illustrate my point. A government official was very hard to deal with in the government office. He was extremely rude and obnoxious, and made life difficult for the people who wanted to meet him. But in the evening, at the Sai Baba temple, during puja time, he went about distributing *prasad* to everyone.

Now this is what I call disconnected living. Being a Sai Baba bhakta, he was enthusiastically offering prasad to everyone. But when it came to following His teachings, such as respecting the people who came to meet you at the office and speaking courteously with them, all that went out of the window.

N: Can I add something here? I was thinking of the role of sadhana in such a case. If one follows the disciplines Baba has shown us, for instance, the reading of the pothis, performing the aartis and meditation—in chapter eighteen, Baba has shown us how to meditate on Him by doing the *Namasmaran*—don't you feel that, if done regularly, these practices could also change one's state of mind and being? See, the mind will get restless and tell you, *Today is a bad day. I'm busy, so I should probably take a holiday from my sadhana.*

But if the discipline and yearning are there, and you still do it, even if it's half-hearted, over time, it is bound to at least weaken these patterns of the mind. Could you shed some light on that, please?

G: Yes. What you are saying happens because of two reasons.

One is that you see that the vibration in the sadhana, whatever it may be, starts permeating your being throughout the day. It's not just restricted to the sadhana time, because it's a vibration which is set in motion and which is ongoing. More importantly, if we have a fixed time every day for the sadhana, the body's biorhythm gets adjusted accordingly, and it will automatically happen. You will notice that at that time, you are more receptive to the sadhana because the timing has been set.

I'll give you a common example connected with meditation.

Supposing you meditate at a fixed hour every day, say 7 a.m. to 7.30 a.m., and one day, you don't meditate because you have to travel for work or you have something else to do. The fact is that, on that day, when you are not meditating at that time, you will find your mind calming down automatically because it has been set; the rhythm has been set.

Hence, there is tremendous benefit in discipline and sadhana because they permeate your daily living. If sadhana is regular and prioritized, it is bound to impact your daily living.

N: Wonderful. Thank you.

Questioner #4: Everyone knows Sai Baba as He is such a common figure. But as a child growing up, I used to only hear about His miracles and the stories about Him.

I'd like to ask, Do you think that these are true? Does reality have a space for this kind of thing, or are they just fables that grew with time? So, how do I approach this seriously, if I want to really go into the teachings and also have an open mind towards all the stories?

G: Sure. That's a nice question you have asked. You'll agree with me that God is all-pervading, all-knowing, all-powerful and all-loving because that is the definition of God. There's nothing excluded from God. Right?

Now, when a representative of God, of that omnipresence, omnipotence and omniscience comes along, in this case, Shirdi Sai Baba, there's nothing that can be beyond His ambit, as He is a representation of the Absolute. There's no doubt that these miracles happened because even a master such as Ramana Maharshi sent His devotees to record Baba's miracles and teachings. He wanted Baba to be known to the Western world.

So, let there be no doubt because, in the realm of Consciousness, anything is possible. It is Infinite Consciousness, so how can anything not be possible?

The point is, you are so right in saying that the focus was on miracles being catalogued because, at that time, Jnana Yoga was less prevalent. The bhakti bhava was more dominant. People were prone to bhakti, especially the simple people.

So Baba used the miracles as examples because they would be set in people's minds; they would be recorded. When you read the Satcharita, of course, you read about the miracles, but then you also try to understand the teachings through the miracles, the Knowledge that they are giving you. That is when your true journey with the Satcharita begins, you see.

So, do not doubt the veracity of the miracles, but do not get lost in them. That is what we do. We get so taken up by the miracles that we want those same miracles in our lives, and we completely miss the point of the lesson.

The reason why we are being told a story is totally missed. I have received so many emails from Baba devotees saying, for example, 'Baba did a miracle in this one's life, but in my life, I have no job, I have no girlfriend. I am waiting for a miracle.'

You see, this is what happens. We just keep waiting for miracles. It is truly a pitfall, which the seeker needs to watch out for.

So, I am glad you brought this up. Study the essence of the stories. What is being pointed at? All this has to be looked into. It is a multi-dimensional teaching, in that sense. This is how you can approach the stories seriously as a sincere and earnest seeker.

To view the corresponding video, scan the QR code.

44

Developing One-Pointed Devotion to Baba

Nikhil: Today, I would like to discuss one-pointed devotion to Baba as well as spiritual life and devotion not being a matter of convenience.

The example of one of Baba's most intimate devotees, Megha, is very inspiring for all of us because he was the very embodiment of one-pointed bhakti towards Baba, and he crossed every threshold of inconvenience to worship his master, whom he regarded as God. And as a result, he got the fruit in the end. When he left his body, Baba wept for him, which speaks volumes about his devotion and his relationship with Baba.

In this regard, yesterday, I had a conversation with Vinny Ma. She shared some details which may not be mentioned in the Sai Satcharita, but I felt everybody might want to know about them.

When Megha would go to collect *bael patra* for Baba, he used to walk about eight kilometres into Kopargaon and back. He would go into the forest, which was dense and full of dacoits. At that time, there were no roads. Out of fear, those who came to Shirdi for Baba's darshan would come together in a group, with *tongas* lined up one behind the other. A single tonga would never go by itself.

That speaks volumes of the dangers that Megha faced. But for his master, with complete one-pointed devotion, he would go without fearing for his life. And this was a regular affair. Flowers and leaves were not easy to get for worship. It was not like how we get them today, where we step out and buy them from the market. Megha had to travel far to get to the forest where he plucked them.

What lessons can we learn from Megha's inspiring life and apply them to our devotional practice? Could you share your views on that?

Gautam: Sure.

How do we bring these lessons into our daily living? I think it's pretty simple. If we make the teachings our focus twenty-four seven—and not just a kind of a half-an-hour practice in the morning of doing a reading or japa chanting and forgetting it the rest of the day—we would be one with Baba's teachings. If we live the teachings, if we reflect upon them in our relationships, that is how we could get close to Baba, isn't it? Because, after all, Baba is His teachings, which we can relate to today.

We live in a very fragmented world with many distractions. We wear various hats: the social media hat, the one we wear at home, at work, and so on. So it's all the more important that we live Megha's example today by our dedication and devotion to Baba's teachings. Because that is what is left with us, you see? That is the main thing which I have been trying to communicate on your channel: live the teachings, breathe the teachings and implement them in your daily activities.

N: That's a very good point you raised about the fragmented personalities one adopts in today's world.

Talking about the devotion and sincerity of Vinny Ma and Pawar Kaka, I'll just share a little story that happened recently.

My editor, Anand, who has been with us for about two or three years, suffered a very deep loss about four months ago. And then we had the Covid pandemic, followed by the lockdown.

I knew Anand was in a very difficult situation, but I told him, 'See, a lockdown is imminent. If you feel it is possible for you to go today to both Vinny Ma and Pawar Kaka, and we can do the shoots, then we will have content to share with the community for the coming months.'

And believe me, he went for the shoots, without any questioning, in the most difficult of times he was going through. I don't think anybody else in his place would have done it; it would not have been easy at all.

And even Vinny Ma, who has a lot of pains and bodily aches at the age of seventy-eight, said yes, despite it not being convenient for her in any way. Pawar Kaka, I believe, had fainted the day before because of the heat. He had gone to Pune and something had happened.

But they were all so committed to Baba, that Baba took priority over everything else. The very next morning, the shoots happened.

I feel they are all shining examples of one-pointed devotion. This was something I was inspired by, and I thought I should share it with the community.

G: Yes, that's beautiful.

N: One aspect that I see is the convenience factor creeping into our sadhana. Could you speak a little about that?

G: See, there are two things here. One is a practice which we may or may not have, such as reading the pothis or whatever it may be. Many people compromise on that by saying, for example, *Oh, I woke up late*, or *I'm on holiday today*. So that is one way of looking at it.

However, I'm focusing more on the teachings in our daily living. That is more important. Whatever comes to me in the course of the day, be it pleasure or pain, how do I handle it? What is my relationship with all the people I come across during the day?

Now, even there, it can be very convenient to forget the teachings. Let's say someone pushes your buttons, and you yell and scream at them and go on a rant; it means the teachings have gone out of the window. But when it suits you, you remember the teachings. That is called convenience.

N: Absolutely.

There is this tendency to shift from one master to another, read books on various teachings and watch multiple YouTube channels, which only creates confusion in the mind of the seeker.

Could you talk about that also, please?

G: Well, you see, it is a natural process. We begin by exploring and wanting to absorb what's out there. That is all fine.

However, the confusion arises when we continue doing it for a long time because then we don't really know what it is we are looking for. We keep jumping from one master to another and from one video to another.

So while it is good in the initial phase, because we get a sense of what appeals to us, in the long run, we cannot ride two horses; we can ride only one.

Nisargadatta Maharaj said that we will get water, not by digging shallow wells all over the land but by digging one deep well. [Refer to talk 4.] But in our impatience and, perhaps, in our unconscious greed to consume and absorb more, even if it be knowledge, we dig shallow wells all over the place, losing interest very fast. Our attention span doesn't last, and then we miss out on getting the water because we don't dig deep enough.

N: For this, we certainly need our ghada upright and not upside down. [Laughter.]

One last question on this. Supposing one has spent many years in that initial phase, and now they wish to settle for one master; for instance, they realize that Baba is where they find their peace. So what could accelerate that process, or what would be the beginning steps to deepen the experience of being on that path?

G: You have to stay with it, you see. If you hold on to one thing, or let's say, one support, through all the vicissitudes of life, then you're going to be more stable. But if you keep grasping for other supports based on whims and fancies and convenience, you're going to be going from one support to another at the risk of drowning.

It's as simple as that.

N: I was exposed to many teachings in my younger days, and what helped me in difficult times was one particular teaching, which became a filter through which I was looking at life. And that cemented it for me.

G: Yeah, that's a good point.

I wanted to add one more thing. Megha's devotion to Baba is of great importance. See, devotion comes from the heart, right? And that is why Baba wept when Megha passed on, as it touched His heart.

Similarly, I think we all know what touches our heart the most. So this becomes a good measure of knowing what is important for each of us—a thing, a message or a person that has touched us. And that which touches your heart is worth holding on to, in my opinion.

N: Absolutely. When you stick to that thing for a prolonged period, you experience peace and joy. So could this experience be a good yardstick?

G: Yes, in fact, that is the only measure, and that is why it has touched your heart because, deep down, all human beings know that what they want most in life is true happiness; not happiness, but true happiness. And true happiness is happiness which does not depend on pleasure because pleasures come and go.

Happiness is nothing but peace of mind. So if something has touched your heart, you need to understand that it is so because it has brought you peace.

N: Thank you so much for this. Now, would you like to take a few questions from the community?

G: Sure. I'd love to.

Questioner #1: My question is about Prarabdha and Advaita. In the chapter concerning Pundalikrao, Baba tells him not to take the guilt upon himself as the coconut was broken due to His wish. However, in many other places in the Satcharita, Baba talks about Prarabdha. So, how do you reconcile the two? Because the very basis of Prarabdha is that you are doing something and reaping the result thereof in your next life or sometime later.

G: Well, to start with, you have to keep in mind that everything is said in context. It wouldn't be appropriate to pull something out of a chapter and apply it to all situations.

The fact is that you are here because of Prarabdha. And Prarabdha Karma is that which has to be faced. However, if Prarabdha needs to be tempered, the grace of the Sadguru comes into the picture.

Now, how does this question help your peace of mind in daily living? Why do you feel you would get more peace if you understood this? Could you elaborate on that?

Q #1: So, how do I get Prarabdha if I am not the doer?

G: That is your understanding now. When the karma, the action, happened, did you have this understanding at that time?

Q #1: No. So after the understanding, there is no Prarabdha?

G: After the understanding, the Prarabdha will continue because you are in the form of the body. Although the understanding may be there, the Prarabdha, which is an accumulation from the past, still has to get exhausted in this life, you see.

More importantly, you are not creating fresh karma based on doership. When you live with the understanding that nobody is the doer of their actions—the Satcharita and even the Bhagavad Gita stress this point—and when you see that every individual you encounter is playing their role based on the script, which is their genetics and their conditioning, you stop blaming, accusing and condemning the people you meet. And when that happens, you are not creating fresh karma, because you are out of this loop of finger-pointing and accusing people. You are out of the unconscious action-reaction loop in the sense that karma is pure action and not 'my action' or 'the other's action'.

That is what happens when you understand the concept of non-doership. The whole dynamic of the relationship changes. That's the beauty of it. Thus karma becomes pure action and not 'my action' or 'your action'. Nobody is the doer; God, the Source, is the original doer.

Questioner #2: Regarding your comment about following one guru and one teaching, I am a Gemini and I tend to drift away from one thing to the other. I follow multiple gurus, such as Sai Baba and Ramana Maharshi.

I do all the yoga practices taught at a foundation run by a certain guru, but I have difficulty surrendering completely to him when I see some videos, about which my mind judges. So I feel I am definitely not behaving the way a disciple should.

DEVELOPING ONE-POINTED DEVOTION TO BABA

When I watch Sai Baba's serial, I end up in tears, seeing Baba's compassion, and I feel that Baba is my guru.

So how can I come to terms with this nature of mine? I know it is not good, but I find it difficult to sort it out.

G: As you rightly pointed out, being a Gemini, you have this tendency. So it is clearly something not in your control.

Now, see, the word 'follow' means different things. You could still know where you belong and absorb different things from different masters. In my case, I was going to my teacher Ramesh Balsekar for nine years, and during that period, I met so many masters, so many yogis, so many psychics. I met all kinds of people; I enjoyed it, and I got something from everybody.

But, at the end of the day, I knew that I would always go back to my guide's living room where he used to give satsang, because that is where I found peace of mind.

Now, you see, that could be missing from your life. You may do practices which you benefit from, or maybe some things spoken by certain people appeal to you, but you must identify for yourself where you belong. And if you don't have that answer, it's nothing to feel bad about. Keep asking this question, and the answer will unfold.

But without knowing that—as I pointed out earlier—you could be going all over the place endlessly, and that does not have much benefit in the long run.

So it's all right to do a yogic practice, but which is that one pillar, which you feel is your support? That needs to be identified, if not now, then at some point in your journey.

I remember about ten years ago, I gave a talk in Poona, and a gentleman who was perhaps in his late fifties, was in the same boat. [Refer to talk 4.] He told me, 'I've done Reiki, Pranic Healing, past life regression, Kriya Yoga; I've done this workshop, that workshop. So now, what do I do next?'

And I replied, 'But have you asked yourself, *What is it that I'm looking for by doing all these practices?*'

He said, 'No, I never asked that.'

I said, 'That is why you'll keep doing various things.'

LIVING WITH FAITH AND PATIENCE

He was taken aback because, up till then, nobody had told him what I told him. And he was so grateful, because he said, 'Now, at least I know that before I enrol for the next course, I have to ask myself what I am looking for.'

I told him, 'See, there are two possibilities. One is that you have already found it, but didn't know you found it, because you were unaware of what it is you were looking for.

'Let's say you were looking for peace of mind. You met twenty different teachers. Think about them, choose the one who makes you feel, *My God, actually, this is what has appealed to me the most*, and go back there.

'Or since you've still not hit the target, so to speak, continue looking, but now you have a reason to look, and you'll get the answer. It's as simple as that. Okay?'

N: Wonderful.

There is something I wish to add here. After spending some time with your master and the teachings, you develop a bhava for them: you tend to have a relationship where a feeling of caring arises naturally. I think the flowering of this relationship is also a very important sign that you are on the right path.

G: Yes. You are unconsciously thinking of the master all the time; in your mind, you say, for example, *Oh, what would he have said about this?* because he has become part of your consciousness. That again is a good sign.

N: With the Sai Satcharita and the work that is happening, I feel that, whether you know it or not, it will become the filter through which you will look at life. I mean, it goes so deep within.

G: Exactly.

N: We see these shining examples in the Satcharita, like that of Megha. Could you speak on how we can emulate them to turn our life around?

G: We can choose anyone in our life to inspire us. Or anything where we can give selflessly, where there's no personal interest involved. Seva is very important because the whole secret of this is that when you give of yourself selflessly, whether it is your money or time, the ego is getting diminished as it is not getting any tangible benefit. It doesn't enhance the ego, because the ego is in the giving mode.

Usually, the ego demands from the Universe; it wants to receive all the time. However, seva turns the focus away from the little me and onto something else, whatever it may be, and that is a very important part of the spiritual journey.

So Megha's example of selfless giving entailed walking eight kilometres and all the other things he did to serve his master. We need not walk eight kilometres, but we can see for ourselves where we can give selfless service.

This attitude of giving—selfless giving—is what we can get from the Megha story.

To view the corresponding video, scan the QR code.

45

Penetrating the Veil of Maya

Nikhil: These days, although we are physically far away from each other, technology is bringing us together virtually. Ironically, the topic for today is maya, and I'm going to discuss a few things with you about the changes that have taken place in the world, such as artificial intelligence [AI], and how they correlate to Baba's devotees in particular.

So, with AI rapidly gaining dominance, it's going to be very difficult to differentiate between truth and untruth. There are technologies with the help of which one can, for example, literally clone your voice. One will not be able to tell whether it's you or an AI-generated voice.

Now coming to Sai Baba, He said, 'If you forget Me, maya will lash you.'

Also, there was a video we had put up, 'The Kali Yuga Has Begun Accelerating Its Pace', in which Dharamdas Baba says, 'Kali Yuga has come out of the cradle, and it has jumped and caught people by the neck.' These were his words.

With social media quickening its pace, can you put this quote as well as what Baba said about maya lashing you, into perspective for devotees?

Gautam: I think we need to broaden the scope of Baba's statement a bit so that it becomes simpler to understand. When Baba is saying 'Me', He is referring to Source Consciousness, the Totality, and not just Himself as an individual. It's a very important statement because maya is the divine hypnosis, where you could say we are lost in the illusion of separation, the illusion of fragmentation and the illusion of me and the other. So Baba's statement has to be seen in this light. He is not asking you to remember Him as an individual all the time but as the Godhead, the Source, and see maya for what it is. Because, if you don't, it will lash you, in the sense that you will be mired in it; you will be going into quicksand and sinking in it.

You mentioned social media. Let's say you are projecting an image of yourself on any of the social media platforms and you want appreciation for it. For example, I have friends who, when they are travelling abroad, post pictures saying that they are at so-and-so international airport or that they are dining in Switzerland. They will not post a picture of themselves at Jabalpur airport or something, you see. Now this is not a judgement. My point is that we try to project the best version of ourselves in the virtual world so that we are liked and appreciated. In the process, our sense of self gets enhanced.

So this is maya operating through social media where you could get lost in this projection. That is the context which I have to place before the listeners.

Another factor is the most recent development of AI.

I will give you a case in point where I requested someone to help me with a certain paragraph in a new book I'm writing. So it required some research, a fair degree of research—visiting two or three websites. Now, what came back was, no doubt, comprehensive, but I had a feeling that it was not a unique voice. It was not something which had labour or extensive research behind it. And I found that it was generated by ChatGPT.

So I concluded that the person helping me on this task took the easy approach, fed in my requirement into artificial intelligence and got an output. So what has happened in this case? The individual *buddhi* [wisdom] and the individual effort got compromised in the process. Though detailed, the information was so general, that I realized this voice was not authentic.

But this is just one side of technology. The flip side is that these social media platforms and AI are helpful also. I know people who are not good at drafting emails and therefore use ChatGPT to do so. Their clients get very impressed, little knowing that these emails are not drafted by the person who sent them.

So you see, technology is a double-edged sword because, while it can help, it is also maya. While we can use it so that we stay in the background and don't have to put in much effort, we can also get overtaken by it or get mired in it.

And once again, 'Maya will lash you' means that you will be so lost in this maya which is coming, that you won't be able to find yourself.

N: Now, when you say, 'find yourself', you know what I'm going to ask you next. [Laughs.]

G: Yes.

N: So please speak a bit about that.

G: Who are we without our identifications and projections?

Once again, I belabour the point that Baba's teachings are so simple that they get missed. They are pointing to a way of being in daily living. But we are so much into projecting and wearing a mask all the time that with social media and AI, we are now getting more and more opportunities to display various masks.

Our true Self is pure Presence, the simplicity of Being, without becoming something in the other's eyes, something grander than ourselves. But we are trying to put on this whole show instead of being just pure and simple, and resting in our innate nature, which is not separate from the other. In essence, we all are the same, and the fundamental teachings are always there for us.

But the point is, Which of us will have this awareness when we are dealing with the world today?

I repeat, Sai Baba's teachings are very subtle. It's not about reading one story in the Satcharita, closing the book and going to sleep. The simplicity of these stories, their essence—you could call it a way of dealing with people and situations, with equanimity and calmness—shows us how to abide in our Self. Pointers towards this end have been given to us in the Satcharita.

I think you've struck a very appropriate note because maya is coming headlong at us, in a sense. What we have today was not there ten years ago. There was no social media.

Imagine if, in Baba's time, there was all this video filming and everything. We would have a beautiful record of Baba's life. So that is the value of the resources available to us.

The point is, Is humankind going to abuse this privilege, this basic gift of communication which has come our way? Is it going to turn through distortion and identification into something which makes us who we are not?

N: Yes, there are two sides to this coin.

Also, I feel this is a great opportunity because what we conceptually knew as maya earlier is in our face now, and it's only going to get worse. The sages have said that everything is ever-changing; it is transient.

So if we see it in the light of these teachings, it's also an opportunity, right? Could you speak a little on that, please?

G: Sure.

This opportunity most likely gets missed. It's an opportunity only for the person who is aware that they are dealing with an illusion, which is amplified in this day and age. It's like a test; you know, how the masters test us all the time. Are we getting lost in something, or are we holding our space and our presence? So you can't say that the opportunity is for everyone. It depends on how immersed one is in their master's teachings.

Once again, I would like to clarify that it is not about remembering Sai Baba in the morning for an hour or doing japa and then being entangled in everything else for the rest of your day. Awareness has to be practised throughout the day in whatever you are dealing with, in the work you are involved in. You need to have the awareness that you are dealing with this manifest world, to what extent you are identified with it and how much you are witnessing it as Being and Presence.

Even the Gita advises us to be a witness and not get sucked into all the drama. And there's so much drama today. Consider the way the news and media are geared: all the sound and visuals are created to entrap you into the drama of life, which, coming back to our topic, is maya.

So awareness of the master's teachings and living the teachings is what can take you through this haze called maya.

N: So sincerity, here, is a virtue to cultivate because, sometimes, life could become overwhelming. On one hand, you may have so many things coming together, such as a health crisis or a financial crisis, and on the other, you have all this social media stuff going on. Besides, it would not be an exaggeration to say that our society is disintegrating, and by that I mean relationships between people. So while we have technology and it's easier to communicate, there is a major difference in the depth of bonds today, compared to what they were a hundred years ago when Baba was there.

G: Absolutely. And that is because we've distanced ourselves due to technology also. Earlier, the relationships were more humane. It was more about being there for each other.

I'll give you an example of a friend who migrated to London and fell ill there. When she informed her friends circle there about her condition, they said, 'Oh, that's very sad to hear. Get well soon and call us when you're back on your feet, and we can catch up for a meal.' This shook her up. She said that if she were to fall ill in Mumbai, three of her friends would come running to her house to help her out, bring food, or simply be with her.

Now, because we are so lost in our individual worlds, that quality of being there for one another and offering one's time has evaporated because too much is going on.

N: One important pillar of Baba's teachings is seva because that puts the attention on giving and caring. And they say charity begins at home, so, in that sense, there is no excuse for not offering service.

As *sadhaks* and as Baba's devotees, I feel this also is something to deeply reflect on as this is something Baba has shown us, examples of which the Satcharita is peppered with. One may say that what is happening today is the 'new normal', but this normalization is not okay. If we are Baba's devotees and are committed to Baba, regardless of how the world is, would it be valid to say that seva is a prerequisite?

G: Yes, and you specifically mentioned charity. With charity, a very beautiful thing happens, which gets missed. We feel we are giving something to the other without expecting anything in return. That is the broad definition of charity. But what is actually happening is that the focus is no longer on the me; it is being turned around and placed on the other.

All through the day, all my life, I'm obsessed with myself, right? About who I am, how I look and how people perceive me. But giving is such a great gift because it's shifting this obsession with the self onto the other in a selfless way because I know I am giving where that person, at the most, can only appreciate me. They do not have the resources to return the favour. That's why I'm giving whatever it is, in the first place.

When we do charity, we think we are doing a favour to others, but, in fact, we are the ones who are being favoured. It's a process of being 'un-selfed', whereas today, with technology and all these platforms, we are enhancing our sense of self and our image.

Yes, sincerity is important. However, one more word I would like to add is 'earnestness'.

N: Yes.

G: Nisargadatta Maharaj said that earnestness is the key. A master knows which devotees are being earnest, and that is a very undermined quality.

N: The next factor, if I may add, would be discernment, because in the context of maya specifically, one can learn how to discern. In the Satcharita, there are certain pointers given on discerning between what is right and wrong.

So could you speak on discernment?

G: Yes.
The one who is lost in maya will not be able to discern.

N: I would like to believe that the people on our channel are people who are interested in the implementation of the teachings and going forward on the path. It's not just about the miracles. Baba would expect us to be discerning; to be aware and alert.

G: Yes, I would say discernment can go a very long way.

If one is aware at each moment of the day as to what they are saying or doing, that is also discernment. For example, *Am I saying something superfluous? Am I projecting an image just to impress someone? Or am I being myself, my authentic self, without this need of approval?* So discernment comes in such subtle ways.

Another example. Let's say you meet a friend from school or college after a long time. You enjoy meeting your friend, but beyond a point, there's nothing to talk about because you are on your spiritual journey, and your friend is still reminiscing about the good old days and mundane things which don't interest you.

Now where's the discernment in this case? *Is it worth my time, my effort, to spend time in this relationship? Or would I rather be enriched by a different kind of relationship where I am on the same wavelength as the person I'm meeting?*

So in this case, what do I do? I meet my school friend, by all means, to honour our friendship, but I may not meet him as regularly as before. So I have to discern because my time is precious. Where am I being enriched at the soul level? At a level of feeling, at a level of Beingness, where can I contribute my time, and where can I save my time from being consumed by that which is not serving me in any way?

This is how discernment pervades one's daily living in different ways.

N: That's a very important phrase you've shared—'pervading daily living'.

One of the practices Baba made His devotees do was the spiritual practice of reading, or the parayana, of certain books, such as the Vishnu Sahasranama. The Hanuman Chalisa was also dear to Baba, and I found one verse in it, which I felt if one contemplates, there's much to learn and implement in our lives.

There was this incident in the life of Hanumanji, where He was given the responsibility of guarding Lord Ram and Lakshman, who were in a cave. Ravan had evil intentions, and Vibhishana had found out about this. Vibhishana even told Hanumanji that two demons who have been commissioned by Ravan have this power whereby they can take any form they wish. So He was not to let anybody in, whomsoever it may be, because it could be these demons in disguise.

Remaining true to His word, many people came but Hanumanji did not allow them to meet Lord Ram and Lakshman.

It was decided that Vibhishana would take a circle around the mountain, while Hanumanji would be at the entrance to the cave and not move. So a little later, after they had their interaction, Vibhishana told Hanumanji that he wanted to go in and check on their wellbeing. And Hanumanji let him pass.

After a few minutes, Vibhishana again reached the cave and asked what was going on. Hanumanji immediately realized that the demons, having taken the form of Vibhishana, had entered the cave.

So the takeaway from this story is that discernment is not easy. I feel that if one takes to heart Baba's teachings and ponders on them, it's not that easy.

G: Not at all. As I said, it's not about reading a story and keeping the book aside. It's about applying the lesson in daily living.

Sincerity, earnestness and discernment—these are our safeguards against the lashings of maya.

N: Over the last few years, I've seen a major change. The amount of content coming out is more like an avalanche, and it's not just in the Baba community but everywhere else too. In such a scenario, people can say anything they want. So how does one distinguish between what is right and wrong?

Another topic I would like us to talk about is the difference between charisma and one's character. This is something I observed while I was editing the videos of Vinny Ma and Pawar Kaka, which are on Baba's param bhaktas and their lives, their devotion, their character, the faith they had and how they would present themselves in front of Baba. There is a stark difference between them and some of the examples we see online now. It's very charismatic today.

G: Yes, this is an important point, and we will have to delve into some details here, but before that, I would like to just close the previous point. Too much content out there, as you rightly mentioned.

I have people coming to me who watch YouTube videos of many teachers. So I say to them, 'Look, that's all fine when you are in the realm of exploration, but when you're doing that, ask yourself, *What am I looking for?*

I believe everyone's looking for Sukh-Shanti, peace of mind, as my spiritual guide would say. So then, review those channels, videos or teachers you've seen, pick one you feel you are getting some satisfaction from—one with which you feel comfortable and at peace—and then dig deeper into it. This is also my suggestion for those who are watching this channel. I do feel your channel has delved into all aspects of Baba's. There's the leelas, or chamatkars, there's the *gyan* and then there's the bhakti. It's a very holistic channel.

I'm not saying this to promote your channel. All I'm trying to convey to the listener is to reach one place and then dig deeper because you will find that it may appear simple, but there's always the hand of the teachings behind every incident in your life. Something will come to support you. And that is grace. Sainath's grace, for example.

So I just wanted to close on the previous topic that there is too much out there and there's going to be more and more, but do ask yourself, *What is in it for me?* And you will find that whatever takes you deep within yourself, through inquiry and contemplation, is really what is meant for you.

N: To add to this, Baba has said that if you read too many books, you'll only get confused. Now the same applies in today's context with the surplus of content available online.

Maybe in a subsequent podcast, we can speak about the practices that Baba advocated and their implementation. Baba made a very important point in the Gyaneshwari, and I love it because the whole essence of the teachings is right over there. In the Gyaneshwari, Baba says that it's very important for the human soul to know what the purpose of life is. If you ask for *moksha*, you will be given it. If you ask for life, you will be given it. If you ask for death, you will be given death. Though it may not happen instantly.

I don't want to leave the listeners on a gloomy note because it could be depressing to hear about maya. Obviously, technology is going to grow leaps and bounds, but at the same time, I feel it's a great opportunity to awaken. It's a great opportunity because the teachings are available; you can put them into practice when difficult situations arise.

If you have faith in Baba and are focused on your practices, you can always stand up again and keep persevering. As Baba says, shraddha and saburi, but I feel many people see saburi as only patience, but it's also perseverance.

G: Yes, you're right. It's not all doom and gloom. That's only true if we get sucked into maya, as Baba warned.

But when we meet every new challenge with the grace and support of Totality, God, Consciousness, Source, Sai Baba, then, as my teacher would say, why would you consider your glass half-empty and not half-full? If God has brought you this far, why do you feel He will drop you here?

So yes, you're right, we don't want to be pessimistic. We are saying that if we are truly following the master's words of wisdom and his actions, with bhava and bhakti, then we will be navigating our boat through the waters of life in a very efficient manner.

To view the corresponding video, scan the QR code.

46

What Can We Learn from the Param Bhaktas?

Nikhil: Continuing from the earlier podcast, I would like to discuss the terms 'character' and 'charisma', and the difference between the two from the perspective of Baba's devotees, especially in the light of the param bhaktas. As I said earlier, when I was doing the edits of Vinny Ma's and Pawar Kaka's videos, where they pay tribute to the param bhaktas, it was very clear to me they were people of very deep character. Could you say something about this?

Gautam: Regarding our talk about social media earlier, it is the first time that this platform is available. Earlier, it was very difficult to come on television. You either had to be part of a series or in the news for some reason. But now we can put up whatever we feel like, let's say, a video on a channel on YouTube.

So there's a lot of projection now. This has its pluses and minuses because people can either benefit from a platform, such as this one, or they can get taken in or impressed by the projected image.

I'm reminded of the time I met a psychotherapist friend of mine, around tea time in the evening. He was wearing a very colourful shirt and after commenting on the shirt, I asked him if he was coming from work. He replied in the negative and explained that he would not wear this shirt to work because he doesn't want to project anything when he is meeting his patients. Hence, he does not wear anything attention-grabbing.

Now what struck me was that my teacher said something very similar. He used to give satsangs in his living room wearing a simple white *kurta-pyjama*. When someone asked him the reason for his choice of attire, he replied that people were coming for the teachings and not for him, so he didn't want any projection. He used the same words as the psychotherapist did, you see, which brings us to this topic of character and charisma.

According to me, character rests on two factors—simplicity and humility. And when I say character, I mean the refined qualities in a person. If you find that these qualities are present in someone whom you are interacting with, then, to my understanding, that person possesses character.

Now someone with character can also be charismatic. However, that charisma is not dependent on projection. So, I could be simple, but the way I speak, the things I say and my actions make me charismatic, although I'm not doing anything deliberately to be so. That's a very important point because someone simple and humble may also be charismatic. However, that charisma is pure charisma. It is not dependent on an outward appearance.

In Baba's time, as you were mentioning, wouldn't you say that His devotees were the epitome of humility and simplicity?

N: Some of the great devotees, such as Khapardeji and Buttiji were so humble and respectful towards Baba that they would only look at Baba's feet. The way they would present themselves in front of Baba would also reflect what was inside them.

G: Absolutely.

And that is again a very important point. If you knew deep down that you were presenting yourself before God, before a representation of God, or the Source, or Totality, only reverence would arise; there would be no room for anything else. The attitude would be one of looking down reverentially. It would be natural.

But we tend to lose sight of these very basic things. That is why I feel that, in those days, because life and people were so simple, it was perhaps easier to be like that.

Regarding our earlier talk about the lashing of maya, today, there's so much to look out for, which the people didn't have to do back then in Baba's time. Of course, they had to, to a certain extent but not to the degree we have to.

N: One important difference I see between character and charisma is that the latter often needs validation from the outside. On the other hand, even if you leave someone with character, on an island, it will make no difference because they are established in themselves.

Take the example of Kaka Dixit. Baba told him not to leave his wada for nine months. It says a lot about Kaka Dixit's spiritual ripeness. He was the epitome of an ideal sadhak.

When you hear of the great devotees, not just Baba's but others too, you realize that devotion was a very private thing. It was not put out there for others to see.

This takes me to the next topic that I would like to bring up.

In the earlier years, the leelas were shared by devotees out of compassion for others to come to know about Baba. So there was certainly a need for it. But I also feel sometimes that now what is happening is that the experiences are happening by Baba's grace; they are not really brought about by the devotee themselves. So this blowing-one's-own-trumpet syndrome, which some people indulge in, could you talk a bit about that? I'm only saying it so that we can become more self-aware. It might happen to us as well, who knows?

G: Sure.

In connection with doing charity, the Mother of Pondicherry said that charity is best done when it is done without any exposure. To give an example to the contrary, you want to name the wing of a hospital after yourself because you're donating money to it. Giving such examples, she said that when we are looking for name and fame by doing charity, then it is not charity.

You want to project an image; you want to show everyone how charitable you are. The ego has walked in through the back door. You are doing a good deed, no doubt, but you want attention for doing it.

Whereas when you do charity quietly, without any tamasha, then it's honourable and respectful because you're doing it simply for the joy of helping others with your money. There is no identification in that act.

Now coming back to technology, social media and all that, we can show others what we are doing. So when we are being charitable, we announce it to the world to derive our sense of self from it. In that case, are we using the technology we have today to enhance the ego with its projection and drama? Or are we using it constructively to reach out to the masses to influence them positively, instead of using it to boost our identity?

N: If you're doing some charitable deed, one thing you must ask yourself is, *What if I were at the receiving end? Would I like to be photographed?* You need to be sensitive. It's nice that you're doing something charitable, but does it need to be recorded and shared?

G: Yes, you are quite right; nobody asks. I've seen many videos where good-hearted people are doing charity on the streets and filming themselves doing it. I doubt that these people must have asked those they were helping if they were okay with being filmed. This point which you have raised is noteworthy.

N: There is a family I'm very close to in Goa, who are devotees of Lord Dattatreya. A temple was built about eighty years ago through their grandfather's efforts. One of the younger members of the family told me that this happened many years ago, but this old gentleman has never mentioned it to anyone. His name is not connected with the temple, and he never speaks about it. And when you see this old gentleman, he is very humble, very much like Aai.

I feel that sharing such examples would serve as reminders for living humbly because, unfortunately, there's a tendency to normalize immodest behaviour. Our society is rewarding such trumpet-blowing; social media even monetizes it.

I came across a story of some rich guy who was robbed. The village panchayat, when they found the robber, said, 'Fine, we will punish him. But you are equally responsible because you created the temptation.'

G: Yes.

N: I feel the prevailing system is encouraging unconscious behaviour. And then we wonder, *Why did it happen?* Through podcasts like this, if people begin to even reflect on such behaviour, maybe it can make them more aware, and as a result, help them make better choices.

G: To carry on in the spirit of the last podcast, the words used were 'earnestness' and 'sincerity'. I think these go a very long way because, where devotion to someone like Sai Baba is concerned, it is our actions that speak louder than words. We should reflect on how we behave with people in today's environment, how we project onto social media and how we get sucked into this dream of projection, and whether we are maintaining our simplicity and humility while doing so.

This kind of cross-checking, I think, really helps. At the end of the day, take five or ten minutes to review your day—how it went, whom you met, what you spoke about—and just ask yourself, *When was I at peace? When was I not at peace? Was I saying something I didn't believe in just to impress the other person?*

Because, in the final analysis, it all comes down to peace of mind for myself and others. If I am following my master's teachings perfectly, then it does follow that I would be at peace, and more importantly, I would try my best not to take away another person's peace.

We do a very good job of taking away other people's peace but we don't realize it. We say something, knowing that it hurts them or upsets them; we pass judgement or condemn them. It's important to remember that we should not take away someone else's peace—at least not intentionally.

So to wrap up this topic of charisma and character, if the signs of character are humility and simplicity, then it does follow that one would be at peace in daily living.

N: It is said that when one is absorbed in the master's teachings and the contemplation and remembrance of their master, they imbibe the qualities of their master.

We see devotees like Aai, who is very simple in her ways, very honest, very much like Baba. And these qualities have been visible even in the most difficult of times that she has gone through, as is evident from certain stories we've mentioned in the book, *Sai Baba and Aai*. So it runs deep. I feel you become like your master.

G: I would like to mention two things here.

One, you used the example of Aai, which is very apt. She is someone who couldn't care whether you filmed her or not for YouTube, you see. [Laughs.] On the other hand, people might say that Nikhil and Gautam are trying to project something through this channel about who they are and all that, but when we are in this space, we have to be open to criticism as well as compliments. Coming back to the example of Aai, it is exactly what I was trying to point out—simplicity and humility.

The second thing is that you touched upon a very beautiful point as part of your closing statement. When you follow your master's teachings, you become like the master.

Do you know, I read in some book years ago that someone who is immersed in their master's teachings even starts looking like the master? And this is beyond gender. I could have a male master, let's say, Sai Baba, and I could be a woman.

But that certain quality . . . it's not just the physical. We are looking at the physical, but we have other subtle layers and those get imbibed.

Now you might laugh at this, but this is true: owners of dogs can start looking like their dogs, and vice versa. Don't take this literally, but you do see these qualities.

I'll tell you something quite funny. When I had my home in Goa, a couple came over with their dog. Now, you know, a dog's nature is to run into each room, sniff around, and come back. You'll be surprised to know that the boy also went into each room as soon as he walked in, unaware. Unaware, you see. The dog went into one room, while he went into another. The person or the being we are around the most imprints us the most. We automatically go into that dimension.

And so this is true of anyone with any master, be it Sai Baba, Ramana Maharshi or Ramakrishna Paramahansa. When we are immersed in their remembrance and their teachings, we take on their qualities.

N: Even Ayurveda says that you become what you eat. What did Swami Vivekananda say? 'Show me a person's company and what he eats, and I'll tell you everything about him.'

G: Yes.

N: While we have so much exposure to media, it would do well to become more mindful about it. That is why I realize more and more the importance of Baba's emphasis on the parayana of the scriptures without distraction; the mind gets absorbed in it and picks up those qualities.

G: Yes, and that is one aspect.

Furthermore, if you also remember that everyone you encounter today, especially the people who trigger you, are also created by the same Source that created you, then again, that moulds your daily living in a different way.

So that immersion comes into daily living through reading the Satcharita and the scriptures, as you said, and also through your experiences during the day. *That* is immersion.

N: Also, you mentioned an incident where somebody met you and told you that they've watched all your videos, and also which is their favourite miracle among the ones you shared. So there was a disconnect happening here. Could you talk a bit about that incident and that phenomenon in general?

G: Well, as you know, I have only been speaking about living the teachings because, for me, that is the greatest miracle. The miracle is peace of mind, equanimity and calm.

Now, because we tend to love chamatkars, what may have happened is that this person may have watched other speakers on the channel and got enamoured. We get taken up with all the miracles people experience with Baba even today. People have visions of Baba and all that, but that's not what I speak about.

However, since that was such an overriding emotion and thought in that person's mind, he felt that I too was talking about miracles. Because, for him, that was what was appealing—not peace of mind in daily living.

So I had to correct this person and tell him, 'Thank you for complimenting me, but maybe you've mistaken me for someone else because I am just trying to bring down Baba's teachings to daily living; I'm not talking about miracles.'

The person got a bit flustered; maybe he realized there was a mistake.

If a person wants to be immersed in miracles, there's nothing wrong with that. But here, perhaps, the person was so enamoured with the miracles that he could not comprehend that the person he was listening to—me—does not speak about them.

In his case, the message of living Baba's teachings, which are simple and pragmatic, did not quite sink in. My endeavour on your channel is to share the teachings so that they impact daily living.

As you rightly said, we have to be careful about the content of our consciousness all the time. We have mentioned before that by seeing twenty different channels on YouTube every day, we are digging many shallow wells and not one deep well.

So being immersed in the teachings and putting them into practice is what would pull us out of this living dream of life.

N: I would also like to speak about responsibility. When I look back, I see that it is because of the deeds of these great devotees in the past that Baba's history was recorded and shared, and later on, through the efforts of the next generation, namely, Narasimha Swamiji and, thereafter, Vinny Ma. All by Baba's grace, of course, but the fact is that they took the responsibility to share all this in such a beautiful way.

I also feel that what we do collectively today is going to influence the next generation. Many people don't even know, to date, about which version of the Satcharita to read. Maybe we should do a podcast on that because that was, interestingly, the first topic I discussed with Vinny Ma when I met her. So we have the abridged version and then the complete version, which is a word-for-word translation having all of Baba's words and teachings. In many cases, people read the smaller book, in which case, the teachings are missed. Of course, it has its role to play in the propagation of Baba's life story, but the teachings are not given their due worth.

G: Yes.

N: Great people like Narasimha Swamiji, Vinny Ma, and the devotees who set up the Sansthan, such as Kaka Dixit, were people of such high character that I have no words to describe them.

G: And hard-working. Hard-working, to do all that they did!

In this age, we are lost in our own lives. There's so much distraction, so much coming at us from so many different directions; our attention is fragmented.

You know, it's a very common sight: you go to a restaurant and everyone's on their mobile phones, instead of talking to each other. That fragmentation is immense, and the hard work that was put in by the previous generations, or let's say, even recently by someone like Vinny Ma, is becoming even tougher today because of fragmentation.

So I can hear your call to go back to that—to put in one's time responsibly through hard work, dedication and devotion. To wrap this up, it's again, to not get sucked into maya.

It is written in our scriptures also, that to keep the company of saints is of tremendous merit. How do we keep the company of saints? It doesn't mean only physical company. It means being immersed in their teachings, reading the scriptures, if one is inclined to do so, and reflecting upon them during the day. *That* is keeping the company of saints. Then one is really living a life of dedication and devotion.

To view the corresponding video, scan the QR code.

47

Getting Closer to God

Nikhil: On this auspicious day of Guru Purnima, we will be discussing the topic 'What steps are you taking towards God?' But first, I would like to share a little background about how it came up.

A few days ago, a friend introduced me to a very beautiful temple and a trust of Baba's in Bangalore. As you enter the temple, you see some inspiring quotations of Baba's, which are very much what He has said in the Satcharita. One of them said that if you take one step towards God, God takes ten steps towards you. So I felt it was a beautiful saying, around which we could have a discussion.

Gautam: Of course, it would be a nice topic to discuss.

N: I believe even Ramakrishna Dev said the same thing using different words. This speaks for the effort made by the devotee to get closer to God. It could begin with a sincere yearning followed by practice.

G: Yes.

We take a step towards God because we want certain things. I don't think that is the step being referred to in Baba's quotation. What is being referred to is the acceptance of the will of a Higher Power, of the Source, which we call God.

When we take a step toward God in that sense, with an attitude of acceptance and surrender, then this quotation, that if you take one step towards God, He will take ten steps towards you, comes into play.

Normally, it is only when we have setbacks in life that we think of God. As the great Advaita sage Ramana Maharshi said, if not the first blow, if not the second blow, then eventually, with the third, fourth, or fifth blow, one starts asking what life is all about. You could say that is taking a step towards God.

N: Could we discuss this also in the light of practices, especially since it's Guru Purnima? I felt, from the perspective of worship and remembering Baba all the time through the reading of the Satcharita, singing bhajans, etc., that we have a choice about what we do with our time, the most precious thing we are all given.

So could you shed a little bit of light on that, please?

G: A very beautiful thing comes into play when we are immersed in all that you mentioned. All these are different ways of remembering God. If we take a closer look, normally, during the day, we are obsessed with ourselves—with what we can do for ourselves, who we are and the masks we wear. When that turns around, when the spotlight is moved away from ourselves to the Source, as represented by Baba in this case, it is called 'the process of being unselfed'. Because now our spotlight is on this divine power which knows best.

The little I is in conflict all the time. Either we are not happy about what someone said or did, or about a certain happening. We are always unsatisfied. But when the content of our mind is full of God and Divinity, there's no room for that dissatisfaction.

If, throughout the day, our remembrance is of God, through ways, tools and techniques which appeal to us, then what is the content of our consciousness? Rather than the 'me and my story' and all our worries and fears, the content is divine; it is sacred. We are tapping into the Source, and that is when we realize that things are in harmony.

If you look at the word 'guru', there are various definitions given for it: 'remover of darkness', 'giver of light', 'remover of ignorance', 'spiritual weight', etc. And what is this darkness? It is the ego with all its antics.

Guru Purnima is such a sacred day, especially for anyone who's on the spiritual path. It is on this day that grace flows the strongest. Since you spoke about taking that one step on Guru Purnima, you will be quite surprised to know how much grace does for us.

N: I also wish to speak with you about satsang. When all of us, Baba's devotees, as you say, brothers and sisters, or guru bandhus, are in the company where everything we do or share is about Baba, it gives great joy to the heart. I have felt that the bond is very special with those few devotees or friends from whom you sense that love for Baba emanating.

So, I feel that also aids one's sadhana. We walk towards Baba together.

G: Yes. I must say that you've raised a very pertinent point again.

When you meet some friends from your past and, in that circle, you discuss things such as the holidays you all have gone for, the restaurants you have visited or the movies you have seen, there's no harm in that, but that is where the level of communication is in that group.

But with satsang, it is different. What is satsang? The company of Truth. In this case, it is Truth that has brought people together in different ways. One person, through a chance encounter with someone, becomes part of a group. Another one, who was seeking a group desperately to belong to, finds it. Whatever it may be, it is the quest for Truth that brings people together: What is life all about? There's definitely more to it than what meets the eye.

So no masks are being worn because we are not trying to impress our guru bandhus. We have been drawn to the Light. This is a very special relationship, and this is something to take note of because then we can support each other on this path.

I'll give you an example. I knew someone in Delhi who was extremely drawn to Nisargadatta Maharaj and his teachings, but he could not find anyone in his neighbourhood who had the same interest. They were only engaging in mundane conversations, which he was getting tired of. So the yearning for satsang was intense for him.

Now this is a very beautiful sign because you could say that his inner calling had been awakened. I gave this example because those who are already part of a *sangha* need to understand it's immense value, as it is supporting each of its members on their life's journey.

And satsang does not just mean people. The company of Truth means the company you keep in your mind throughout the day. If, during the daytime, we find we are condemning people, judging people and criticizing them, then that is the content of our consciousness. Now is that the company of Truth?

Whereas if we see that everyone is an instrument of God and has been designed by God, then we don't take things personally anymore. We know that we are nobody to pass judgement. We are nobody to condemn others. If we find flaws in others, then we most certainly have flaws in ourselves too, although we don't recognize them.

Joel Goldsmith shared something very beautiful. He said that the word 'neighbour' does not just mean your physical neighbour. Who are the neighbours in your mind? They are closer to you, in fact. What thoughts are you harbouring? Are they thoughts of harming someone, of conniving, judging, blaming, condemning, hating and harbouring ill will? Or is the satsang with your neighbours [thoughts] imbued with the quality of Truth?

So here the point is that Sai Baba's devotees have to be quite watchful of what is going on throughout the day, not just in their relationships with people but in their mind too.

N: It is Baba's assurance in the Satcharita that wherever His leelas are sung, day and night, He is there, ever-present. Hence the importance of *kirtans* and bhajans, which bring people together, something that is experienced by millions of devotees throughout the world. Sometimes, one needs a bit of a spark just to remember Baba's assurance. If one is immersed in the Satcharita and Baba's bhajans, with the faith that Baba has given this assurance, then that is a very important step that one can take.

G: And it's all the more important in this day and age because we are so fragmented from morning to evening: we are multitasking, doing hundreds of things; social media is consuming us.

But when the whole focus is on one master, Sai Baba, and that too constantly, then that bhava starts permeating our daily life. That overrides what has otherwise been our default setting of being too distracted and fragmented.

So this constant remembrance is as if we are summoning our consciousness to come back to some wholeness, something which is full, something which is beyond the little I.

I remember reading somewhere that a devotee told Ramana Maharshi that when he was at work, he completely forgot about the Self, the Source and all that. So the Maharshi told him that whenever he was at work, he should remind himself that it was not he who was working, but rather, that it was the current working through him.

So what is that? That is the process of being unselfed because, till then, you feel that you are the doer. So you say, *Okay, Baba, whatever happens during the day, it's very clear to me that You are guiding it. You are the force behind it. I am only the instrument.* Consequently, you find that you become less entangled in the work and it becomes less of a burden to you because then the strength comes from the Source.

So this also is remembrance; this is satsang. Every time you find that you are too involved in a situation, too caught up, anxious or wound up, it's a sign that the little I has taken possession of it. And when you relax and surrender, and step back, saying, *All right, there is an intelligence which is far more intelligent than I am; let me allow it to do its job,* that is when Baba takes over.

However, that space has to be created, and remembrance is the key to that.

N: There is a very beautiful line in the Aarti: *'Jaisa bhava, vaisa anubhav,'* meaning, 'As is your bhava, so is your experience.'

While I was working on the book *A Jewel of Sai Devotion*, I found that Dr Gawankar [about whom the book is written] specifically had satsang on this one line. He would tell devotees to reflect on this line in the Aarti.

G: Very true, and if your bhava is compromised, feeble or fragmented, that will be your experience.

N: So that automatically takes me to the next point: even if you realize that, okay, it is fragmented, that awareness itself is a great starting point.

G: Of course. It's a very big thing because, mostly, we are not aware.

We are running on old patterns and conditioning, with blinkers on, and we could do that for the rest of our lives. So when the awareness comes, it is truly a gift from God.

We are human beings. We are going to falter, we are going to trip, no doubt about it. But by and by, we will find that our remembrance is becoming more effortless as a result of our sadhana, our earnestness and our sincerity. It becomes our new default setting, which brings with it a degree of peace, equanimity and calm, which we did not have earlier. That is truly the test of our sadhana and efforts.

If we are able to navigate our boat through choppy waters, trusting the hand of the Divine, we will be more at peace than if we thought we were doing it ourselves.

N: One other beautiful saying by Baba in this temple in Bangalore is related to this: 'As is your relationship with Me, so will your experience be.' You may see Baba as your parent or you may see Him as your Guru, for instance.

Now Aai has also spoken about this in detail in her interviews. She advocates that we keep one specific relationship with Baba and look up to Him through that lens. Just to make it clear, we are not saying one is better than the other, but it helps to have one particular relationship.

Baba Himself has told His devotees many times in the Satcharita that this is a beautiful practice one can inculcate—to make Him part of their daily life. For example, if you're cooking, think, *Baba would like this dish. Let me dedicate it to Him.* Or, if you're going out, pray, *Baba, please come with me. Be with me, guide me, protect me.*

So, when every action in your daily life is thereby surrendered to Baba, you remember Him.

G: What you just said is beautiful but very hard to practise unless we are really dedicated because what you're talking about is constant remembrance of Baba. The reality is that we don't think before we step out. We just open the door, run down, go here, go there, do things.

When Baba says that if you take Him as a friend, He is your friend, and if you take Him as a parent, He is your parent, you have to consider this carefully. Now the thing is that I have many friends. So am I taking Baba as only a friend? Baba has kept everything open. He is saying that whatever you take Him as, He is that. So that is established.

No doubt, it is easier to identify Baba with one relationship—perhaps the one we cherish most. Now let's consider another possibility. If you take Baba as the guru, then Baba becomes all your relationships. He becomes the friend, He becomes the parent, He becomes your co-worker; it is all-encompassing.

You may feel that, for example, you are someone who doesn't believe too much in the concept of a guru. Let's say you are new on this journey and you say, 'Oh, I prefer to consider him as my friend.' That's all right. Wherever you're standing, you build that relationship.

But the point here is that you have a representation of Divinity, which is nothing other than your Higher Self. And if you embrace Sai Baba as the Sadguru, then He will define all the relationships in your life.

So, I think that by saying He is who you want Him to be, Baba is doing something beautiful,. He's wide open. However, are you wide open to taking Him as everything and not just one dimension of the relationship?

N: I would like to add something here.

Aai, of course, sees Baba as her guru, but when she was young, she would see Baba as her grandfather. But you see, that was so complete and whole. That dependence was so complete that she would never do something without His consent. By that, I mean prayer and remembrance.

So I would not want to undermine any relationship by considering it is lesser than the other, but I come back to this point of bhava, complete remembrance and complete faith. This is why I feel the reading and understanding of the Satcharita is so important.

Something as simple as cooking, which we consider a chore, too can become sadhana. While you are immersed in your day-to-day responsibilities, so long as whatever you do is dedicated to Him, then you can rest assured that He is running the show. Then it is His responsibility.

LIVING WITH FAITH AND PATIENCE

G: Yes, and let's take cooking as an example. One is more joyful and looking forward to this activity when one has this bhava. We are so pulled down by the burden of life that we think everything is a tiresome chore. That is the energy we bring to the task; in this case, cooking. But as you rightly said, if we are cooking for Baba, then what will be our approach? We are not going to be grumbling about it. [Laughs.]

N: I would like to add something, and this applies only to Baba. We are so fortunate that He rewards devotees through the little miracles. He rewards you as if you are a child. We've all experienced it.

So, as one goes forward on the journey, Baba shows that if you take that first step, Baba will take ten. These are signs of encouragement. Obviously, we don't get stuck there, but that is so beautiful. As we go towards Him, He too shows signs of His presence, which everyone here has experienced in some form or the other.

G: Then what we find is that one step on our part becomes two, three, four, five [laughs], you know. It's like it's just expanding all the time; it's so beautiful.

And just to reiterate this point, when that starts happening, we are no longer living our lives as the little I, the small ego with its problems, trying to survive, battle and navigate relationships and situations, and wanting certain outcomes. We become more and more open to whatever happens, knowing that the results have never been in our control. All we can do is do our best.

That is why Nisargadatta Maharaj said, 'The road is the goal.' [Refer to talk 3.] But we are so burdened by wanting to reach somewhere and desiring a certain outcome that we forget that.

And this approach of you taking one step towards Him, and His taking ten steps towards you is this: If you dedicate all your actions to Him, if you remember Him all the time, knowing that He is there, you needn't worry like you've been worrying. Then the Source is going to greet you with Its arms wide open and embrace you.

N: There is an assurance given by Lord Krishna in the Gita similar to that given by Baba in the Satcharita: that a devotee who remembers

Him over everything else—food, water, clothing, relatives, loved ones—and remembers Him alone, to such a one He is indebted, and that person is His true devotee.

So what more can one ask for? Baba has given us so much. He's always there with all of us. So I would like to end it with that. And I hope that with these assurances of Baba's, we will always remember Him. For me, Guru Purnima is always New Year.

G: I would like to wish everyone a most auspicious Guru Purnima. May it be fulfilling at all levels; may it provide an impetus for one's spiritual journey in the year ahead, and may the grace of the Almighty, of Sai Baba, fill your life, fill your cup, fill your heart, and fill your awareness.

Om Sairam.

To view the corresponding video, scan the QR code.

48

We See Things the Way We Are (Gautam's Talk)

Namaste!

I would like to share with you all a beautiful example that Joel Goldsmith gave of how we see things in a particular way: A man walked into a bar, sat at the bar counter and ordered one drink after another. After a few drinks, he turned to his left and saw somebody else sitting there, sipping a drink. He looked at that man intently, drinking away. And then, he told that man, 'Excuse me, sir.'

The man looked at him and replied, 'Yes?'

The first man said, 'Sir, I have some advice to give you. You better stop drinking because you have started looking blurry.'

As we all know, it was not the other person's but the first man's vision that had got blurred after consuming drink after drink.

This is who we are—this man, constantly drinking and then telling the other person he is looking blurry. We judge people based on how we see them, which, in turn, is based on our conditioning: what we are taught as children, how our parents treat us, the school we go to and the religion we are born into. All this shapes us.

Then we start judging people. In fact, the Sai Satcharita begins with this: Hemadpant and somebody else are having an argument and quarrelling. [Refer to talk 42.] Sai Baba steps in and expresses His disapproval of what is happening

We have lost sight of one basic thing—we take decisions based on our conditioning and our nature, and so does the other. So who is right, and who is wrong? The same Consciousness flows through all of us, just as the same electricity flows through all the gadgets in the kitchen. Each gadget is designed a certain way. There is no right or wrong.

If someone has had a childhood where there is an abusive parent, they will think a certain way. Someone who has been brought up by loving parents will think differently. So when we accept that everyone says and does things based on their genetics and conditioning, we no longer start taking things so personally. We no longer start blaming, condemning and hating people for who they are.

In fact, the opposite happens. Compassion arises. If I see a flaw in someone else, I now know that just as that person has some flaws, so do I. In that sense, we are both equals. I may have a different point of view from his. But I agree to disagree without being disagreeable. We move on.

This is called living the teachings, and it starts from the beginning of the Satcharita. We have to keep our judgements aside and understand that if we find faults with others, it is our vision which is blurred, just like that of the drunken man.

When people accept who they are, there is no longer this compulsive need to change others. We are always obsessed with wanting people to be different from who they are: 'You should be more generous.' 'You should be more loving.'

Rameshji said that what he considered the original sin, in terms of Advaita, was that we, both you and me, are two objects in manifestation. But I assume I am the subject and you are the object, and start pronouncing judgement on you. Just like I assume this sofa is an object, this glass of water is an object, and I am the subject. I forget that just as you are an object, I too am an object, and the only subject is God.

We have assumed this role where we start telling people how to act and behave, saying, 'Do this, do that. You should be like this, you should be like that.' And then the realization dawns on us: *God doesn't need me to control this relationship; I too am an instrument like the other.*

The whole dynamic changes. This conflict we have with people, this action-reaction tennis match that we are constantly playing—'You said this, so I said this to retaliate'—changes.

You say your point of view, and you put your racket down. You get disengaged from this drama because the more the drama, the more the rnanubandhan in the relationship keeps perpetuating itself. You find relationships going on and on in the same abusive, unhealthy ways. When we accept that this is how the person is, this is how I am, a certain space is created; the bandhan is no longer engaged in incessantly.

Sometimes, relationships improve; sometimes they end. Whatever happens—because it is no longer perpetuated by my wanting something or someone to be in a certain way—I am open to it as Baba's will.

All this is most important because the Satcharita begins with it. If you find yourself arguing, know that you can only constantly argue if you feel you are absolutely right. But if the humility is there to accept that maybe you are not, then you allow Baba to take over.

So, any time we find ourselves judging someone, I hope this story that Joel Goldsmith has given us will help us take one step back and *reinterpret* what's happening.

To view the corresponding video, scan the QR code.

49

Traits of the Ego

Nikhil: If devotees become aware of the traits of the ego, they can become alert to its arising and try to nip its antics in the bud. I have prepared a few points which I would like to discuss with you.

Gautam: It is an excellent idea to take a look at how the ego functions, but before that, let's not forget Baba's teaching, which is mainly about surrendering to Him, and that means the dropping away of the ego along with its identifications.

A devotee needs to understand that you cannot surrender to Baba and still have an extremely strong identification with the ego because both cannot happen together. Submitting to Baba's will means giving up your will because Baba knows best.

So, before we start, I want to make it clear that to have any negative quality, such as pride, arrogance, hatred or malice, is an indication that the surrender has not happened. The ego is still strongly identified.

Now, depending on what you ask me, we can explore this in various ways.

N: One of Kabirji's *dohas* sums up very beautifully the important point you just made:

> Jab main thaa, tab Hari nahin
> Ab Hari hain, main naahi
>
> When I was there, God wasn't
> Now God is here, and I am not

G: Exactly.

N: So the ego and God cannot coexist.

G: Yes, but today, what is happening is that we are trying to make both coexist. [Laughter.]

N: Many people ask me in their emails, 'How do you identify these wonderful devotees who are featured on the channel?'

To start with, I am wary about bringing onto the channel someone who feels that they are special. Because the ego loves to feel special.

G: That is why my teacher, Rameshji, would say, 'True humility is never recognized by the one who has it.' It means that if someone says that they are humble, they are not, because they are trying to proclaim, *I am humble.*

Humility is reflected in one's actions and words. But those who claim to be humble do so because they want recognition: *Look at me! I am so special in my humility.*

That is the ego with its identification. In this case, it is spiritual identification.

N: Yes.

G: Normally, someone will buy a fancy car, and their 'Look at me' means 'This is *my* car.' But the spiritual ego will say, *Look at me. I am blessed with certain experiences. I, for some reason, by divine command, am the chosen one.*

So, one has to be very careful of that. And from what I have seen, the personalities on your channel, Aai being a prime example, have no such airs. On the contrary, their demeanour is very matter-of-fact.

N: The other side of the coin is that one can have a negative impression of themselves, and even that is the ego at play.

G: True.

N: Someone who's extremely introverted can have a poor self-image, which, in turn, becomes self-destructive. That also is the ego.

G: Yes. Let's say you feel that nobody looks at you. That is the inverted ego because you've built a 'poor me' identity around it: *Nobody loves me. Nobody looks at me. Nobody appreciates me.*

It's the same thing because life is duality of every conceivable kind, and these two are polar opposites. So, either way, it is *Look at me*; one is outside, and the other, within. It's the same ego.

That is why I'm particularly fond of the Buddha's teaching because he always advises us to take the middle path. The beauty of the middle way is that it makes it easier for you to reach stillness.

These polar opposites are like a pendulum. When it swings to one side, it is already gathering momentum to swing to the other, and that is what happens with most of us—we swing between pleasure and pain, ups and downs, non-stop.

So, the middle way is to be aware and witness the ego and its antics. See what positions the ego takes, whether as the 'poor me' or the 'great me'. Both are positions; so peace is to be found in stillness, by being alert, and not in taking positions.

N: On the Baba path, one thing that happens often is 'special' experiences. It's one thing to have an experience and write it down in your diary. But sometimes, there's over-eagerness to share it or that feeling of specialness creeps in: *I have had this experience.* Can you speak about that?

G: There are two ways of looking at it. One is that you are sharing the experience because you want to be seen as someone special or as the chosen one. And two, you are sharing it so that others on the path can benefit from your experience.

Only the one who has the experience knows what the intention behind sharing it is. I will give you an example.

When my mother went through a spiritual awakening, she was seeing visions of the energy movement in her body, of which she drew illustrations. She was not an artist. Her drawings were very raw, but what she saw, she drew.

Now the question was whether these drawings should be shared with people. When people familiar with the subject saw their uniqueness and asked her to share them, she felt that the only reason to do so would be to provide a road map for those who were going through a similar process. They should not feel that they are losing their mind or be bewildered by the movement of energy in the body. That was the intent. The intent was not *Oh, I am so special. I've had this experience. Now I want to tell everyone about my drawings.*

So the person who is having similar experiences needs to see what the intent behind sharing your experience is. Do you want people to acknowledge you and look at you? Or do you genuinely feel that sharing it would benefit other seekers?

N: It's a very fine line because sometimes one may not even be aware of the reason for sharing.

Sometimes, I can sense in people who approach me, a keenness for wanting to be featured on the channel, and they are the ones whom I keep at arm's length.

On the other hand, we need to plead with devotees such as Aai to give their time. They are not by any means interested in being featured. In fact, it is a bit of a bother for them because they like their solitude and remaining anonymous. They don't want to be in the limelight at all; it's just the opposite.

G: This reminds me of something very funny. Someone asked Siddharameshwar Maharaj, Nisargadatta Maharaj's guru, 'How do you feel when someone touches your feet?'

Siddharameshwarji replied, 'Don't ask me; ask my feet. I don't know, and I don't care.' [Refer to talk 8.]

So that is the whole point.

The reticent behaviour of devotees such as Aai is understandable. If I am a devotee, and I trust that whatever happens is Baba's will, then I don't need to do anything. The Universe will come to me and ask me about my experiences, and then I'm ready to share them because they are there for sharing.

Or, the other way is that if I have these experiences to share, and it happens effortlessly and smoothly, without my having to draw peoples' attention, then it is meant to be.

So whatever happens naturally with the least amount of doership involved is what is meant to happen.

The person with the experience can see for themselves, with some degree of awareness, where they are coming from in the sharing of the experiences. But, as you said, if the awareness is not there, then nothing can be done.

N: Yes.

If we think about it, the leelas and the experiences are, after all, Baba's. It could happen to anybody. The person, whoever it's happening to, is almost irrelevant. Baba is important.

G: Yes.

N: So when the sharing is done with the intention that the main subject is Baba and not the person themselves, and where Baba's compassion is being shared, then the instrument is almost irrelevant.

G: Yes, that is well said. You will know whether the one sharing the experience is directing the spotlight on Baba or themselves. That's a good point you raised.

N: Another aspect of the ego is a disproportionate sense of reaction to an event sometimes. It might just get triggered by something which does not even warrant it.

G: If I'm strongly identified with the position 'This is me and this is what I believe in. How dare you challenge my belief?' I will react and may even explode. That shows that my identification is so strong that if someone says something, I get very upset.

But if I accept that everyone has their own point of view, I will agree with some and disagree with others. But I do acknowledge that their point of view is as valid as mine. That is the middle way.

So, this is another good pointer: Do you really get upset and triggered all the time by people? If so, it has nothing to do with that person because, after all, you are the one feeling upset and not the other person.

N: Yes.

G: So, you have to look at it carefully. Someone said something to me I didn't like. *I* didn't like. That's the problem, you see. The I with its sense of doership. So either I blame the other for doing something which I don't like, or I blame the whole act of something happening on the other, with me being at the receiving end with my identification: *He did this to me.*

You see, this point gets missed in the early days of one's spiritual journey. What is missed is that the centre of attention is the me.

So—I'm stressing this point again—any reaction which arises is an issue that *we* have to deal with and not the other person.

The listeners of this podcast need to see what triggers them and what makes them react. It becomes a beautiful exploration of the spiritual dimension. That is what a sincere seeker and devotee starts doing on the path.

So it's actually a gift.

I tell people who attend my talks that if you are getting triggered, rather than fighting it or getting triggered unconsciously, be thankful because you are now given an opportunity to look at these things which are triggering you and question them instead of suffering endlessly by constantly getting triggered.

N: Can you give a few questions that we could ask ourselves, some pointers, so that we can become more alert to what's triggering us? Something we can do as an exercise?

G: If you can take stock of what has upset you during the day, that can become a sadhana. *Why was I upset? And who really was upset? The I with which identification was upset? Was it truly a valid reason to get upset about?*

It will be a beautiful spiritual practice because you will see in each and every instance that you have circled back to the me. So what happens is that, earlier, the dialogue is *Something happens to me.* Or, *Something has been said to me.* See how we pull back to the me?

But with spiritual understanding, it starts shifting to *Something happened.* Full stop. Not *Something happened to me. Something was said.* Full stop. Not *Something was said to me.*

So when that starts happening, the I gets freed from this crust of toxic material which has got built around it. Then pure functioning, pure witnessing, starts happening, and it makes life much simpler.

N: One other point is that, in bhakti, it is important to have a relationship with your *Ishta Devata*, in this case, Baba. But at the same time, it's pretty similar to what we said in the beginning about feeling special.

This is something I've seen commonly among devotees, where they say, 'I am Baba's special child,' or 'I am Baba's most special devotee,' or they will add Baba's name before theirs.

So it can get tricky when you are having a relationship with Baba and feel that you are the centre of it, because it can swing both ways. When things are great, I've seen that they are ultra happy, but when something doesn't work out, then it's 'Oh, Baba let me down.'

G: You see, this may be their truth. Supposing they know on what grounds they are saying they have a special relationship. We don't know. So, let's say it is their truth. Now they make an identity out of it, that they are Baba's special one.

You also mentioned adding Baba's name. I presume you meant putting the prefix 'Sai' before one's name. Now, this is an interesting point to explore. See, sometimes people change their names or take on a new name. The reason is that the old ego has shattered, and a new person is born, so to speak. Nisargadatta Maharaj's earlier name was Maruti Kambli, and then he took on the name Nisargadatta when the transformation happened.

Now, that's the turning point. But what happens if there's no transformation, and I just put a prefix because I am a disciple of someone? Then, it could become another identification. But, as you know, many masters change the names of their devotees too.

N: Correct.

G: The whole idea is that your associations and identifications with your old name fall away. But the problem occurs when you have built a new identification without the old identifications falling away. So, I have all the old identifications connected to my name, my beliefs, my judgements and my concepts. And now I have added one more name as my identification with a divine personage.

Sometimes, people don't understand this; they go and put the prefix or whatever, but they must understand it is not a small thing because now they have to live up to that prefix. And are they living up to that? Is the transformation happening?

So the decision has to be taken carefully. If the motivation and the intention are right, then, by all means, you can go ahead. You can take a decision that, now, since you feel you are a new person, or you are on the way to being one, this will help you in your practice. If you feel that's for you, why not? But please look at it as not just another identification.

N: One day I was sitting with Aai, talking about something, and she mentioned that she doesn't consider herself Baba's devotee. She said, 'I am the dust of His feet.' She believes that we are beggars in front of Him and that we cannot consider ourselves devotees unless He says, 'You are My devotee.'

Now, someone so close to Him, someone so devoted to Him, says this, and on the other hand, you have people who claim they are Baba's greatest devotees.

So, you see, the contrast is so apparent.

I just feel it's always safer if you take Aai's approach, though one cannot instil humility. I mean, as the saying goes, 'The bigger they are, the harder they fall.'

G: Yes.

N: I thought to myself about Aai, *This is a true devotee. There is no sense of entitlement at all.*

G: Yes, and that is why I'm so glad that you have these beautiful people you have exposed all of us to, and, hopefully, these videos will be around for a very long time. It's a great service that has happened. It's all His play unfolding.

N: Yes, I'm sure.

G: I would be very happy to explore the topic of the ego in subsequent podcasts also, if your audience feels it would benefit them.

N: There is one point which I feel could pretty much become a podcast in itself. It is reaction and response.

So maybe we could consider that a sequel to this particular episode because one of the traits of the ego is that it's always reacting.

To view the corresponding video, scan the QR code.

50

Reaction and Response

Nikhil: The response to the first episode of the series *Traits of the Ego* was very sincere and rather encouraging. People asked some meaningful questions, so I felt it would be nice if we could continue this series. It will provide devotees with a framework to know what to look for on their spiritual journey.

Gautam: It is the journey of unravelling the ego and all its projections, defence mechanisms and ways of controlling and dominating others.

I'm very happy that the audience has responded well to the first podcast. It shows there is a sincere effort being made to understand oneself and what life is about.

N: Every human being undergoes challenging situations to which they either react or respond. So, in today's episode, can we talk about the difference between a reaction and a response? We can discuss the various aspects and maybe you can give some tips as well as questions that the audience can ask themselves to help them differentiate between the two.

G: Yes, this is a very important point you have raised because most of us are reactive in nature, especially when our buttons get pressed. We just react according to our past patterns of behaviour. Irritation or anger may arise, and we keep repeating this reaction endlessly.

Spiritual inquiry, as well as sincerely following a master's teachings, is about looking at these past patterns: why we do the things we do and say the things we say. This beautiful opportunity is always available to us because any moment that we face brings forth either a reaction or a response, you see.

Now let's go a bit deeper into this.

All our reactions are based on our past conditioning: who we think we are and how life has shaped us.

Supposing someone irritates us, that irritation is a reaction, and that reaction is appearing within us. It really has nothing to do with the other person. We think that someone says something, because of which we get irritated. But the fact is that the other person is just a trigger. This irritation is lying dormant deep within us, and it is waiting to surface. So, although it may seem counter-intuitive, we should be thankful for someone irritating us because they are giving us an opportunity to take a good look at our inner picture.

Let's say that something happens, and we react in unawareness. It's a knee-jerk reaction. Something else happens, and we react again. Thus, life goes on and on in this reactive mode. It is a life lived in unawareness.

Now let's talk about a response. It has a different quality and energy to it. A response is not knee-jerk. That is an important distinction between a reaction and a response. It is not based on the accumulation of past conditioning, who I think I am and what the world has done to me.

That is why we find that a sage mostly responds, whereas an ordinary person reacts. The sage is open to what the next moment brings, which includes what someone may say or do to the sage. But the sage's response is not based on doership—*Someone is doing this to me*. The sage views the person as an expression of Consciousness. Maybe the person says something, which the sage may not like, but as the sage is not carrying the baggage of doership related to hardwired conditioning, the sage accepts that whatever the person says, they are entitled to say it because it is their right.

Whether or not we take delivery of what someone says is up to us.

N: Yes.

G: So you can see the difference between a sage's response and an ordinary person's reaction.

It is a matter of acceptance, if we go back to the teachings. Baba asks us to see the Divine in all. As simple as that. If we just live that teaching, we accept that the person in front of us is equally an expression of God, just as we are. We don't set ourselves up in opposition to the other and, therefore, we don't react with criticism and condemnation. We accept that the other person's view is based on their conditioning and nature, just like it is the case with us. If this acceptance is total, if we have truly imbibed Baba's words, then we will respond and not react to the situation. There will be no animosity, no negativity and no targeting of the other person, saying, 'I'll get even with you.' All that drops away.

This whole action-reaction loop, in which the ordinary person gets stuck, becomes like a tennis match. For instance, you can see couples or any two people arguing endlessly. And that is what perpetuates the I-am-right-you-are-wrong cycle.

Nobody is right, and nobody is wrong. When we live this understanding, our life becomes more of a response to life, a response to what the next moment may bring or to someone we may encounter. It may be pleasure or pain, or someone whom we may or may not like, yet we find that we experience a certain equanimity, owing to which our approach to life undergoes a tremendous change.

N: Supposing someone working in an office feels they are not given their due acknowledgement or appreciation on completing a task and that the credit is given to someone else, a reaction can arise unconsciously in that person, which could be emotional, physical or mental. Now if the person is a sincere devotee and they start watching the reaction as a practice and nip it in the bud, would that awareness help?

G: Yes, it would certainly help. There's no question about it, and that is what I refer to as witnessing.

So even if I felt I did a great job and I'm not acknowledged, and I feel a sense of resentment for being unappreciated, even that feeling is witnessed. It is not judged that I should not be feeling this, because that is the ego coming in through the back door. Witnessing creates a gap between what I am feeling and who I truly am. It creates this separation where I'm able to watch what goes on within me.

Now what happens? I witness that I am feeling unappreciated. This does not mean I bury it under the carpet. There are two things I could possibly do.

One, I can accept the situation: *Okay, I am unappreciated, and I feel so. And that is how it is.*

The other thing is that I may feel that since I have witnessed this feeling of resentment, I'd like to talk to my senior and explain to them that this is how I view the situation; in other words, I put my cards on the table.

The point is that in both cases, it is a response and not a reaction. It is not a situation where I storm into my senior's cabin and say, 'I have done so much work, and you are being unfair to me. I certainly don't deserve this.' That is the approach of a reactive mind based on doership. It doesn't leave any room for considering the senior's point of view about my feeling of being unappreciated.

So one can see the difference between the two, and that is what I mean when I say that the quality of our life starts changing.

Even if I am moved to raise my point of view or my feelings, I put my point across in a more understanding and equanimous way. Perhaps there was a misunderstanding and the senior did not realize my crucial role in the work done, because of which my colleague took the spotlight. What has happened is that my *attitude* has been transformed thanks to the teachings.

We all face disturbing situations, and it is not that they are going to stop occurring. But how we deal with them based on how deeply we have imbibed the teachings is what is important. The teachings are meant to be applied in our daily living.

I am so happy to see that the audience wants to explore this troublemaker, the ego, which takes away one's peace of mind.

N: Yes. That is how beautiful this teaching is.

Coming back to the Satcharita, Baba said that if someone asks you for money and you don't want to give it, say no. Don't bark like a dog at them. [Refer to talk 1.] Even that is an example, where Baba is teaching us to respond rather than react.

Another example is that of a couple where one partner has a tendency to provoke and the other, to get provoked. But let's say that the person who is on the receiving end doesn't play along and responds consciously, then gradually, the conflict will lose steam because, as they say, '*Tali ek haath se nahin bajti* [It takes two hands to clap].'

G: Exactly. In any situation of conflict, if one person is the witnessing presence and is not in the reactive mode, the tennis match cannot be played because it takes two to play tennis. It doesn't take both people in the situation to have a certain understanding or awakening. Even one person having it is enough.

Now just because acceptance is there, it does not mean you get walked over. Every individual has to decide for themselves to what point they are okay to take the other's provocative behaviour: *Do I subject myself to what is coming at me from the other person? Do I subject myself to it indefinitely? Or do I share my point of view and see if there is a transformation in the equation? If not, and if I find it unbearable, then maybe I should walk away from the situation.*

This depends on one's nature and one's conditioning. Some people may not feel they are capable of walking away, especially those who are timid.

But, to clarify, this teaching does not mean that one becomes a doormat.

N: Correct.

G: It means accepting people the way they are. Thereafter, as Krishna says in the Gita, do precisely that which you think and feel you should do.

So this is an important point to consider.

N: One other aspect of the ego, specific to reaction and response, is the consistent unconscious thinking that people indulge in. I don't think this is widely discussed in the Baba circle, but in the normal case of a person who is not a sadhak, the mind, if left alone, starts going in circles. Would you say it's true of most people?

G: Yes, it is, because it is the unaware mind that is lost in the stream of incessant thoughts.

N: Correct. So now, I do feel that if devotees also take this as a practice—to watch the mind—even before they are in a situation of reaction or response, then the likelihood of them being more responsive in life will depend on how many gaps they have in their thinking process.

G: Yes, and as Osho rightly said, hell is not a place. Hell means to not be aware. Because when we are not aware, we create hell for ourselves as well as for others, you see.

And to not be aware means we are lost in the past or the future, and more importantly, we give in to the habitual thinking based on doership, resulting in condemnation, hatred, malice, jealousy, envy, blaming people for what we think they have done and blaming ourselves. This is what hell is because these thoughts perpetuate the antics of the thinking mind, which keeps going on and on like a Ferris wheel.

However, witnessing enables us to get off this Ferris wheel of thinking and creates a gap. That is the beauty of it.

And so, to sum this up, as you said, one finds that the reactive mode is either diminishing in one's life and one is becoming more responsive, or even if there's a reaction—because, after all, we are products of our conditioning—it is momentary and doesn't get perpetuated and extended into a long-drawn-out argument. The understanding, which is the greatest gift of the teaching, immediately kicks in.

So let's say that reaction is purely spontaneous and it gets cut off thereafter. The load which the reaction was earlier carrying is no longer being carried. For example, even in a sage, anger may arise in the moment, but there will be no involvement in it. The anger will not continue over time. The sage will also be quick to offer an apology if the other has been hurt.

N: Can we go back to the earlier example where the person in the office feels they are not getting their due recognition?

So if I'm in a situation where something like this arises, given my nature, I would first ask myself whether what I am thinking or feeling is true. Then, if I have received any communication, such as an email, I would think over my initial reaction to it and delay my reply.

And if there is an emotional charge that arises, especially if someone is rude to me, I would give myself time to sit with the sensations and watch them. Then the chances of me responding rather than reacting are much higher.

And as you said, I can always be assertive without reacting if I find that what is happening is not agreeable to me.

G: Yes. In fact, you have recommended a wonderful practice. It reminds me of my younger days at work. When I felt an injustice was being done by a client who was, let's say, unjustly questioning a bill after approving the estimate, or who was rude to my colleagues, what I would do is I would immediately write out an email, but I would not send it. I would send it the next morning, and before sending it, I would look at what was written. I would be so surprised to find words that I would not normally use!

After having looked at the email with a fresh responsive mind and not a reactive mind, I was, in effect, giving myself the opportunity to be more objective, more neutral, and to make the appropriate changes. *Then* I would send the email.

N: Yes.

G: This awareness had kicked in.

Now let's go forward, say, five or ten years.

In a similar situation, I write an email, and now when I say 'I', I am referring to anyone with the understanding. I don't send it, I wait for some time, I reread my email, and I feel nothing needs to be changed. At that point, I know that the teaching has set in deeply because even the email I wrote prior to checking it was a response and not a reaction.

That is how one can gauge one's progress; by the words one uses, whether verbally or in writing. Then you look back and say, *My God, a transformation has indeed happened!*

N: Those people who are more emotional than rational could look within themselves in terms of their feelings, which could help reduce the intensity of their emotions.

G: Yes, that would help because it is extreme emotions also which take us away from our centre. And this whole process is the journey back to the centre.

N: When people have noise in their head, most of it is repetitive garbage. I think people would be ashamed if there were a loudspeaker which could play the contents of their mind on the street. Then everyone would get enlightened that very same day.

G: [Laughs.] Well said.

N: The question, 'How do I know this is true for certain?' gives you time to ponder.

Baba talks about saburi because we tend to react to anything, without being patient. So, Baba's teaching here is so important. If we have the patience to question the integrity and the very foundation of our thought, or the string of thoughts, we may realize that either what we are thinking doesn't matter or that it may not be true. Then, in that case, where is the question of either a response or a reaction?

But I feel that it has to be a constant practice because when a situation comes up, and you are not practising regularly, it may have the power to pull you down.

G: True, because the new conditioning has to also get established in one's being. That takes time because it's replacing the old patterns of conditioning, you see.

N: Despite the helpful discussion that we have engaged in today, I feel there is one exception to this reaction and response rule. You know what it is?

G: What?

N: It's humour. When someone cracks a good joke, you must react and not respond like a sage.

G: [Laughs.] True. That's a good one.

N: Apart from humour, we must stay in the response containment zone, so to speak.

G: It shows that laughter is a natural process. It's quite beautiful that you raised this point. It's a natural response.

N: Yes.

G: One could say that the reaction of laughter is a natural response.

N: Yes, so we leave it at that with some laughter after a very serious talk. [Laughter.]

To view the corresponding video, scan the QR code.

51

The Ego Loves to Feel Special —Part I

Nikhil: In continuation of the series *Traits of the Ego*, today, I would like to discuss with you something characteristic of the Baba community. It is the tendency one has to feel special due to having experiences, sometimes, even to the extent of blowing one's trumpet about it.

I remember that in one of the previous talks, you mentioned that those who don't have experiences are even more blessed.

So I felt it would be nice if we could discuss this very subtle sense of feeling special, also from the perspective of sharing experiences: whether they are done to inspire others, whether they are considered Baba's leelas or whether people feel they are the cause of the leelas?

I feel this is an important point because, sometimes, when the experience, which is Baba's leela, is received and shared, some people may almost feel that they have caused it, or that feeling of being special creeps in.

So I think this would be an interesting discussion.

Gautam: It is a tricky thing, to be honest, because as you rightly said, the point is, if someone has an experience, what is the motive behind sharing that experience? Is it to enhance the listener's life? What is the essence of the experience? What was Baba trying to tell the person? And if He was trying to tell that person something, what is He trying to tell others through them? What can that person share with others? Where are they coming from when they are sharing an experience?

Only that person will know—and if they are unaware, they may not even know it—whether they are just boasting about their experience, that Baba came to them and such-and-such a thing happened, or whether their motive is compassion. They don't know why Baba chose to bless them with this experience, and now they must share it so that others can benefit from it as they have.

What tends to happen is that we ordinary people who don't have experiences look up to those who have them. It's natural. And then we feel, *I wish I had such experiences. Why don't I?* The ego feels a lack, and then thinks, *I am less worthy, and therefore I don't have experiences.*

Now this is not true.

This is something we have to really understand because it could be a blessing not to have experiences. Many of us get lost when we have experiences because the ego operates like that; it feels special, and then it wants more and more of these experiences.

The spiritual journey of the one who has had the experience is sometimes derailed because now they are after experiences, whereas the import of the experience, the purpose of the experience, is lost.

So I would say, be diligent in your sadhana and live the teachings every day. By all means, look up to those who have had experiences, but don't get so enamoured by them. See what you can learn from the experiences, what value they can add to your life, and live it accordingly.

I am reminded of something I saw on TV about Tulsidas. His Ramayana became hugely popular when he wrote it in his time.

In those days, you could not photocopy the Ramayana and print thousands of copies; it was all handwritten. Tulsidas used to read from the only copy he had. He would go from place to place reading from it, and it was so beautiful that people started memorizing the Ramayana.

Now it so happened that his competitor, someone else who was very famous in the field of *prachar*, was jealous. He wanted to steal Tulsidas's copy, so he hired the local thief to steal it in the middle of the night, for which he paid the latter some gold coins.

When this thief went to steal the copy, Tulsidas was sleeping, and so were two of his students, on the veranda. It was a great opportunity to fulfil his task. But suddenly, he saw the shadow of a guard, and he wondered, *Where could Tulsidas have got him from, to guard his copy?*

When he took a closer look again at the shadow, he saw that there were two shadows. And then he saw the shadows in detail. He could see the shadow of a quiver of arrows as well as that of a monkey's tail. He realized that those whose shadows he was seeing were no guards. It was Lord Rama Himself who was guarding the copy, with Hanuman by His side. He went into a state of shock when the realization sank in completely. He could not move from that spot.

In the morning, when Tulsidas woke up, he saw this man quivering. The thief told him, 'I have committed *paap*.' Tulsidas was taken aback. *What is this man saying? What paap?*

The thief went on to explain: 'I came to steal the Ramayana, and I had darshan of Lord Rama and Lord Hanuman. I saw them protecting your copy.'

Tulsidas thought to himself, *How fortunate this thief is! Lord Rama doesn't give me darshan!* Now although Tulsidas was such a devoted bhakta that beautiful poetry just flowed from him, he never had the experience that the thief had. But when he heard the story, he said, 'I know Lord Rama is here.'

So, perhaps, it was to make Tulsidas humble that Lord Rama didn't appear in front of him at that point. Maybe he did so later. But that is the essence of the story, you see: just because you don't have the experience does not mean that the Lord is not with you.

It does not mean Baba is not there in your life. We always want an effect. We want to see something, and then we miss what's important. But if we are living under God's grace, under Baba's grace, if we are trying our best, we may fail, but at least the effort is there to live by the Satcharita and to lead by example.

That's all we can do. We are mortals, we are human beings. But that is enough.

So that is what these stories are about, you see. These experiences may or may not happen. Please do not make that a goal because then you are missing out on the journey.

N: What a beautiful story you have narrated! I actually forgot what was the starting point of this talk. Maybe it doesn't matter.

G: [Laughs.]

N: On an ending note, it's always easier to see these traits in somebody else first than in yourself. So, sometimes, even when you observe them without criticism in another, it's easier than seeing them arise within yourself. But at least that can be a starting point for awareness because then it can shift to yourself.

G: Yes, because whatever you observe in another is an invitation to look at what is happening in your life. Let's take something simple as an example. Let's say I find that a certain person is a miser. Now the word 'miser' and its meaning is in my consciousness. I have imposed it on the other, that this person is a miser, but I need to know what being miserly is.

So it's an invitation to look at yourself whenever you observe something in another. *Do I have this quality of miserliness? What do I know about miserliness?* And then, do you understand that a person does not choose to be a miser? Who knows what experience they had in life, perhaps when money was scarce? All this exploration is part of the sadhana.

To view the corresponding video, scan the QR code.

52

The Ego Loves to Feel Special —Part II (Gautam's Talk)

The ego loves to feel special. That is how the ego is designed. It really isn't anybody's fault. It just has to be seen in the light of clarity.

It is very easy to start feeling special when we get experiences, whether in dreams, meditation, or whatever it may be. It happens because the ego's sense of self gets enhanced. *Wow! I am the chosen one. This experience happened to me, and it doesn't happen to others generally.*

So this is a classic pitfall on the spiritual journey, and one has to be very careful not to get caught up in experiences.

I remember, a while ago, since we started these interviews on the channel, a very beautiful person started writing emails to me: 'Baba came to me in a dream and He said this, and then He said that.' It was all very nice, but I found that the emails were limited only to this aspect. It didn't go on to 'Based on the dream, this happened in my life; this is what I reflected on.' It was always this talk of Baba coming in a dream, wearing yellow clothes, and so on.

It has its place, but you see, one thing about dreams is that by and large, they are also psychological reactions to the waking state. So if something is on my mind all the time, it is likely to reflect in my sleep as a dream.

Now if you lose sight of this, you start feeling special about Baba coming in your dreams. You feel that you are the chosen one, and then the ego starts wearing this robe of 'Look at me!'

These emails kept coming. I kept getting an email every ten days, and I found that there was no learning, no growth. Was the person contemplating the message in the dreams?

This is not to belittle the dream experience. I brought it up to just show that Baba may or may not come to you in your dreams or your meditation. It does not mean that someone who does not dream of Baba, or in whose meditation Baba's vision does not appear, is in any way inferior to those who have had the experience.

The whole point is that in which scenario are the teachings being lived? Whether you are at work or home, are you following in Baba's footsteps? Baba may come to you in your dream, but if you are not following the teachings, you are not following in His footsteps. Then what is the value of that dream? What is the value of that vision?

Some experiences are given to us because they act as catalysts; they encourage us on the path. But if we get attached to them, and our daily living is still a mess, then we are repeating the same patterns, our relationship dynamics are not undergoing any transformation and we are no more at peace than we were earlier. Then that has no value. Absolutely no value.

But if we find we have a dream or a vision, and we can benefit from it in our equations with not only people but also challenging circumstances in our life, then that vision or dream has been translated into an experience of essence.

So this is a message to you to not be discouraged if you are not the 'chosen one' because, for all you know, your life is more peaceful than someone who has these visions and is not at peace.

Ultimately, it boils down to living the teachings day by day.

If that happens, then you can rest assured you don't need dreams and visions of Baba because He is with you throughout the day. Otherwise, you wouldn't be at peace.

To view the corresponding video, scan the QR code.

53

The Ego Wears a Mask

Nikhil: Namaste.
All through the Satcharita, Baba pointedly spoke about the ego. For example, he never approved of people reacting, criticizing others, being impatient or being argumentative. In fact, the beginning of the Satcharita starts with the Hemadpant incident. [Refer to talk 42.]
So I thought, today, we can talk about the false sense of self, or the ego.

Gautam: Yes, that's beautiful. I'm so glad that the audience is delving deeper into the subject of the ego because this directly impacts daily living. And by talking about the traits of the ego, it's not like we are finding fault. We are only trying to understand how the ego operates. What does it derive its false sense of self from? All we are doing is looking at the way the ego operates in awareness. We are not trying to say, 'This is right, this is wrong,' because, after all, the ego was not created by us. It was created by God. Ego is identification with name and form as a separate entity. *This is me. This is me and my story.*

So how does the ego operate, what are its habits and what are its different patterns for different people based on their conditioning? We can explore these questions so that everyone can become aware of them in light of their life, their issues, their projections and so on.

N: Could we begin with the concept of the false sense of self?
As you had explained in one of your talks, a newborn child doesn't have that sense of 'me'; it doesn't refer to itself as 'I'. Sometimes, children even refer to themselves in the third person, but later, when

the parents condition them into saying 'I', then that sense of self starts developing.

G: Yes, it becomes 'me' as separate from 'you'. My conditioning, the way my parents treated me, the school I went to, the college I went to, the religion I was born into, my economic status—this is 'me'. So all this has accumulated over time. This is who I think I am.

I start operating from this centre, as separate from the other person. That is what happens when the ego gets encrusted with conditioning. We become very rigid. We don't realize that our views are based on our conditioning. Someone else may have a different conditioning, because of which their perspective may be different, but we feel that ours is the right one.

N: This reminds me, in chapter one, Baba specifically said that one should not be rigid about their own views and put someone else's down.

G: That's it. When we look at the ego and the way it operates, a transformation takes place. We are no longer fixed and rigid about people or events in our lives.

N: Could you give certain pointers to become aware of this false sense of 'I'?

G: You see, there are various ways we can look at it. Let's take some basic daily living instances. I'll tell you one.

I was with two friends, and one of them asked, 'Have you seen this new movie?' And the other friend had no interest in the subject of the movie. So the first one said, 'Oh my God, you haven't seen it! How could you not see it? Which world are you living in? You're missing out on it.' He went on and on as if to say, 'I've seen this movie. You haven't. And therefore you don't know what a good movie is all about.'

Now this friend who was at the receiving end started shrinking—energetically, of course. I could actually see it. He felt he was being talked down to.

We have to be careful about not thrusting our opinion down someone's throat. We have to be alert to this in our own lives. Are we also doing this? Are we putting people down if they don't have the same tastes or point of view that we have? If so, it means we are operating from a false sense of self. Let's say, in another instance, we have identified with a movie, which we think is great. Someone else may not. But are we open to that person's point of view?

Let's see what would happen in an awakened man. He will see the movie, may really love it, and may share his viewpoint that it was great. But if someone else didn't think much of the same movie, then he would say, 'Fair enough.' He is not going to operate from a sense of authority, saying, 'I know best. How could you not like it? That means you don't appreciate good movies.'

That is what the ego operating from the false centre does. These are giveaways, with the help of which we can catch ourselves indulging in such behaviour. Or we can look at something entirely different. What are we identified with which we are projecting onto others?

Now let's take social media, which is a very big thing, today. Am I always posing in these fancy nightclubs and restaurants? Or if I'm travelling to some exotic locations, am I, for instance, posting photos, saying, 'I'm at Paris airport.' See, the feeling may be great, but I'm deriving my sense of self from the fact that I'm at Paris airport. I want people to see the picture and say, 'Wow! You are at Paris airport.' And it makes me feel good.

So, I've added on to myself something that is external. Now an exalted sense of self, derived from being seen in Paris, has been attached to pure being, pure living. Now I depend on being seen in Paris for who I am. There is nothing wrong in sharing our joy with others. We just have to see where we are coming from in the process.

This is how the ego operates. If an awakened man wanted to share with his friends that he was enjoying his visit to Kanpur or Nagpur or wherever, he would be equally comfortable posting pictures of his trip to Kanpur as well as his trip to Paris. That is the point. There is no differentiation there because the sense of self is not derived from a projected image of 'Look at me.'

So, as I began by saying, we are not putting the ego down. We are trying to just look where we derive our sense of self from.

We are always adding things to us. This pure being that we are, precisely the way God made us, and shaped us, is now seeking something from outside for validation. I want other people's approval. So will they approve of me if they see that I'm wearing a fancy brand of shoes? Because then this is who I am. All this becomes extensions of the ego.

The beauty is that if a spiritual seeker or anyone drawn to any spiritual path is listening to this video, it will open up and expose the traits of the ego.

N: If an aspirant begins to notice this with awareness in their day-to-day living, they will find that it need not be restricted only to posting photos. They could even derive their sense of self from a relationship or some pain or certain patterns. But just to have that awareness, is the first step to change.

G: Well said. For example, I could be so identified with my past. Supposing I had a past where I struggled a lot, where I didn't have enough money, I had to work very hard for my money and I find myself bringing up this past in conversation every time. 'You know, when I was young, I didn't have enough money to have a meal in a fancy restaurant.' It means I am invested in the story. Though the past is dead and gone, what I keep telling people has become my script today, in the present. If I keep replaying the past, that means I derive my sense of who I am from my past. But we are here and now in front of each other.

So this is a great pointer: How much are you living in the dead past or an imaginary future? That means you are not available right now. You are not present to what the moment has to offer. That is a classic trait of the ego—the avoidance of the present.

If we find that we are avoiding the present, unconsciously, of course, by always glorifying the past or putting down the past, or saying things which are very much in the future, which may or may not happen, then we know that we are operating from this false dimension.

N: I'm reminded about a pointer Nisargadatta Maharaj would give devotees, where, as an exercise, you avoid using the first person pronoun in conversation, just to create space around what is happening. For instance, you don't say, 'This is happening to me.' You say, 'It is happening.' If done intentionally for a week or so, you begin to become aware of how much of your attention is on the me and the I during the day.

G: Yes. Maharaj says that the internal dialogue should switch from the active voice to the passive voice: *I see something*, becomes *Something is seen*. *I hear something*, becomes *Something is heard*. [Refer to talk 2.]

It brings a sense of neutrality and objectivity to what is seen and heard. Otherwise, we are in this mode: 'You are telling me this. How dare you tell me this! I disagree with you.' You see, we are so 'me-centric' that we lose sight of the fact that the person may be saying something which means something entirely different from our interpretation, but we take it personally. 'You are telling this to *me*.' So what Maharaj is suggesting here is that we lose this 'me-focus'. Because the me keeps adding on: 'I see something; I hear something; I touch something; I smell something; I taste something.' And also, 'I like this, I don't like that.'

So the quality of passive witnessing brings about that gap where we will find, over time, that we are not as invested as we were earlier, which was building up this false sense of self. We become more neutral and less reactive. We are more equanimous with what is seen and heard.

This is an exploration which can go across many videos, but I'm glad that it's a start, and I do hope the subscribers to your channel explore this in their own lives.

It's actually quite a gift. They will really find things opening up.

N: The fact that some are sincere and following these pointers, does show that they've gone through a series of good and bad experiences. But then, this is what takes you ultimately to peace.

Miracles and all are signs of encouragement, but even Baba says in chapter three that it's only when you go past all this wavering of the mind and have that stillness that the door opens. It's the beginning, but it will take you to where Baba wants to take you.

G: Yes, and you see, the thinking mind is swinging like a wild pendulum; for example, swinging between points of pleasure and pain. When that swinging starts reducing, you don't get swayed by pleasures as much as you used to. You don't get swayed by pain too. By pain, I mean psychological pain. So when the pendulum slows down and comes to the still point, which is in the middle, that is where peace is to be found.

To view the corresponding video, scan the QR code.

54

The Ego Loves to Criticize and Complain

Nikhil: Knowingly or unknowingly, people engage in the habits of complaining and criticizing, and this is something that Baba certainly did not like. There are many leelas in the Satcharita that point to this. In one leela, two devotees were massaging Baba's hands and feet, when one got critical of the other, and Baba was quite displeased about it. He didn't like this trait at all.

So could you shed a bit of light on these two specific traits?

Gautam: Let me give you an example about complaining—a typical one.

I know someone very wealthy, and yet, whenever we meet, she complains all the time. It could be about the weather or the streets of Mumbai—how dirty, filthy and noisy Mumbai is. But the conversation is mainly a complaint about this or that. [Refer to talk 6.]

What is a complaint? 'I don't like how things are.' And when that becomes a habit, it means we have not accepted how things are. We are complaining about them all the time.

So the complainer is the ego, which feels things should be different from what they are and wants to enforce its point of view all the time because it has got lost in its self-created position that I don't like things the way they are and, therefore, I am going to complain about it.

So, for a master, if they have a student who is complaining all the time, while another student isn't, it's a pointer indicating which of the two has got lost in the story of the me and its wanting things a certain way and getting stuck in that position.

In your life, what are you complaining about all the time? It's an invitation to look at that. Are you complaining about a particular situation? Then do what you feel you can do best in that situation. That's all you can do. Thereafter, it's God's will.

A boy who used to come for my talks was having problems with his job, and he used to complain about it all the time.

So I said to him, 'Look, I understand that many of us are not happy in our jobs, yet there's no other alternative. But if this dialogue is going to be a dialogue of complaint incessantly, we are making life miserable for ourselves and the others to whom we are complaining.'

So what is happening here? You are not happy with what *is*. Now, you can try to do something about it. In this case, you can speak to your supervisor. If you feel that door is closed, then look for another job. If you feel that door is closed too, then stop complaining. Is the complaining achieving anything? Is it making things better for you? It's not. In fact, your state of mind is a mind full of complaints, a complaint against God eventually: *I don't like where You have placed me*. That is what a complaint is, if you look at it objectively.

Even teachers like Eckhart Tolle have said that it is better to walk out of a situation if it's driving you up the wall, rather than complain constantly. It is of no use because you are actually harming yourself.

It appears that you're complaining about something outside of you, but the content of your consciousness is one of complaint. That is how split we are. Ultimately, what is the content of our consciousness? What we are thinking about all the time. So if we are complaining all the time and not accepting of what *is*, then our consciousness is one of complaint. That which is within our consciousness is our vibration, and that is what we are sending out to the world. In this case, complain, complain, complain.

N: Could you speak a little bit about criticizing?

G: Criticizing and complaining have very similar roots because both have the me operating at the core. I don't like something, so I criticize it. It's the same. I feel I know better. I feel I am the subject, the other is the object, and so I criticize the other, thinking I know best.

This is how the ego functions. This is a classic trait of the ego. Whom are you criticizing, and what are you criticizing? You are ultimately criticizing God's Creation.

Whether it is another person or a situation, a situation comes into your life only if it is meant to. You may call it your destiny, you may call it the hand of the Divine—whatever. The fact that a situation has manifested means it was meant to manifest.

Now how does one meet that situation? Does one meet it with criticism and complaint, or with the acceptance that, here and now, how best do I deal with the situation without coming up with this whole 'I don't like it' story and criticizing what *is*, till kingdom come?

So you can catch yourself doing it. If you are with friends who are criticizing someone, and you add your opinion in agreement, then you also become party to it.

How quick are we to criticize others? This is a good measure for gauging where we stand on our spiritual journey. If we are honest with ourselves, we will find that we are criticizing, often because of peer pressure. If some friends get together, and let's say they are criticizing the government, or a friend who's not with them, or someone rich who's run off with money, then the mob mentality comes in, and everyone joins in the criticism. If we are alert, we will realize that we are lost in the maya. We are so invested in these stories that we are criticizing all the time.

So the awakened man is able to watch this as a play of the ego, and when that happens, he takes one step back, being aware that God knows best how to deal with His Creation. He lives his life day by day, and his main concern is peace of mind in daily living. And where is that to be found? It is not to be found in complaining or criticizing.

So that becomes the way of living life, and it's quite a beautiful journey because it's one of disengaging from all this activity. It's like a reverse journey. You are coming back to your centre, which was, at the time of complaining, out of place and stuck to things, such as your opinions, views, and judgements. This process is more like a centring—being present, being available, with a vacant mind and not a dull mind; a vacant mind which is not full of the garbage that we have collected from society. And when our internal dialogue is not one of complaint and criticism, we become available to people.

The greatest gift we can give another is our presence. Imagine someone comes to you, or you go to someone. Wouldn't you love it if that person's full attention is on you, listening to every word you speak? It's beautiful. That person is available to you. So when we explore these traits of the ego, we start becoming more available.

N: As seen in many instances in the Satcharita, Sai Baba would appear to his devotees in any human form. And if this pointer you have given is taken to heart by Baba's devotees, they will realize that when they criticize others or pass judgement, they are really doing it to Baba as He resides in all. Often, it is done unconsciously, but if the devotee becomes aware of it, then that itself, I think, could be the turning point.

G: It is. And as Maharaj would say, to criticize anything or anyone is to criticize the affairs of Brahman. [Refer to talk 1.] God knows best, right? He doesn't need you to criticize His Creation.

That's the point. And as you were saying, Baba would come in any form in front of His devotees. That is actually a test. Because if we truly believe that Baba is omnipresent, omnipotent and omniscient, that means any form which presents itself to us is a representation of Baba's.

So this is how the masters test us. They may come in a form which immediately triggers us. That's the test. In our lives, we have people who push our buttons. But when we see that they are acting out their script, their blueprint, which God created, we no longer start pointing fingers at them because we see Baba in all forms.

We may not like some forms; after all, we are not saints. But when we see things objectively, it removes the sting of personal doership, which is what my teacher used to say. When the sting of the false notion *He did this to me* is removed, we don't react like we did earlier with all that anger and venom directed at an individual. We accept that the person is playing out their script.

Yes, we do get triggered based on our conditioning. But when that sense of personal doership is removed from the equation, because everything is Baba, we find that our reaction is now more of a response. And even if there is a reaction based on decades of conditioning, the involvement is cut off pretty much immediately. So we don't go on and on like a stuck record, which becomes our constant dialogue. We may still react, but when this understanding comes that Baba is behind EVERYTHING, that involvement gets dropped.

The result is peace of mind and harmonious relationships. And that is why this saying is one of my favourites: 'We can agree to disagree with people without being disagreeable.'

We can agree to have different points of view. We are not here to enforce our point of view on anyone. We are not here to put down another's point of view. We agree to disagree. We don't have to agree all the time.

We are human beings, but even if we disagree, we don't make an enemy out of that person. We may not get along only on one aspect, but we get along on other aspects. Hence, we are no longer disagreeable.

We have this life of duality, of polar opposites of every conceivable kind, of me and the other. What has happened is this 'me and the other' became 'me versus the other'. My view against your view, my thoughts against your thoughts.

When we start seeing that all forms are Baba's, the 'me versus the other' gets healed and comes back to its original polarity.

To view the corresponding video, scan the QR code.

55

Restlessness

Nikhil: Especially in the Baba community, there is so much emphasis on 'special' experiences that, sometimes, the basic self-awareness of one's restlessness is missing.

Could we speak a little bit about restlessness, of both body and mind, which is another trait of the ego.

Gautam: Let's say you have a vision, which was a gift. The memory of the experience stays, and that memory creates the experiencer. *I had this vision.* It was a pure experience. It came, it went, you had no control over it. But now the burden of memory is there because you are starting to live your life wanting more such experiences. That is how the ego operates. I had this experience, and now that I have the memory of it, I want more of it.

So one has to be very careful about it. Although the experience was meant for a purpose, it got usurped by the ego because it made the ego feel special, and now the ego is hankering after that experience.

I just wanted to clarify this point.

Now, regarding restlessness, if your thinking mind is restless, it is going to manifest in the body. In some way, you will find yourself fidgeting, or in the case of the younger generation today, they will get distracted by social media.

I remember this girl telling me that she can't sit still anymore. If she sits still, her hand immediately goes to her mobile phone. She opens WhatsApp, and when she is done seeing the messages there, she starts clicking on the display pictures of her friends to see the pictures they have posted. [Refer to talk 34.] And thus it becomes an endless activity. This is restlessness. There's so much fragmentation, there's so much distraction, that even to be still is a challenge.

You may not even be aware you are restless. But if you find you can't sit still or that you're always switching on your TV or some streaming service, or you're constantly drawn to being engaged with social media or whatever, then that is a sign of a restless mind.

And peace cannot be found in restlessness. It is the absence of restlessness which is peace.

So it is important to look at this because if you find that peace, you will become aware that you are very happy at times, doing nothing but maybe just sipping a cup of tea, sitting, relaxing and being present. And then when you feel it's time to check your posts on social media, you do that. Both are honoured. It's not that we have to live a monastic life. It is all about balance—the middle path, as the Buddha would say.

N: As one advances on their spiritual journey and makes true progress, one of the measures would be inner silence, not experiences—stillness of the mind. So you made a very important point that, sometimes, to cover up the restlessness, there is involuntary activity, such as being constantly addicted to social media.

One measure as to where you are on your journey, I would say, is that you can sit for one hour in a room without the compulsive need to hear or see a podcast or YouTube, or something. Because, otherwise, it's very easy to say, *Oh, I can be by myself,* although your mind is engaged in some activity.

G: Yes. Actually, peace is the only measure.

N: It reminds me of two instances where Baba had asked certain people to stay in confinement. One of them was a devotee, Kakasaheb Dixit, whom Baba told not to leave his wada for nine months as a form of advanced sadhana. Kakasaheb was a sadhak who was religiously engaged in his sadhana, and he was transformed after that experience.

Similarly, there was another gentleman who was told by Baba to stay in the chavadi, but the restlessness got to him. After a few months, he ran away, thinking he was a bit smarter than Baba. And then a leela happened where he got into trouble and had to come back crying to Baba. No doubt, it was a bit extreme, being confined for a few months, but Baba would not do it without a reason.

This reflects the restlessness of a non-sadhak and the difference between them and a sadhak. It is a giveaway that the ego is at play.

G: Yet, it is also the nature of the mind to be restless. It's always trying to create, to become, to move, to flow here and there. The point is that peace is a still mind. Peace is the acceptance of what *is*, and reflects our relationship with it. And when that happens, as opposed to restlessness, we find that, as you said, the inner silence, the inner peace, gets revealed. And that is actually what gives us the strength to deal with life situations. As Ramana Maharshi said, the state of equanimity is the state of bliss. And equanimity is the absence of restlessness.

Then, if I am restless, and this restlessness is a physical manifestation, what would I do if I felt that the body needed to expend energy? I would go for a long walk or a swim. I would indulge in physical activity. I would not sit like a statue at home and say that I have to be still. And that is because the natural flow of energy needs to be expended.

But if I find that the engagement is in the mind—for example, if I am playing video games all the time—and I'm restless, then that has to be looked at.

And so that, in itself, is a beautiful sadhana for all of us, to just reflect during the day how much activity and restlessness there is in our minds. I think Eckhart Tolle gave this example which I often use. He said, 'If you are walking on the streets, you might see what you think is a madman blabbering away. Ask yourself what is going on in your own mind. The only difference is that with you, it is covert. You're not blabbering it out, but can you imagine if you started speaking all that's going on inside your mind? Who would look worse, the person blabbering on the road or you?' [Laughs.]

That is the nature of our minds, you see. It's always wheels upon wheels of stories: *This happened to me, that happened to me. This one did this to me, this one did that to me.* It's non-stop.

N: You know, it's interesting you mentioned physical symptoms as well. Sometimes, when you go to the airport or a public space, you can see that certain people can't sit still. They're always fidgety. It gets a bit better when they have a gadget, as their energy is all directed towards that. But in the absence of this distraction, they just can't seem to sit still.

It's important for a devotee, particularly, to become aware of these symptoms as a sign of restlessness of the mind.

G: Sure.

N: If the witnessing starts, it's the beginning of the journey. So I hope these pointers help.

G: Yes. As I was saying in an earlier video, we are not fault-finding here. We are just showing how the mind operates, how the ego operates and what to look at. We are just exploring these aspects of the nature of the mind.

To view the corresponding video, scan the QR code.

56

Contemplating the Teachings (Gautam's Talk)

There are two aspects you could consider while following a teaching: contemplating and living the teaching.

Now let's explore how this works. I'll give you my own example.

In his satsangs, my spiritual teacher, Rameshji, would tell everyone to have ten minutes to themselves at the end of the day, when they could just sit by themselves with their cup of coffee, or whatever, and be comfortable.

The main thing is that this is not a rigorous practice. Be comfortable. Think about the main events that transpired during the day. You crossed the street and saw something, or somebody called you and said something, which impacted you negatively or positively.

The point is to think of these events and then investigate what exactly happened. I saw something, heard something, touched something, tasted something, smelled something or whatever it may be.

Consider, I saw something. Let's say I was crossing the street and saw an old lady at the opposite end. Seeing that she needed some assistance, I helped her cross the street. So, seeing something, a reaction arose within me, which resulted in an action—the action of helping the lady across.

Now if I had not seen that old lady, the action would not have happened. Therefore, is it truly my action? If my action depends on something that is seen, over which I have no control, is it truly my action? Also, someone else could have seen the old lady and continued

CONTEMPLATING THE TEACHINGS (GAUTAM'S TALK)

walking away. In my case, I decided to help her, based on my nature, which God has given me.

So Rameshji called this process a process of self-investigation. Let us call it contemplation.

If you read a chapter of the Sai Satcharita every night, that is the first step. Then you contemplate it: *What is this story telling me?* You don't just leave the story in the book, because then that is just mental reading, which is yet the first step. It's important to ask yourself, *What do I have to look at as far as this story is concerned?* And during the course of the day and the week ahead, maybe this story will keep coming up in your mind, and you will see the essence of it: *Where does it fit in, in my daily living?*

You may still be working on your past patterns, habits, etc. because that is hardwired conditioning, which is not going to disappear overnight. This process of contemplating a story—not once or twice but a few times—is a very important step. This leads to living the teaching. When you find that the lesson you have learnt from this story is being naturally lived by you, then you are living the teaching.

Rameshji said that you will find that nobody truly is the doer of actions because you cannot control what happens and your reaction to it; it is based on your genetics and conditioning.

I saw that all the major events in my life, such as my father's passing away when I was young, simply happened. I had no control over them. As a result, I took very naturally to this teaching that he presented. I didn't have to go through the process of contemplation.

Although some of the other spiritual seekers did not take to it naturally, it did appeal to them, somewhere within themselves. And so they would go home in the evening, sit with their cup of coffee, and look at what happened during the day. That was their process. Till they realized, by and by, that they were looking at daily living now through the lens of the teaching.

So this is what happens when we read the Satcharita regularly. It is possible that it can stay only at the mental level, as if you have read a story of some bygone era, without it impacting your daily living. On the other hand, you can turn the reading into, one could say, a meditation: *What is in it for me? How does it impact my daily living?*

How does it impact the peace that I can touch in daily living? Then that becomes a very crucial step because that reading and contemplation now have value, which has a direct impact on your daily living.

And so when you start finding that you are naturally living the teachings—in the way you respond to what happens during the day and to the people in your life, especially those you don't get along with—and that your understanding is now changing and more accepting of what *is* and of people for who they are, then that contemplation has got delivered.

That is why my teacher would say that it is like getting a driving licence. You first learn to drive, then you get the licence, but you're still nervous, especially when driving through heavy traffic. But two years later, when you're driving through heavy traffic, you realize, *My God, two years ago, I would have been so stressed driving through this. Now it is a breeze because I have practice. I'm used to it.*

When you find that comfort level with Baba's words and teachings, you will know that you have been living the teachings. Your life may not have become easier, but you will feel it has certainly become *simpler* and less complicated. You will find that you are dealing with problems from a different level—from a position of peace, equanimity and calm. You will find that life is no longer a problem that needs to be solved every day. You will find that life is simply the living of it with the blessings and grace of the teaching.

Then the prayer changes from 'May I live the teachings' to 'May I be lived by the teachings.'

To view the corresponding video, scan the QR code.

Appendix

Sai Baba of Shirdi—The Hidden Jewel of Advaita

Sai Baba of Shirdi is renowned as the Master of Miracles, but few have been exposed to His diamond teachings of Advaita (non-duality). Sai Baba's philosophy was based on Advaita Vedanta, which also includes elements of Bhakti. However, the phenomenon and magnitude of miracles that occurred during, and even after, His lifetime was so overwhelming that, in their incessant narration over the decades since His death, His teachings have been largely overlooked, overshadowed and forgotten. With the deeper understanding prevalent today that extends beyond the fascination and hope for miracles and moves in the direction of Self-enquiry, digging out these precious gems of Advaita from the sacred soil of Shirdi is essential to understanding the deeper significance of this colossal spiritual figure in our life. For Sai Himself said, 'I give people what they want in the hope that they will begin to want what I want to give them.'

Although we have built temples dedicated to Sai Baba on almost every street corner in Maharashtra, Western spiritual seekers inclined towards Jnana have, unfortunately, not been exposed to Sai's teachings as there is hardly any awareness of literature that is primarily devoted to expounding His teachings. This is in sharp contrast to what happened in the case of other realized masters, such as Ramana Maharshi and Nisargadatta Maharaj, who had a steady stream of seekers from all over the world visiting them because they had been exposed to their teachings that had spread far and wide through books published on their talks during satsangs. Perhaps the time has now come for the world to recognize and accept yet another gift of the highest teachings of Advaita Vedanta—as espoused by this avatar.

Sai's life (–1918) itself is a manifestation of non-duality: There is no definite account of the date and place of His birth. He is supposed to have been born of Hindu parents and raised by Muslim foster parents. He is regarded by both Hindu as well as Muslim devotees as a saint, and in His life and teachings, He embraced both faiths. He lived in a dilapidated mosque, which He named Dwarkamai (the sacred city where Krishna lived), was buried in a temple and taught using concepts drawn from both traditions. What could be more non-dual than that? Ironically and unfortunately, a large number of His followers still squabble over whether He was Muslim or Hindu, whereas in the light of His life and teachings, such bickering is a non-issue, not worthy of even a discussion, let alone a debate!

The Sai Satcharita (considered the most important account of His life, teachings and miracles) contains some of the most lucid statements on Advaita made by a saint whose motto was '*Sabka Malik Ek.*' Sai clearly did not mean to emphasize that there is only one God (as in an embodied form) for everyone but rather that 'Everyone's Master (God) is One,' which is what the aphorism means. One—not two, non-dual. One—the One Unicity, One Source, One Consciousness.

This makes it hardly surprising that He was considered an incarnation of Lord Dattatreya and Sant Kabir.

Here are some of Baba's Advaitic sayings:

> Who is this Me? You need not go far in search of Me. Barring your name and form, there exists in you as well as in all beings, a sense of Being, or Consciousness of Existence. That is Myself. Knowing this, you see Me inside yourself as well as in all beings. If you practise this, you will realize all-pervasiveness and thus attain oneness with Me.

Sai clearly points out that you are not the ego, which is identified with name and form. You are that Consciousness that enables you to Be—'I Am,' not 'I Am this or that.' You are that same Consciousness that functions through everyone and brings about life as we know it, just as it is the same electricity that functions through different electronic gadgets. This understanding annihilates any notion of separation that exists between 'me' and the 'other.' All there is, is only Consciousness. And it is not something to go in search of, as it is already there within us. Only the veil of ignorance needs to be removed. Sabka Malik Ek.

> Why should you take responsibility for your actions upon yourself? Do not entertain the sense of doership in doing good as well as bad deeds; be entirely prideless and egoless in all things, and thus your spiritual progress will be rapid.

Here, Sai clearly states that God is the only doer of all actions that we supposedly think are done by us. All actions are divine happenings and not deeds done by anyone. No pride or arrogance for our so-called successes, no guilt or shame for our so-called bad deeds. God is the only doer.

> You see, mysterious is the path of action. Though I do nothing, they hold Me responsible for the actions which take place on account of Prarabdh (Destiny). I am only their witness. The Lord is the Sole doer and Inspirer. He is most merciful. Neither I am God, nor Master. I am His obedient servant and remember Him constantly. He who

casts aside his egoism and thanks Him, and he who trusts Him entirely, will have his shackles removed and will obtain liberation.

From the above statements, we can see that Sai is constantly giving us pointers to liberation, enlightenment, or Self-realization. In the following paragraph from the Sai Satcharita, Sai Baba has covered some major milestones on the Advaita road, including being the Witness, the illusion of separation, the will of God and enlightenment.

Let the world go topsy-turvy; you remain where you are. Standing in your own place, look on calmly at the show of all things passing before you. Demolish the wall of difference that separates you from Me, and then the road for our meeting will be clear and open. The sense of differentiation as I and thou is the barrier that keeps the disciple away from his Master, and unless that is destroyed, the state of union or atonement is not possible. 'Allah Malik'; i.e., God is the sole Proprietor; nobody else is our Protector. His method of work is extraordinary, invaluable and inscrutable. His Will be done, and He will show us the way and satisfy our heart's desires. It is on account of rnanubandhan (former relationships) that we have come together. Let us love and serve each other and be happy. He who attains the supreme goal of life is immortal and happy. All others merely exist; i.e., they live so long as they breathe.

Clearly, the supreme goal of life that Sai Baba refers to is enlightenment, or Self-realization. By 'immortal', He does not mean that we (the body) will live forever but that we will realize that our true nature is immortal, eternal Presence, beyond the pleasures and pains of life and, hence, the shackles of time. It is ever-shining and, never having been born, it can never die.

Since His passing, Sai Baba has been worshipped by millions of devotees in the hope that miracles will occur in their lives. Few worship Him for the miracle that is His teaching. It is in itself a direct path to Self-realization, a path that takes us beyond the pains and pleasures of daily living and anchors us in peace of mind. Other than this, there is no greater miracle that this Diamond of Advaita could bestow upon us.

Although there are thousands of temples dedicated to Sai Baba today, it's time to worship His timeless teachings as well, for He said, 'Meditate always on My Formless Nature, which is Knowledge Incarnate, Consciousness and Bliss.' It is this statement that we should remember the next time we bow down in front of the stone slab at Dwarkamai, upon which Baba used to sit. Let it be a reminder of His formless form. Sai had also said, 'My bones will speak from My tomb.' [Refer to talk 1.] They certainly are speaking but, the point is, are we willing to listen? Or are we going to Him with our heads and hearts stuffed with our hopes and wishes for miracles in our lives, assuming that what we want is going to be good for us in the first place?

The dhuni at Dwarkamai has been burning ever since Baba's passing over. May it consume our ignorance and burn brighter as Baba's teachings blaze forth across the world in time to come, lighting up the road for all of humanity. For, truly, Sabka Malik Ek.

Glossary

Words appearing in italics can be cross-referenced within the glossary.

A

aarti	A Hindu ritual of worship in which lamps are lit and offered to the deity while singing songs in its praise
Advaita	A Sanskrit word that translates as 'not two' or 'no second'. This gives the idea that the inner Self, or Atman, is the same as the Absolute Reality, that is *Brahman*
Advaitic	Pertaining to *Advaita*
Aghori	A follower of a Shaivite Hindu sect mostly comprising ascetic *sadhus*. They seek spiritual liberation through intense discipline and the transcendence of societal norms. Their rituals, including dwelling in cremation grounds, wearing ash from funeral pyres, and meditating among human remains, aim to cultivate detachment and understand the true nature of Reality
Aham Brahmasmi	One of the four principal *Mahavakyas*, or Great Sayings, of the Vedic scriptures. It appears in the Brihadaranyaka Upanishad and means 'I Am Brahman.'
ajapa japa	'Ajapa' means 'without *japa*'. Hence, the term literally translates as 'effortless repetition' or 'constant awareness of the *mantra*'
Ajna Chakra	The Third Eye *Chakra*

akhand jyot	'Akhand' means 'uninterrupted' or 'unextinguished', and 'jyot' means 'flame'. It also refers to a *diya* lit for the entire duration of the festival of Navratri, symbolizing the removal of darkness from one's life
Anahat (Chakra)	The Heart *Chakra*
annadaan	Donation of food
ashram	A spiritual hermitage or monastery; a place where one strives towards a goal in a disciplined manner (such a goal could be ascetic, spiritual, yogic or any other)

B

baba; Baba	A father; grandfather; wise old man. An honorific term used in several West Asian and South Asian cultures; Sai Baba
bael patra	A leaf from the bael tree, used in the worship of Shiva. This three-pronged leaf is believed to symbolize Shiva's trident
bandhan	A relationship bond, which is also a bondage as one's karma with the other person has to be fulfilled to be free of it
Bhagavad Gita	A seven hundred–verse Hindu scripture, which is part of the epic Mahabharata. The work is dated to the second half of the first millennium BCE and is considered one of the holy scriptures of Hinduism
bhajan	A devotional song with a spiritual or religious theme
bhakta	A devotee
bhakti	Devotional worship directed to one supreme deity; a religious movement emphasizing the mutual intense emotional attachment and love of a devotee towards a personal god and of the god towards the devotee

bhava	A feeling or emotion
Brahma Gyan	Knowledge of Creation
Brahman	In Hinduism, the ultimate reality or supreme cosmic power, often described as the unchanging, infinite, immanent and transcendent reality that is the divine ground of all matter, energy, time, space, being and everything beyond this universe. Brahman is considered the source and essence of the universe; *Consciousness*; Self
buddhi	Intellect

C

chadar	A sheet of cloth
chakra	A wheel or disc; in yogic literature, one of the several centres of consciousness located in the etheric body, usually depicted as a lotus flower. They are high-powered vortices of energy, which receive the cosmic energy and act as transformers to regulate the force of that energy so that it may be used by the various organs of the physical body
chakravyuh	A multi-tier defensive military formation depicted in the Mahabharata, which looks like a disc (*chakra*) when viewed from above; a challenging situation that is difficult to exit (figuratively)
chamatkar	A miracle
charita	Life story
chavadi	The village public assembly venue, later used by Sai Baba as a resting place
chitta	Pure Consciousness (also referred to as the Heart)
Consciousness	*Brahman*

D

dakshina	An offering made by a disciple to a *guru* who imparts knowledge

darshan	Beholding a holy person or a deity, thereby receiving their blessings; presenting oneself for viewing by devotees
dhuni	A sacred fire. In ancient India, the *rishis* guarded their sacred fire most carefully and kept it clean, as it was believed to be the residence of divinity. Sitting by the dhuni is believed to 'purify one's vibrations' and to have a beneficial impact on physical and mental health
dhyana	Meditative absorption
diya	A small cup-shaped oil lamp made of baked clay
doha	A couplet consisting of two lines, each of twenty-four instants (matras) used by Indian poets and saints of North India probably since the beginning of the sixth century CE
dukkha	'Suffering', considered the first Noble Truth in Buddhism
Dwarkamai	The name given by Sai Baba to a dilapidated mosque that He took to be His home

F

fakir	A Sufi ascetic who renounces his worldly possessions and dedicates his life to the worship of God

G

Gayatri Mantra	Found in the Rig Veda (3.62.10), the Gayatri Mantra embodies the collective wisdom of the entire Vedic revelation and takes its name partly from the gayatri metre (twenty-four syllables divided into three lines of eight syllables each). But 'Gayatri' also means 'she who protects the singer' (from 'gai'—'to sing', and 'trai'—'to protect'). Thus, Gayatri is a name for the Divine Mother who protects Her children and leads them toward *Self-realization*

ghada	A water pot
ghamand	Arrogance or excessive pride
guru	An imparter of knowledge; one who dispels the darkness of ignorance; a spiritual guide
guru bandhu	A fellow disciple or student, studying under the same teacher or *guru* that one has
Guru Purnima	A religious festival dedicated to offering respect to all the spiritual and academic *gurus*
gyan	Knowledge

H

Hanuman Chalisa	A Hindu devotional hymn in praise of Lord Hanuman, attributed to Tulsidas. The word 'chalisa' is derived from 'chalis' which means the number forty in Hindi, as the Hanuman Chalisa has forty verses
havan	A Hindu fire ritual that involves offering substances to a sacred fire while reciting *mantras*

I

Ishta Devata	The term in Hinduism for a worshipper's personal preferred deity. As Hindus worship many gods and goddesses or their incarnations, they may choose one beloved deity as their focus for devotion

J

japa	The repetitive chanting of words or sounds (*mantras*) which liberate us from the mind
-ji, Ji	An honorific suffix attached to names, or used by itself, to indicate respect
jiva	In Hinduism, jiva is a living being or any entity imbued with the life force. The word itself originates from the Sanskrit verb-root 'jiv', which translates as 'to breathe' or 'to live'

GLOSSARY

Jnana Yoga	The path of Knowledge; one of the four yoga systems of Hinduism, the other three being *Karma Yoga*, Raja Yoga and Bhakti Yoga
jnani	A Self-realized master
jyot	Flame; *diya*

K

kafni	A long flowing robe, such as the one worn by Sai Baba
Kakad Aarti	A ceremony that signifies waking Sai Baba at dawn and getting Him ready for the day. It involves the waving of lamps, singing songs in His praise and washing and clothing His *murti*
Kali Yuga	The fourth and present age of the world cycle of Yugas, or 'Ages'; the end of the four Ages that comprise a cycle and is often referred to as the dark age. In Hindu belief, the Kali Yuga leads to the destruction of the world and, subsequently, to the creation of a new cycle of the four Yugas
karma	Actions or the consequences thereof; destiny
Karma Yoga	The path of right action; one of the four yoga systems of Hinduism, the other three being Jnana Yoga, Raja Yoga and Bhakti Yoga
karmic	Pertaining to *karma*
kirtan	'Kirtan' is a Sanskrit word meaning 'praise' or 'eulogy'. It is used to describe a form of call-and-response chanting involving *mantras* or hymns. The chanting is carried out alongside instruments, such as a harmonium, cymbals or drums
Kriya Yoga	An ancient meditation technique of energy and breath control, or pranayama. It is part of a comprehensive spiritual path, which includes additional meditation practices along with right living

Kundalini	The manifestation of the Dynamic Female Cosmic Energy within the individual body, lying nascent in a coiled form at the base of the spine
kurta-pyjama	A two-piece garment which is the basic clothing of men in India
Kurukshetra	'Kurukshetra', meaning 'land of Kuru', is the place where the famous war of the epic Mahabharata took place

L

leela	Divine play

M

Mahasamadhi	The state a yogi enters when they consciously make the decision to leave their body. This is only possible once they have already achieved God-realization, or nirvikalpa *samadhi*, in which the yogi recognizes and experiences their true oneness and unity with God
Mahavakya	The word translates as 'grand saying' or 'great pronouncement'. It is typically very short and highlights the main point or wisdom of spiritual texts or concepts
mahout	A handler of elephants
Manipur Chakra	The Solar Plexus *Chakra*
mantra	A word or sound repeated to aid concentration in meditation. 'Man' means 'mind' and 'tra' means 'to liberate'. A word or sound having a mystical power
mantra deeksha	The act of initiating a disciple into a mantra by a guru
mantra japa	*Japa*
masjid	A mosque
maya	Powers of illusion and creativity associated with Vishnu; a veil that prevents the realization of

	spiritual truth; lack of knowledge of the Self; appearance or illusion
mayajaal	Net of illusion; trickery (figuratively); refer to *maya*
moksha	Salvation; *nirvana*
Muladhar (Chakra)	The Root *Chakra* at the base of the spine
murti	An image of a deity, which itself is considered divine once consecrated

N

Namasmaran	A spiritual practice of remembering God's name
namaste	A customary Hindu non-contact manner of respectfully greeting and honouring a person or group; done with a slight bow, with palms touching and fingers pointing upwards, thumbs close to the chest
Nath Yogi	A yogi of the Nath tradition
nirvana	Enlightenment; *moksha*; *Self-realization*
Nisarga Yoga	The Natural (Nisarga) Yoga of practising harmlessness and living in peace, harmony, friendliness and love, as taught by Nisargadatta Maharaj. The fruit of it is happiness, uncaused and endless
Nithya	The Absolute

O

ovi	A verse form in Marathi poetry; the Sai Satcharita is written as a series of ovis

P

paap	Sin
paduka	An ancient form of wooden footwear in India, consisting of a sole with a post and knob which is positioned between the big and second toe

palki	A palanquin
param bhakta	A *bhakta* of the highest order
paratha	In Indian cooking, a flat, thick piece of unleavened bread fried on a griddle
parayana	Repeated chanting or recitation of a scriptural text as a spiritual practice
Pawan Putra	Another name for Lord Hanuman, son of Vayu, the wind god
pothi	A religious or spiritual text
prachar	The dissemination of religious or spiritual knowledge
prana	In yoga, Indian medicine, and Indian martial arts, 'prana' is the Sanskrit word for 'breath', 'life force', or 'vital principle'. It permeates reality on all levels, including inanimate objects. In Hindu literature, prana is sometimes described as originating from the Sun and connecting the elements
Pranic Healing	A no-touch method of healing yourself and others by using powerful and simple energy techniques given by the school's founder, Grand Master Choa Kok Sui
Prarabdha Karma	The part of Sanchita *karma*, a collection of past *karmas*, which is ready to be experienced through the present body (incarnation)
prasad	A devotional offering first made to a deity, typically consisting of food, which is later shared among devotees
pravachan	A spiritual discourse
puja	A ritual of worship performed to offer devotional homage and prayer to one or more deities, or to host and honour a guest, or to spiritually celebrate an event

R

rahasya	A mystery or a secret
Ramdasi	Often links to Ramdas, a name whose meaning is 'Devotee of Ram', 'Servant of God', or 'Devotee and Servant of Ram'
Reiki	It comes from the Japanese words 'rei', meaning 'universal', and 'ki', meaning 'life energy'. It is a type of energy healing
rishi	A sage; he who sees (spiritual insight)
rna	A debt
rnanubandhan	A cosmic debt of former relationships. An invisible chord that ties or, rather, binds one in relationship with others, due to undischarged debts which are brought forward in this life from past lives. '*Rna*' means 'debt' and '*bandhan*' means 'bond' or 'bondage'

S

saburi	Patience
Sadguru	The *guru* within; the true *guru*; in some Eastern religions, Sadguru (or Satguru) is a person who is considered to have achieved enlightenment and who can help others achieve the same
sadhak	A practitioner of spirituality
sadhana	Disciplined and dedicated spiritual practice or learning
sadhu	A holy man, sage or ascetic
Sahasrar (Chakra)	The Crown *Chakra*, which is not a *chakra* but a centre
Sai Satcharita	A record of Shirdi Sai Baba's *leelas*, teachings and incidents as they occurred during the tenure of the writer's association with Him
samadhi	The tomb of a holy person or saint in India; a union of the individualized soul with infinite

	spirit—a state of oneness and complete absorption
samsara	The endless cycle of birth, death and rebirth
sangha	A Sanskrit word meaning 'association', 'assembly', 'company', or 'community'. It is mostly used to describe the Buddhist community of ordained monks and nuns
Sansthan	The Shri Saibaba Sansthan Trust, Shirdi, the governing and administrative body of Shri Saibaba's Samadhi Temple and all others temples in this premises
sashtanga namaskara	A type of namaskar (gesture showing respect) where you lie flat on your stomach with all the 'angas', or body parts, touching the ground
Sat	Truth; the Absolute Reality
satsang	A Sanskrit term derived from two roots: '*Sat*' meaning 'Truth' and '*sangha*' meaning 'community', 'company', or 'association'. It can be translated as 'associating with good people' or simply 'being in the company of Truth'
Self-enquiry	It is the constant attention to the inner awareness of 'I' or 'I am' recommended by the scriptures and sages, particularly Ramana Maharshi, as the most efficient and direct way of discovering the ultimate reality
Self-realization	It denotes a state in which an individual knows who they truly are and is fulfilled in the understanding that they are one with the omnipresence of God; Enlightenment; *moksha*; *nirvana*
seva	Selfless service; an act of compassion and care for others above oneself
Shanti	Peace
shraddha	Faith

siddha	It means 'One who is accomplished'. It refers to perfected masters who have achieved a high degree of perfection of the intellect as well as liberation or enlightenment; an individual who, through the practice of *sadhana*, attains *siddhis*
siddhi	Psychic and spiritual abilities and powers
sthan	A place
Sukh-Shanti	Happiness-Peace
Swadhisthan (Chakra)	The Sacral *Chakra*

T

tamasha	A source of entertainment (literally); a hullabaloo or brouhaha (figuratively)
Tat Tvam Asi	The *Mahavakya*, 'That I Am.'
tonga	Horse-carriage

U

udi	Sacred ash, especially that offered by Sai Baba

V

Vishnu Sahasranama	A Sanskrit hymn containing a list of the 1,000 names of Lord Vishnu, one of the main deities in Hinduism and the Supreme God in Vaishnavism
Vishuddhi (Chakra)	The Throat *Chakra*

W

wada	A large mansion, typically found in Maharashtra, India

Disclaimer

The interviews and talks were a spontaneous series of recordings intended to delve deeper into the teachings of Sri Sai Baba. There are many historical references made, and while best efforts have been made while editing the videos to remove or edit any historical errors, we do not recommend that any of the material ever be used or cited for historical reference.

Sai Baba's Original Paintings and Photographs

At HouseofSai.com, an archive of all the original images of Sri Sai Baba has been compiled over the years. These beautiful images are printed on high-quality canvas and are available to devotees through the website. This seva is not for profit.

The cover image used on the book cover is also listed for those devotees who may be interested.

Podcasts

The talks in the series *Living the Teachings of Sai Baba* are available on Spotify, Apple Podcasts and other leading platforms.

Please scan the QR code below for details.

For information on Gautam Sachdeva, visit:
www.gautamsachdeva.com

The author may be contacted on email:
info@gautamsachdeva.com

For further details, contact:
Yogi Impressions LLP
1711, Centre 1, World Trade Centre,
Cuffe Parade, Mumbai 400 005, India.

Fill in the Mailing List form on our website
and receive, via email, information on
books, authors, events and more.
Visit: www.yogiimpressions.com

Telephone: (022) 40115981, 22155036
E-mail: yogi@yogiimpressions.com

Join us on Facebook:
www.facebook.com/yogiimpressions

Join us on Instagram:
www.instagram.com/yogi_impressions

www.ingramcontent.com/pod-product-compliance
Lightning Source LLC
Chambersburg PA
CBHW071743150426
43191CB00010B/1677